Rosa Fa⟨...⟩

£6-95

Bank.
with love from
Buck.
2/9/88

HORSESWEAT AND TEARS

A year in John Dunlop's racing stable

Also by Simon Barnes:

Phil Edmonds – A Singular Man

HORSESWEAT
AND
TEARS

*A year in John Dunlop's
racing stable*

SIMON BARNES

HEINEMANN KINGSWOOD

Heinemann Kingswood
Michelin House, 81 Fulham Road, LONDON SW3 6RB

LONDON   MELBOURNE   AUCKLAND

0 434 98152 4

Printed and bound in Great Britain by
Richard Clay Ltd, Bungay, Suffolk

To the memory of
Tim Dunlop
13 August 1966–14 May 1987
R.I.P.

LIST OF ILLUSTRATIONS

The author and publishers would like to thank Eamonn McCabe for his assistance in supplying the photographs.

THE CAST

John Dunlop, *trainer*
Tim Dunlop

Tony Couch, *assistant to Dunlop*
Jeremy Noseda, *assistant trainer*
Marcus Hosgood, *racing secretary*
James Burns, *pupil assistant*
Mark Campion, *pupil assistant*

Eddie Watt, *senior head lad*
Tom Hamill, *head lad*
David Kitcher, *head lad*
Robert Hamilton, *senior travelling head lad*

Lads: Raymond Baker   Shona Crombie
      Chris Beavis   Mick Gettins
      Ken Bedford (Scobie)   Stuart Johnston (Angus)
      Chris Blyth   Jane Martindale
      Steven Brain   Eileen McGuffie
      Paul Coombes   Peter Sanderson

Graham Foster, *apprentice*
Willie Carson, *jockey*

Wally Watkin, *driver*
Denis Hartigan, *loose-horse catcher*

Lavinia, Duchess of Norfolk, *owner*
Mike Huntley-Robertson, *owner*
Sue Abbott, *owner and syndicate administrator*
Paolo Benedetti, *agent*

Robert Allpress, *vet*
Michael Ashton, *vet*

ACKNOWLEDGEMENTS

I owe John Dunlop more thanks than I can say for making this book possible. I have been granted unprecedented access, quite exceptional freedom. In what was a difficult and troubled year for him, professionally and personally, he gave me an unfailing welcome. No door was ever closed. I hope I have repaid some of his trust and kindness by writing a book that is, as he hoped, good for racing.

I would also like to thank Sue Dunlop. Throughout my year at Castle Stables, she has been kind and hospitable, and has given me some splendid meals.

To Marcus Hosgood, racing secretary, I owe thanks for his unflagging help. He has acted as a racing adviser throughout the preparation of this book, and it has taken him hours. Also, he produced the appendices. The man is a star.

I owe a debt of thanks to the ladies who run the front office at Castle Stables: Susan Crossland, Claire Wayland and Vera Burgess. They have put up with my telephonic demands again and again, acted as fixers, and made me coffee on the coldest of mornings.

I also owe thanks to just about everybody else at Castle Stables. Everyone whose name appears on the cast of characters has helped me, and many others have done so anonymously.

I would like to add a special thank you to all the stable lads, named or unnamed, who have worked at Castle Stables throughout the year. Their welcome, good cheer and bad jokes have helped make every trip to the yard a pleasure.

I also owe thanks to the great and good Derek Wyatt, for many reasons, most particularly for his constant support.

Thanks to John Pawsey for about a thousand things throughout the year, and for acting as the ace fixer for this book.

Thanks to Margot Richardson, and everyone else at Kingswood.

Thanks also to Eamonn McCabe, photographer. It is always a pleasure as well as a privilege to work with him. I hope he enjoys the 65,000 word caption I have written.

And finally, special thanks to my wife, Cindy Lee Wright. Without whom, and all that.

1

I T WAS BLOODY cold, that January. It was a January when you could see your breath indoors and it froze on the insides of the windows overnight. It was miserable for the townees: a nightmare of frozen points and cancelled trains and jump-leads and AA Home Start. No one who ventured outside for more than five minutes could feel his toes.

All office workers spent that January giving thanks that they worked indoors: the icy rush from front door to car was as much as anyone could stand. How good it was to come home and watch the news: Weather still holds Britain in its Icy Grip. Rail Chaos. More Cold Weather on the Way. Wintering ducks found it harder and harder to find any open water: all their particular places were frozen over.

For a sportswriter like me, it was an odd time: there was no sport to write about. The pools panels, those heralds of doom, plucked the football results from their imaginations week after week. The rugby internationals were off. Undersoil heating failed to cope with these extreme conditions. For weeks, there was no racing: it has to be pretty tough for the jump-racing fraternity to call things off, but when the ground is as hard as the hob of hell, no sane person can think about jumping a horse, and nor can jump jockeys.

No, this was not a time for optimism. The most cheerful thing I could think of was that it probably could not get much worse. Those airy, colourful days of summer seemed now to belong to fiction: had the sun really shone? Had I really sipped cold drinks beneath trees? Had the trees really had leaves on? Surely not. And had I really watched Shahrastani and Dancing Brave duel for the mastery at Ascot that splendid Saturday in July? Flat racing, and with it all the joys of summer, seemed no more than a wild fantasy, an arcadian idyll from a wholly imagined past.

This was how the year began: the year I was to spend with the people and horses of Castle Stables, Arundel. My pursuit of the joys of summer began in the freezing cold, with multiple pairs of socks, gloves, waterproof zipped up to the ears and hat pulled down to the nose, in stamping, shoulder-clapping, freezing, miserable January.

When it is cold, horses turn into dragons. Twin gouts of steam jet from black nostrils as they leave their boxes and skitter about in frantic efforts to keep warm: tap-dancing across the tarmac, striking sparks from their shoes as they mess about in their fidgety efforts to keep out of the biting wind: 'Stand still, y'bugger!' Who would be a stable lad in January? Up in the pre-dawn dark, furiously brushing the hairy backs of their horses in a desperate effort to get their own circulation moving. It is the fingers that suffer most: the blood flees from them and they turn into great clumsy purple sausages. And because you are clumsy you are always barking knuckles and stubbing finger-ends: petty hurts that bite with triple force in the freezing cold.

Why is it impossible to tighten a girth with gloves on? Why is it that, no matter how hard you try, your gloves always get wet and seem to suck the warmth from your hands? Why is a human being born with external ears? After you have been out for half an hour, it feels as if someone has fastened a Bulldog clip on to each ear.

It was so cold that even the great warm smell of every stable in the land had vanished: a great cauterizing, deodorizing chill had taken over. For some reason racing stables have an affinity with wind: the wind chill factor at Castle Stables, which lies at the foot of Arundel Castle, and thus on the top of a sudden and handsome hill, was a phenomenon that challenged belief: the wind seemed to howl in straight from the Urals. Faces pinched shut, locked fingers tried to get some feeling from the reins, shoulders hunched dispiritedly. The training of racehorses for the next far-distant, impossible-to-believe-in summer did not stop for mere Arctic weather. True, no one thinks about flat racing in January save the trainers and their chilblained lads. The owners are more likely to be in Barbados, or Miami. The gallops in January are racing's flipside.

The weather was so bad, it had put the Arundel all-weather gallops out of action. The stable went into its foul weather routine: instead of sending out two lots every morning, they were now sending out four smaller bands of horses. Each lot wound its way to a large aircraft hangar-like building, made of corrugated iron: a large, draughty, ugly building. Anything was better than the merciless cold outside. Each lot assembled in this building, the indoor school, and walked and trotted in circles. Three 15-minute trots, then a good walk to warm down from the exercise, and back to the yard. Hardly inspiring stuff, this: it was the industry in tickover. Little could be done to improve a horse's fitness in such foul weather: good food and such exercise as was possible at least stopped the string from losing condition, from going backwards.

For the lads, it was the most boring time of the year. No racing: no spice of betting: above all, no winners. They sat in the saddles, cold, some of the faces looking far too young to buy a legal drink, others looking improbably ancient, middle-aged faces above boys' bodies. About a fifth of the lads are actually female: but everyone was bundled up into as many clothes as possible, and men and women seemed to vie with each other only in scruffiness of turnout. Above their heads, a loudspeaker blared out, of all things, Radio One: the lads like it, a lot of them were singing along, it helps the time go faster during the boring, repetitive exercising of this boring part of the year. And surprisingly, the horses quite like the music. They don't mind noise: it is sudden noise they hate.

In the middle of the ring stood John Dunlop, the trainer at Castle Stables. He is one of the top trainers in the country. If he walked into a bank in, say, Streatham, I doubt if he would be given an overdraft: he looked, as he generally does on the gallops, pretty disreputable. He has a wide selection of ancient riding clothes, antique anoraks and windcheaters of historical interest. No one looks wholly serious in wellingtons, even if the wellingtons are Hunters. And around Castle Stables, Dunlop generally completes his outfit with a flat cap that looks as if it had been used to rub down a wet dog. His face in January looked angular and pinched, and whose does not? There is an intricate tracery of red veins visible on those high cheekbones: you might, if you were pretty thick, perhaps if you were a bank manager in Streatham, take him for some no-account outdoor worker, a man with a hard luck story, a bit of a loser.

That would be an understandable reaction in a townee. Most people do not expect the owner of a multi-million-quid business to possess that flayed outdoor look. But raise your eyes above the Help-the-Aged riding clothes – and he is a tall man – and the eyes are a complete giveaway. From the first, Dunlop reminded me of M, James Bond's master, he of the 'damnably clear grey eyes', whose job was the passionless plotting of complex campaigns, the aiming at distant targets, the incessant pursuit of victory.

There were 200 horses in Dunlop's care, 200 bullets to fire at the rich prizes of the flat season that would begin in spring. There were 150 of them at Castle Stables, and 50 more at Findon, a few miles away: Dunlop's ambition, his restless quest for winners have seen him burst the boundaries of Arundel Park. Altogether, there were about 15 million quid's worth of horses for Dunlop to train.

These included a great cavalry of unraced two-year-olds. The money paid for them varied from a few thousand to approaching one million. Any one of them, from the cheapest to the most expensive, could be a dud. And any one of them could have rocket power in its lovely, pencil-slim legs. There are the handsome blue-blooded aristocrats bought by Arabs, any one of which might, in a couple of years, grow up to be a Classic winner. But there was no guarantee, far from it, that these expensive darlings would ever even see a racecourse. There were also horses that looked just as lovely to the untrained eye as these long-range Classic hopes, horses that bore the more modest aspirations of less lavish owners.

The three-year-old horses were more like known quantities – if ever a flat-racing horse can be called a known quantity. A couple – don't say a word – carried some quiet hopes for the Classics, a couple of colts that could have their crack at the Derby, a filly or two that could contest the Oaks. A victory in either race would be glory enough for the entire year. And there were the seen-it-all four-year-olds, who included Moon Madness, the splendid Moon Madness, which had won the St Leger the previous autumn. What might he do in the coming year?

It may have been January, and it may have been bloody cold, but there was still hope in the air. There is always hope in the air, everywhere you go in racing. That, and despair: but in racing despair seldom lasts long. For there is always another race, or another horse, or another season. Even in the depths of winter, for racing people hope springs eternal.

2

B<small>UT FIRST THE</small> horse must be bought. Let us fast-rewind
back to October, to the first day of the Highflyer Yearling
Sales, which are held in Newmarket every year. The first day
of the Highflyer is the day that the mystery and beauty of the
horse meets the might of money. Like every other day in
racing.

It is Europe's biggest sale of yearlings. The little, half-formed
horses go to Newmarket every year to parade before the public,
to be sold to the highest bidder. They would be the darlings
and disasters of the next two or three racing seasons: one or
two, we knew already, would be stars of wonder, fortune-
makers, the fulfillers of dreams. The only problem was telling
which, because far more of them, perhaps most of them, would
be heart-breakers. The yearling horses, pop-eyed and spindle-
legged, some bemerding the sale ring in fright, others looking
precociously at ease, were meeting the public for the first time.
Hard and calculating eyes watched them; soppy and sentimental
eyes watched them; the lavish, the greedy, the deeply knowledgeable and the hopelessly ignorant rubbed shoulders and wondered
which was the dud, and which was the horse with invisible
wings.

Tattersall's is custom-built for selling horses: stabling for the hundreds of horses spreads away in every direction, and in the centre stands a neat little amphitheatre. There are extremely comfortable seats for all the extremely expensive bottoms. The amphitheatre commands the attention, but what you are impelled to watch is not the little beauties that are led into the ring: it is the flick and flutter of the eyebrow and hand, the eyes of the bidders slithering here and there looking for their opponents, and more than anything else, the dancing lights behind the auctioneer, the lights that spell out the money being spent in four currencies.

How much is a dream worth? 'Well-made workmanlike filly sire starting to do well in Americah bid if you want hah twenty-seven thousand in the gate twenty-eight fresh biddah twenty-nine and thirty I sell hah now she's an athlete nice walkah and thirty-one selling all the time at thirty-one. . . .'

When the auctioneer announces he is selling, he means the horse has passed its reserve. When that happens, the seller's pulse rate comes down to a mere three times normal: the year's work that began with the fiery conjunction of mare and stallion ends in the sale ring, and the year will probably be counted a success if the reserve price is reached. But the bidding could go much further. Any horse could massively overreach the expectations of his breeders: if two determined bidders like the horse enough, then anything could happen. Bidders, especially people bidding for horses, are prone to rushes of blood: a moment of impetuousness from a bidder could see a small breeder right for a season. Or even a large breeder.

But just as often, or more often, the little horse will leave its breeder wincing and wondering about what has gone wrong. The sales are rumour factories, on a scale Fleet Street cannot hope to challenge. One mutter that a horse looks unsound can cost thousands: one mutter that a horse has a heart murmur will cost money that no vet's clean bill of health can pay back. A simple capricious dislike of the sire can wipe out the year's profit. The result of a race run thousands of miles away can give the seller a magnificent windfall. This is a wild and volatile business:

and why not? Horses are wild and volatile beasts. Do not come looking for sanity where dreams and horses meet.

'I give this colt away it's no money at forty-five thousand. . . .' No money? A hand is discreetly raised: but on whose behalf is the hand bidding? If it is known that, say, an Arab owner has a fancy for a horse, then the price is likely to start climbing. Deception is part of the rhythm of things here. 'Thank you and forty-six and seven and eight. . . .'

Outside, one of the less phlegmatic horses started squealing like a pig. Inside the amphitheatre, the smell of money made the amphitheatre warm and cosy: a pleasant fug of money built up throughout the day. The unwary changed their minds about their upper limit. The litany of money was intoned everlastingly by the auctioneer: always in guineas, to keep everyone slightly confused. Behind the auctioneer, the conversions were flashed in Irish guineas (punts), American dollars and French francs: flickering and frittering away.

'Who's got a hundred for hah she'll make it good gracious me I thought there'd be a show of hands for this one one hundred thank you sir and five in the gate and ten on my left look at hah fine filly by Habitat and fifteen on the rail and twenty fresh biddah. . . .'

Most people were not bidding by raising their catalogues, because the catalogue is about the size of *War and Peace*. Nor is this Europe's biggest sale: just the most prestigious. Lady Beaverbrook bought a rather sweet little thing: the filly's father was Mill Reef and her mother a daughter of Sea Bird II: lordly parentage indeed. She cost more than half a million.

But she did not look half a million pounds better than the horses knocked down for a few thousand. They all looked stunningly beautiful to me: all world-beaters. And as a certain fact, some of the cheaper horses will amaze and delight their new owners, just as some of the expensive ones will be a deathly disappointment. The rockets and the damp squibs look identical.

How can you tell the difference? John Dunlop was there feeling horses' legs. Feeling legs is something horse people do all the time: the mystic pass from knee to hoof is one of the many rituals of racing. Those load-bearing front legs are perhaps the most vital bit of the horse: if something goes wrong there, you can forget about racing. The great cable of the main tendon, the one that runs through the back of the horse's forelegs, is where the weight and power of the horse are absorbed as the horse touches down, and where the spring for the next stride comes from: if it feels as straight and as elastic as a guitar string, it feels like the leg of a racing animal.

But no one knows for certain, no one ever knows at a yearling sale. Every horse bought represents a colossal gamble. Not one of the yearlings at the Highflyer had ever been ridden: they had never been asked to do anything except walk. People come to the sales to buy a Formula One racing car, and make their decision on seeing it pushed in and out of the garage.

John Dunlop takes a look at every horse in the sale. Some he looks at longer and harder than others. I caught up with him as he made his progress around the stabling with his eldest son, Tim. They were working their way round with quiet method, and exchanging observations in racing cryptic with each other and politenesses with the stable staff. 'Thank you very much,' Dunlop observed to each stablehand, with his habitual courtesy, after each horse had been led from its box and walked up and down a few paces for his inspection. And then out of earshot the two compared notes: 'Horrid little horse.'

'Completely cow-hocked.'

What they, and everybody else at the sales, were doing was looking for winners. Nothing less. You might find a horse that is bred 'unfashionably' but which gives you a certain zing: that will do for one owner who has a certain price limit. Another horse, bred in the purple, could be the one for an owner who has no limits to anything save his patience.

There are two methods Dunlop and the rest use to evaluate a yearling: breeding and conformation. Each is subject to an infinite number of variables and interpretations. But then almost everything in racing, as I was to learn throughout the year, is like that. There is only one thing in racing that is *not* like that:

you cannot argue about which horse passed the winning post first.

'Take a look at this one,' a bloodstock agent said to me. 'Typical in its way. Fabulously bred, rotten horse. Looks fabulous on paper. But you can't race bloody paper, can you?'

The second method is conformation: how you read the actual animal. All the clues you get are a long look at the animal standing still, a brief parade of the animal walking, and a little leg-feeling. You look for the heartroom of an athlete, a large gullet that indicates good breathing room, you want the legs to move in clean, straight lines at the walk, you look for a spring and a stretch in the step that might whisper dreams of victory in a year, or in two years.

And then you thank the stablehand, and make a hieroglyph in your programme, and then you walk away with the special Newmarket expressionless expression on your face. 'Didn't like that front leg.'

'Definitely dishing, wasn't he?'

There were more sales to come, sales in Ireland, and in the United States, more sales back in Newmarket. Owners are seeking dreams: and it is through the trainer they seek them. As the flat-racing season draws to a close in late autumn, the yearlings begin to arrive at the training stables: to be turned from gawky, uncoordinated youngsters into race-winning machines. If everything goes according to plan, that is; if the legion of possible disasters is somehow avoided.

Some of the Arab owners had sent nice-looking yearlings down to Castle Stables from the Highflyer, and some more from the States. These included a couple of fairly decent colts, a Caerleon colt with a white star on its forehead, and a Nureyev with a big white blaze. There was a sweetly pretty filly by Lomond.

They didn't have names yet, but that too was part of racing's pattern. If you want to talk to racing people about horses, and especially young horses, it is their pedigree, and particularly their sire, that you have to keep in mind. The top stallions are around for years: each racing animal they produce – and there will be around 40 in a good year – will have a different name. In Dunlop's yard, there are about 100 new yearlings to learn every year. And so, in any racing yard, the trainer and the lads will all talk about 'the Nureyev' and 'the Lomond filly'. Any lad who does not immediately tell you his horse's pedigree through three or four generations is almost certainly an impostor.

And the Lomond, the Nureyev, the Caerleon and the rest looked full of promise. In fact, by November, Dunlop had a stable that was just about filled with promise. Like just about every racing stable in the land.

3

JOHN DUNLOP IS renowned throughout racing for his honesty: 'the most upright man in the game', people kept telling me throughout the year I was with Castle Stables. How delightful it was, then, to learn that he had made his crucial move in racing by lying through his teeth.

He had read in *Sporting Life* that Gordon Smyth, the man who trained for the Duke and Duchess of Norfolk at Arundel, was looking for someone to work for him as an assistant trainer and secretary. Dunlop rang, and arranged to meet Smyth at the races. Smyth then explained that he had wanted someone who could do the paperwork: balance all the accounts, type all the letters, handle all the secretarial work, and also do the PAYE, which is always the dirtiest job in any business. And just as a young actor will tell anyone who asks that he can ride like a centaur, play the guitar like Segovia, sing like a linnet and fence like d'Artagnan, sequentially or, if necessary, all at the same time, Dunlop gave Smyth his great, confidence-giving smile and said: 'Oh yes. No problem.'

'I had never typed a letter in my life, nor written a business letter. I hadn't got a clue. I didn't even know what PAYE stood for, let alone how to do it. Shortly afterwards, someone in a pub told me how. I had a couple of typing lessons and told myself I would get by.'

If I am going to be indiscreet, I might as well continue, and reveal that Dunlop was born on 10 July 1939 and that his middle name is Leeper. His father was a country doctor, but also a racing man, a founder member of Chepstow racecourse.

Dunlop is an Ulsterman by descent, and he did his National Service in the Royal Ulster Rifles. When that was all over, he decided that his future lay in racing: however, he did absolutely nothing about it. He sat about at home doing nothing. Still, we all of us need some kind of momentum to get going: and, in truth, it was to be the last time he took it easy in his life. Finally, bored by inactivity and badgered by his mother, he put an ad in the *Sporting Life*. It told the world he was young, loved racing, and was prepared to do any job in the sport. Never mind about the money.

He got ten replies, and, with his bluff well and truly called, he went off to work for Neville Dent in the New Forest. He lived in a caravan, looked after – 'did' in racing talk – four horses a day, drove the horse-box, ferried about a disreputable stallion to visit mares of equivocal reputation, did quite a lot of everything else that had to be done, and got paid fourpence a week or so for doing it. And it was great and wonderful and marvellous and everything else: the more work there was, the more Dunlop wanted to do it. Racing had claimed him utterly.

At Dent's he had the rootsiest job imaginable, a job that gave him all the street cred, or stable cred, a man could wish for. But after a couple of years, it was time to put the stable cred to better use: Dunlop was, and is, an ambitious man. He was ready for a step up, and his chance came when he joined Smyth as his PAYE wizard. He went to Arundel, where Smyth was training 30 or 40 horses, and was energetic enough to find time for plenty of genuine assistant work as well as avoiding the more horrific errors with the accounting.

By the time Dunlop was 27, Smyth decided it was time to move on, which on the face of it was rather a blow for Dunlop.

But, to his immense surprise, Dunlop was offered the chance to take over the trainer's licence. The Duke and Duchess thought he might have the potential to bring some success from the string of horses that they and their friends owned. They felt he might be able to maintain the standards that had been set: I suppose, on the whole, and taking one thing with another, you might say he has succeeded.

For he is unquestionably a first-division trainer now. He had 119 winners in 1986, more than any other trainer in Britain. He was Britain's top foreign raider, with 13 of these winners overseas. He also trained more horses than any other trainer that season: he kept the strength up to around the 200 mark. The total prize money in the season was £1,315,085, the third highest total among British trainers. He won the Scottish, Welsh and Italian Derbys, a handsome collection of Group Two races and, to his considerable pleasure, he won the St Leger, the autumn Classic, with Moon Madness. 'Nice to show one is still around and still capable of training a Classic winner,' he said. He may be an Ulsterman by descent, but the English habit of understatement is, as I was to learn, an essential part of his method. 'Quite nice', 'fairly pleasing', and 'acceptable' are the Dunlopian locutions for 'over the moon'; 'rather disappointing' and 'not quite what one had hoped for' mean 'sick as a parrot'.

'Especially pleasing to train a Classic winner for the Duchess,' Dunlop added. The Duchess is Lavinia, dowager Duchess of Norfolk, and widow of the late Duke Bernard, for whom Smyth trained, and for whom Dunlop trained when he took over the Castle Stables licence as a 27-year-old. At the start Dunlop was a private trainer. The Norfolks had long been great racing people, and they had for years employed a private trainer to look after their horses, and the horses of a few select friends. Dunlop began as a salaried employee of the Norfolks. His accounts all went through the Castle books, any new owners had to be approved by the Duke and Duchess.

But times change, and owning and training racehorses has got more and more expensive 'in real terms' as the business pages say. Overheads get higher all the time: well, the simple way to bring these down is to expand: the simple way to bring overheads down a lot is to expand hugely. Ideas that simply terrify the life out of most people, but there is a certain force about Dunlop that carries conviction.

He is now a public trainer. He has a vast string of horses. His vast string of owners includes aristocrats, businessmen, Italians and, naturally, Arabs. Dunlop was, in fact, the first man in Britain to train for the Arabs. It was he who introduced the Maktoums to the delights of winning races on English turf, something that has been an addiction to them ever since.

Dunlop is a tenant of both the Duchess Lavinia and of the present Duke: he rents stables, gallops, and estate cottages for his staff. The training grounds are grander than you would believe possible: they lie within the enormous, sumptuous rolling green of Arundel Park. The Park is built on a hill, and you can see for miles all around: that, of course, is why the castle was built there in the first place.

It is all much grander than Newmarket, and there is none of the queueing up for the gallops and the canters that is so much a part of Newmarket life. The downside, of course, is that Dunlop has to maintain the gallops himself; in Newmarket the owners pay 'Heath Tax' to the Jockey Club, who do all the maintenance.

But the facilities for training at Arundel are pretty wonderful: the gallops climb a steep slope in the great tree-filled park, the castle, a folly, and the giant, incongruous cathedral make the backdrops, the indoor and outdoor exercising rings are always available: it feels as if it had been a training centre for centuries, instead of 30-odd years.

But Arundel is a major training centre now, no shadow of a doubt. In 1978, Dunlop trained Shirley Heights here, to win the Derby and then the Irish Derby. The horse won both races by a combined total of two feet: the most important 24 inches in Dunlop's life. A horse called Hawaiian Sound was second at Epsom and third at the Curragh: I remember this because I backed Hawaiian Sound on each occasion. Hawaiian Sound is standing at stud with some obscurity in North America: Shirley Heights is one of the most expensive and sought-after sires in Britain. 'If those two feet had gone the other way, Shirley Heights would probably be standing in New Zealand or somewhere,' Dunlop said. 'But in fact he was a very, very good horse – better than he showed in either of his Derby wins.'

This is a classic illustration of the one thing that matters in racing, that thing being winning. 'This is a numbers game all right,' Dunlop said. 'The more horses you train, the more winners you are likely to get, the more *good* winners you are likely to get.' The evidence of the 1986 season gave all the support you could wish to this theory.

And bearing out this belief has turned Dunlop into a kind of Chinese plate-spinner: a man with an unbelievable number of concerns going on at the same time, all needing more or less constant attention. He has 200 horses, more than 100 owners, just under 100 lads, two assistant trainers, two pupil assistants, five head lads, four travelling head lads, four secretaries, and one bookkeeper. The bookkeeper does the PAYE.

Findon, Dunlop's second yard, a few miles down the road, where Ryan Price used to train, is looked after by a manager and two more head lads. This is used as an overflow, and a place for horses out of full work: the backward horses, the injured, those a touch under the weather. In theory all those at Castle Stables are in full work and capable of running in races. There are particularly good gallops at Findon: every now and then Dunlop will send a few Arundel horses for a gallop there; the break in routine often sharpens them up a treat.

It is an enormous concern, and it takes a man with a card-index mind to keep it all working. I am reminded of my first visit to Castle Stables, when I went down to explain my ambition of writing a book. I was prepared to talk for hours about it. 'I want to write about a year in a racing stable, Mr Dunlop. I want to write about how the industry works.'

He considered for a moment. 'I see. I think it would be good for racing. I'll do it.' If this creates an impression of decisiveness and mental clarity, then that impression is absolutely spot on.

There is a line in Anthony Powell that always reminds me of John Dunlop: 'His face bore that look of sadness with which you associate people accustomed throughout their lives to the boundless unreliability of horses.' Unreliability: this is the curse and the fascination of anything to do with horses, whether you are riding in a dressage test, having a quid on Dunlop's horse in the Derby, or controlling the destinities of the 15 million quid's worth at Castle Stables.

For it is not the love of gain that keeps the racing man in the game. The punter in the shop is linked to Dunlop out on the gallops by the same fascination with the magical, mysterious imponderables of horses. Things go wrong all the time, every day, but every so often they go wonderfully, gloriously right. Horses are enthralling and totally addictive; horses have the power to attract the snobbish and the merely wealthy, just as they have the power to make more than half the nation have a bet on the Derby. Racing is about money and power and snobbery, there is no escaping that fact, but the whole ridiculous business is not *based* on such things. It starts in the horse: in the boundless, glorious and addictive unreliability of the horse.

4

THE ARRIVAL OF the yearlings towards the end of the season changes the mood in the yard completely. There are generally a good few races still to be won, but the new intake brings with it a set of different tasks and a set of different hopes. When the yearlings started to arrive in the autumn of 1986, the 1987 season was already beginning. They came from the sales, from various private deals, some directly from private studs, and they got to Castle Stables during the final weeks of the racing season and the first few weeks of the close season.

As the 1986 season wound down, many of the fillies left the yard 'on their holidays' as the lads put it: they were sent away from the yard to be turned out in a field during the day at a stud farm, strolling about, picking at the grass, and enjoying the change of rhythm and the relaxation away from the stresses of training.

It would be nice to do the same with the colts, but it doesn't work. If you turn a bunch of colts out together, they get stroppy, pick fights, and end up hurting each other. So the colts stayed in the training yard, doing exercise designed to keep them ticking over and in good heart as the feed and good care put on the muscle and aided the growing bones.

The last few weeks of every year are all about the yearlings. Every year a new wave of hope is set in motion with these unnamed little dream-bearers, the Nureyev colt and the little Lomond filly and the rest of them. In an unsuccessful year, they mean a fresh start; in a year full of winners they bring hopes of plenty more of the same. The yard began the job of preparing them for the great leap forward, the day when they are ridden for the first time, and for the still more momentous event when, if things went well, they would actually race. For most of them, this would happen sometime during the next racing season, when they would be two-year-olds. But right now, they were half-ton, million-quid babies, and they didn't know the first thing about anything.

And so the yard set about the task of 'breaking them' as the rather cruel jargon has it. It sounds a brutal procedure, but, naturally, you do not get terribly far with thoroughbred horses if you start brutalizing them. Castle Stables has a special team of experienced lads to break in the yearlings: it is a tough and ticklish job. You want a lad who knows when to be gentle and when to be a bit of a bully: such people are a major asset for David Kitcher. Kitcher is one of John Dunlop's five head lads. The autumn is his busy time, because he is also in charge of the yearling team.

The first step is to get a bit into the horse's mouth: a breaking bit is gentle and jangly: it gives the horse something to mouth and fidget with, something that accustoms him to feeling something in his mouth. One of the breaking team will walk behind him, holding him with reins about ten feet long. The lad will look as if he is ploughing a field. Gradually he will teach the horse to lunge: that is, walk and trot in circles at the bidding of long reins. One of the reins will be tucked in behind the horse: it will be the first time the horse has felt pressure from behind, the first time he has been asked for real obedience from a human, and, naturally, some of them are pretty spooky about the business.

But the real Wild West bit comes when the horses are fitted with a roller for the first time. A roller is simply a piece of padding that fits round where the saddle will go in the fullness of time, but they don't like it a bit. They go completely crazy, bucking and rearing and doing anything they can think of to get rid of the horrible thing. But there is no shifting it. They are stuck with it for the next 24 hours; it remains strapped on as they eat and as they sleep. In the end, according to theory, they should be completely used to it. Needless to say, many remain deeply suspicious about the idea. They will remain 'cold-backed' for days, or weeks, which means they will play up every time you put on a roller or, later, a saddle. 'Oh, I've had some awkward ones,' Kitcher said. 'But it's never been impossible. Some you just have to give more time to. Some will play about a good bit, but they always come. In the end, they always come.'

Once they have accepted the roller, they are asked to lunge in it. After a while, the roller is swapped for a saddle, but nobody sits in it just yet. Everything is done softly-softly. All horse people know that when you take six steps forward, you generally have to take five steps back: nothing happens quickly. If you get impatient with horses, you have no place in the horse business. Patience is the cardinal virtue for a trainer and for a lad; that and understanding. Such virtues are important for all horse people, but they are doubly desirable in racing: racehorses are just not bred to be charming, placid beasts. Charm and placidity are not the qualities that win races. A difficult horse might be difficult because of his champion's temperament. On the other hand, he might possess those qualities because he is just a bit of a sod, and talentless to boot. There is no telling, not yet.

When you have a horse that is more or less happy being lunged in its saddle, you move on to the pretty stage: you take your horse walking in Arundel Park. Each horse is taken out on its own, with no distractions, with a lad walking behind and guiding him gently and tactfully with the long reins. Past the folly, along the avenues of magnificent trees, in the windblown autumn. Raymond Baker has been a member of the yearling team since 1951: 'Done 'em all, Shirley Heights, Snaafi Dancer, the lot. And I'll tell you something, they're a lot better today than they used to be. They've all seen more, been handled more, they've got more used to people. They are a lot less wild. But really I don't mind if they're not all good – I like to see a horse with a bit of spirit to it. I like 'em to have a nice scream and a roar.'

It is at this time of the year that everyone in the yearling team gives thanks that he does not work in Newmarket: Newmarket, with more than 2,000 horses in training at more than 40 training establishments, all of them sharing the same training grounds. You want a yearling to settle down, to relax, to acquire confidence: the fewer distractions he has, the better. Newmarket is a town of spooking horses: if one spooks, they all spook: the herd instinct is based on the principle of safety in numbers.

When you are bringing on a yearling, you find safety in solitude and quiet. Every member of Dunlop's yearling team walks for miles around the empty, rolling spaces of Arundel Park, with his charge slowly getting used to moving at the prompting of some invisible being behind him.

At this stage, the invisible being is still walking like a ploughman. But soon he will be sitting on top. The horse is taught to get used to the idea of feeling a little weight on his back: in the box, his lad will start to lean across him, and to half-lie across his back. The horses get more used to humans every day, and to the weird things that humans do to them: by this time, with a bit of luck, the horse will take this latest oddity without worrying too much about it.

And then, finally, we come to the exciting bit: when a rider sits on a horse for the first time, and gently, gingerly takes up the reins. It is normally about two weeks from the circus act with the roller to the quiet, dignified moment when the animal is first ridden. The performance varies as much as the horses vary, but it normally happens in a quiet, almost anticlimactic manner. If the horse takes this latest event in his stride, then it shows that all the work of preparation has been done to perfection. And that you have a particularly nice horse.

The horses then get used to being ridden in the indoor

school, that aircraft hangar in the park. They slowly grow accustomed to trotting and to turning. They will never be required to learn the extravagant gymnastic turns of dressage horses, showjumpers and polo ponies: they must learn merely to find balance and rhythm as they work in shallow loops and generous circles. They learn to organize themselves, to keep count of their legs as they go around the corners, to listen to the rider. The rider's skill can help a horse immensely: a bad, unbalanced rider will throw a horse's balance out, a good one will help him to find it.

All this work is done under Kitcher's eye. The horses trot gently around him, getting used to being ridden, and getting used to working in large groups of horses, getting used, in fact, to being a racehorse in training. After a couple of weeks of this, they are allowed outside again: this time not with a ploughman, but a real rider. For the first time, they are treated like grown-up horses. They trot up the long cantering paths – at least, they are supposed to trot, though many want to try disorganized canters and sprawly gallops until dissuaded by their riders. A further fortnight on, they will be performing manoeuvres out in the park, trotting in circles and S-bends. The horse is learning to handle himself, learning the essentials of balance, learning basic obedience. But only basic obedience is required. Races are won with a flying atavistic gallop: you do not want to school that out of a horse.

As the yearlings were going through their hoops, Dunlop and Kitcher were sizing them up, already looking for next year's winners, for the Derby hope of two years hence. 'There are some that stick out from day one,' Kitcher said. 'Some that always look nice movers. But you don't know, you see. You really don't know. They come in real scrawny, and by the time they are two-year-olds, they are like a different horse. You might like one right from the start – you never really know, not till you get them out on the racetrack.'

Which brings me, inevitably, to Snaafi Dancer. After Shirley Heights, he is, perhaps, the most famous horse to have been trained at Castle Stables. In its way, the Snaafi Dancer saga is the classic racing story of all time. The horse arrived in a fanfare of trumpets: at the time it was the most expensive yearling ever bought. It was bought by Sheikh Mohammed and it cost an unbelievable $10.2 million. It was the prestige horse, the horse to send a reputation soaring.

There was one slight problem. The horse was useless. 'Rather a sweet little horse, actually,' Dunlop said. 'But unfortunately no bloody good.'

Jeremy Noseda, Dunlop's number three, said: 'The older he got, the worse-looking he got. In fact, even when he arrived he didn't look *that* good. And by spring he was a horrible-looking brute.'

'Mind you,' Kitcher said, 'Moon Madness didn't look much as a yearling. You wouldn't say, there's a nice-looking horse. But he just grew into it, until he became a lovely-looking horse.'

'Everyone I've spoken to said Shirley Heights was the most scrawny-looking thing,' Noseda said. 'No one wanted to do him.'

'Well, he didn't have the best of characters,' Kitcher said. 'He was moody, he had a fillyish sort of a temperament. He messed about all the time. Never wanted to do much. But he just had this engine in him.'

'And Snaafi Dancer didn't,' I said.

'He didn't. We realized that very early on,' Noseda said. 'On the canters, he never looked good. We said, oh, he's just lazy; when he's working, he'll show us something. Then he had problems with his feet. Then he started galloping, and he showed nothing. You'd try to convince yourself that one day he'd spark, we all did. The amount of things he had wrong with him, it was unbelievable. He was club-footed, then he got cow-hocked. He had little ears and horrible eyes.'

'Horses are so seldom black and white,' Dunlop said later. 'There is always hope. But after his first winter Snaafi Dancer really was bitterly disappointing. The writing was on the wall by spring.'

'There don't seem to be any rules in this game,' I said.

'That there are not. No rules, absolutely no rules where horses are concerned. A lot of people think there are. Horses will always give these people a very nasty shock.'

Snaafi Dancer never saw a racetrack. He just didn't like galloping. Eventually he went to stud. But there was only one thing wrong. Snaafi Dancer didn't like mares either. No rules.

5

THERE ARE LIKELY to be 500 or so tubes of Polos in John Dunlop's office at any one time. They are, of course, for the horses. Feeding Polos to 150 horses every day is perhaps the crucial part of Dunlop's life. He will pay a visit to every horse he has at Arundel, slap 150 necks, feel 300 forelegs, and, as the scent of horse and mint mingle, he will have a few words with every lad about every horse. Training is, literally, a hands-on business: every day, if he is not at the sales or the races, Dunlop will touch every one of his charges, and give each one a treat at the same time.

So will just about every trainer in the country. This is one of racing's many rituals, racing's Vespers, if you like: it is called 'evening stables'. The lads knock off at noon, and return at four to prepare both their horses for inspection. Every horse gets a cleaning and a brushing and a grooming of great vigour and fastidiousness, and the lads stand by them as Dunlop ambles his way around from box to box and from yard to yard of his enormous acreage of horses. 'Tommy, how's the big fella?'

'Pretty good, governor.'

'Eating up?'

'Left half a bowl, governor.' Crunch-crunch: the smell of Polo mints filled the box.

'Hm.'

Racehorses are built for speed. Their extreme breeding makes them a little bit more prone to the horsy problems that are a daily part of every horse person's life. But in racing every little niggle is a possible disaster: in the racing season, a tiny touch of not-quite-rightness can mean a race lost, and a reputation squandered.

But horses are never considerate enough to explain where it hurts. Trainers and vets have to work it out from various clues the horse might give you: one of the best of these is food. Horses are creatures of habit and love routine. Some will always eat everything put in front of them, some will always leave a little. If the big eater starts leaving a little, or the smaller eater starts leaving more, then you know that the horse is not fully content. Accordingly, trainers have an obsessive interest in their horses' appetites, and all of them love best a 'good doer', a horse that scoffs the lot and visibly puts on condition as a result.

'All right, all right, just because you won a Classic, you think you deserve all the Polos, do you?' Moon Madness was looking as contented and as sound as any trainer could wish as the flat season approached ever closer. Dunlop is not a sentimental man, but he talks to his horses just as often as any little girl in the Pony Club. So do the lads. So do I, come to that. So does everyone connected with horses, and it drives lay people crazy. As soon as a horsy person gets anywhere near a horse, he starts spouting the most incredible load of horsy drivel: now then old chap, and all the rest. Pass the sickbag, say outsiders, and who can blame them?

But believe it or not, there is a very good reason for all this. If you walk silently into a horse's box, you will make him jump, quite literally. You don't really want half a ton of horse leaping about in a small box: you could get hurt and, far more importantly, as horsy people say, so could the horse. And so you advertise your presence with a few ill-chosen words of horsy drivel. Hallo mate and how is the boy today. . . .

Dunlop passed his hand down Moon Madness's legs, more for satisfaction than from worry. Moon Madness was staying on in training after winning his Classic as a three-year-old. People who love the sport always like to see a good horse stay on in training as a four-year-old: so many times, Derby winners have been snatched out to stud before the sweat of Epsom has dried on their backs. There were several good reasons for keeping Moon Madness going, the first and the best being that his owner, the Duchess Lavinia, is a sporty lady who loves more than anything to see her horses run. There is also the point that Moon Madness's pedigree is about as unfashionable as you could wish: even after his triumph, you probably couldn't get more than quarter of a million for him. When you consider that Derby winners go for millions, this is pretty small beer.

'Of course, the traditional thing to do with a Leger winner is to make him a Cup horse, run him at two miles plus, and aim him at the Ascot Gold Cup. But I don't think he's that sort of horse. I think he's a mile-and-a-half horse. He might be difficult to place, in fact, because he might just not be the *very* top.'

The top mile-and-a-half race of the year is the King George VI and Queen Elizabeth Diamond Stakes. It is often the best race of the season; the three-year-old Classic winners are raced against the older horses, and for a vast prize. The previous year had seen a famous battle in which the Derby winner Shahrastani took on another three-year-old, the great Dancing Brave, and lost.

'We could go for the Diamonds, if there is not the opposition. That would be my thought. Most of his contemporaries have gone to stud, like Shahrastani and Dancing Brave. We'll have to see.'

We were now in February: the two-year-olds had all learned to be ridden, and to accept this with reasonably good grace. They had all learned to stop and to go (guess which is easier to teach). They had learned to go left and right. And most important of all, they had learned the routine of stable life: the morning exercise, the fidgety snooze throughout the afternoon, the feeds, the teatime assault with the body brush, the Polos to follow at evening stables. And after the long night comes the early morning out in the park again, where the horses were now working in long canters.

Some take to the cantering naturally and quickly, showing strong and confident paces. Such precocious animals delight everyone in the yard. But others will have more growing to do, more organizing of themselves to accomplish. Some take a lot longer than others to get fit, and in February will still get knackered after a five-furlong canter. Some grow late, some just carry on growing for longer. All of them, the backward and the forward animals, need someone who can read their state of forwardness or backwardness: it is easy to damage the soft growing bones and those pretty little legs.

'Yes, I think he might be a two-year-old,' Dunlop is wont to say, as he talks to owners agog for news of their babe. I know this sounds a nonsense, all the young horses are two-year-olds now. Dunlop is discussing their chances of running and winning a race as a two-year-old, in the season that is almost upon us.

'OK, keep the bandages on. We'll just walk him tomorrow.' And on to the next horse, Polos in hand. 'Jenny, how's the mare?'

'Pretty good, governor.'

'How did she feel this morning?' Dunlop was squatting at the mare's feet, feeling for heat in the legs, which would indicate that there was something still amiss.

'All right, governor. Felt sound all round.'

So many horses, and so many things that can go wrong with them. So many things that are constantly changing with every horse. Dunlop is playing a 15-million quid version of Kim's game, with 200 items on the tray to memorize. And to make things more difficult still, there is little continuity in the game: every autumn, Castle Stables has its great comings and goings: a hundred new horses arrive, all with their constantly changing quirks and ailments.

'In jump racing, they all love the sense of contuinuity,'

Dunlop said. 'Every season, it's the same old names again and again. I can understand the way they feel. But I don't share it. If you have a middle-rate horse, then it is likely to be a middle-rate horse all its life. But here is a yard full of two-year-old horses, and I know that it is possible – it is not *likely* but it is unquestionably possible – that one of them, almost any one of them, could be the greatest horse that has ever set foot on a racetrack. You know that almost certainly this will not be the case. But you cannot say it is impossible.'

And as the two-year-olds strengthen and grow, and chill February shows its first signs of submission to spring, it is no wonder that the blood of everyone connected with flat racing starts to quicken. The boring bit of the winter is over. Somewhere out there – and this is a certainty – there is a horse that will win the Derby. And there are the horses that will win the Oaks, and the Guineas, and the St Leger, and the King George . . . and the horse that will complete Raymond Baker's 10p Yankee. . . .

Evening stables ended, and Dunlop and I retired for a warming glassful. The lads had buckled their horses' rugs on again, and departed for homes and pubs. The stable settled down for the night, still smelling faintly of the horses' minty breath. And perhaps one of the Polo-eaters really was the greatest racehorse that ever lived. We would learn soon enough.

6

MARCH: SPRING WAS a promise, but not much more. Racing was a certainty: the season was due to begin on 26 March. John Dunlop was beginning to look for racing fitness among his horses. Out on the gallops, things had stepped up a gear: Arundel Park was a place of real purpose of a morning now.

And in bud in the sharp, still chill mornings the park looked prettier than ever: rolling, sculpted countryside, England tamed but still left with plenty of wildness in it, a good model for a racehorse.

The horses move out into the park at around seven every morning. On a ship, the time is in watches, in a racing stable it is in lots: I'll see you before first lot; I should be there sometime after second lot. The first lot is mostly the older horses, though the 'older' in racing still doesn't mean terribly ancient. Most of them are three-year-olds: Love The Groom, the possible Derby horse, Three Tails, the rather good filly, and the rest. There are a few four-year-olds, with Moon Madness easily the pick of the bunch, whose task each morning is to brighten the Duchess's day. And there are a few five-year-olds, like Efisio, the stable's leading eccentric, and good ol' reliable Patriach, who won the Royal Hunt Cup the previous season.

The second lot goes out at around ten, and is mostly the nameless two-year-olds: the Caerleon, the Shirley Heights colt and the rest. (Actually, they have all been given names by now, but no one at Castle Stables is using them yet.) Each lot is sent out by brusque commands through the tannoy: 'Ride away now! Ride away!' and the horses clip and clop and skitter their way across the stable yard and into the park, the odd one trying to run away at once, the odd one throwing in a few bucks to keep his lad warm.

Arundel Park is more famous for cricket than it is for horses. The last but one Duke caused a gorgeous cricket ground to be built in the park, and every year the touring Test team plays its first match there, against a side gathered from all over the place and called Lavinia, Duchess of Norfolk's XI. It is beside the cricket pitch that the horses first gather, in a wooden 'O' roughly made with post and rail, and there they walk in circles for 15 minutes or so. You don't take a horse from his stables and gallop him straight away, no matter how much the horse himself might fancy the idea, any more than Sebastian Coe will hop out of bed, run a mile and go back to bed four minutes later. Athletes warm up and warm down before and after training; they do so with great care and circumspection, doing everything they can to avoid pulls, stretches and tears to the muscles. And if a race-horse is not an athlete, I don't know what is.

The horses are taken through a good long period of walking, followed by a solid piece of trotting work. In fact, as the start of the season loomed close, Dunlop decided that after 20 years he was going to change his routine. He decided to give all his horses an extra trot, taking them all up a good long sand canter. The more warm-up you give a horse, the better it should be for him.

After the trotting comes the cantering. The horses set off, in groups of four or five, and bowl along the cantering path. This is woodchip, laid and maintained by Dunlop, though not with his own hand. It is supposed to be an all-weather surface, but for that, as we know, we must read most-weather surface. Dunlop watches all the horses go by with great attention. Normally he does so from the back of his hack, or work-horse. The hack does not have a name, he is just called 'the hack'. Dunlop gets on him and gets off him. The hack. Dunlop is not a sentimental sort of chap. (Chris Beavis, the lad who does 'the hack', calls him Charlie. Beavis, in fact, is the only person at Castle Stables –probably in the entire racing industry – who makes Dunlop look idle. Beavis gets to the stables around five, and does not leave until late evening. In the depths of winter when the snow made the roads impossible for his gallant little Honda 50, he made a train journey from home to stable and walked four miles a day to and from stations. Beavis simply loves working and being with horses. The hack is a lucky horse.)

When he has visiting owners, Dunlop leaves the hack in his box and drives them across the grass in a big Mitsubishi Range Rover thing. I spent many mornings of the year swooping across the grass and bouncing along the avenues in the machine with Dunlop explaining the mysteries of his craft as we went. By the time the March weather was showing signs of promise, I could think of nothing better in the world than leaning against the parked Range Rover and watching the cantering horses go past, the great lines of trees behind them. Some of the horses relax and settle into a good economical rhythm, others fight like mad for their heads and try to set world records. 'This one,' Dunlop said, 'never does anything but try to run away. And when you let him, he doesn't go terribly fast.'

Tim Dunlop, John Dunlop's eldest son, was riding out that day. He was working in a merchant bank for a while, and was not enjoying it overmuch. All he wanted to do was train race-horses. Sergeyevich went past; he seemed to be with the younger horses that morning. He cantered by coolly enough, but spoiled his looks by letting his tongue hang out, a particularly undignified habit some horses have. The Nureyev colt stood out, as always, because of his big white face, and he was beginning to look really quite promising.

'Here's a nice filly by Lomond,' Dunlop said. 'I'm really rather pleased with her.'

'She's a beauty,' I said as the devastatingly pretty bay cantered by. 'What's her name?'

A pause. Then Dunlop said disconcertingly: 'I don't know. I can't remember.'

I laughed. 'I thought you knew everything.'

'Well, your illusions are shattered.'

They go past in their small groups to guard against the well-known domino effect of horses in large groups. If one horse starts racing, they all start: if you started with 70 horses cantering in a line, you would end up with the charge of the light brigade. With small groups, you have a chance of getting them to canter decently, and of stopping them at the top. There, you find another ring for walking the horses. Here, you will see one of the most important parts of the training process. But it doesn't look like this, it all looks terribly casual and arbitrary. 'How did he feel, Chris?'

'Still a bit thick in his wind, governor.'

'That'll do, then. Scobie, he looked fine.'

'Very well-behaved, governor.'

'Give him another canter then. Eileen, that didn't look too good.'

'Didn't seem right at all, governor.'

'All right, cricket pitch tomorrow, and that'll do today.'

Those consigned to the cricket pitch are restricted to walking exercise. If you detect a hint of lameness, a fraction of off-colour, then the first thing to do is to take the horse away from the stress of hard training. Those that need or that flourish with further training will get a second canter. Some horses need to do more work than others to get and to stay fit. Some seem to thrive on as much work as you can give them, others will find too much training stressful and distressing, and will lose condition if they are made to do it. Knowing which horse needs what, and when, is one of the great arts of the business: with 200 horses, this takes some doing. But Dunlop can recognize every horse in his yard when it is walking away from him in thick mist. And he will recognize the lad, too, and call him by his right name.

Stable lads all work terribly hard, but they only call it Work on Tuesdays and Fridays. These are nothing less than Work Days. Work, in a racing stable, means galloping. Sebastian Coe doesn't go for the burn every day, and equine athletes don't seek to bust world records every day, either.

'The horses can tell when it's a Tuesday or a Friday,' said Chris Blyth, one of the lads. 'They seem to have a clock in their heads. You jump on their backs on a Friday and you feel a little bit extra in them as soon as you walk out of the yard.'

The most important part of a racing stable's work is Work. It is through Work that a horse's abilities and its racing fitness are worked out. It is the nearest a horse gets to showing its true ability outside a racecourse. But all the same, a horse is not galloped flat out. The Work is good and brisk, and pretty demanding, to be sure, but there is absolutely no point in draining the horse to the depths to see how much it has got in its tank. Save that for when it really matters.

Again, it is a matter of doing all you can to avoid stressing and straining the horse. A horse that races at two miles will never be asked to gallop two miles at home. He will do his five or six furlongs like everybody else. Work is not a racing trial, it is a preparation for racing.

Dunlop traditionally starts the season fairly gingerly. Arundel is on the edge of the downs, but it is not real downland, and it doesn't drain like downland. And there are a few clay pockets, too, which always make for trouble: galloping through clay wrenches legs and lames horses. The ground is not good enough at the beginning of the year for real fast Work, and consequently, as the season began, Dunlop was not expecting to go out and set the track ablaze in March. Autumn, though, is a different matter: work up to it and crash them all into the winner's circle in the autumn, that is Dunlop's racing rhythm.

Because of this, he is doubly tender with the two-year-olds. They were not even galloping, or Working, as yet. Instead they were doing a double canter three times a week. But the three-year-olds were beginning to come into stronger Work, and the entries for the early season races had been made. They do their

Work in pairs, and the idea is to assess one horse against the other. One rider may be told to work alongside another horse that is known to be a slower animal, and then to pull away at a certain point: if he does so easily, then all is as it should be. If he fails, then maybe the horse is not as good as was thought. On the other hand, maybe the other horse is better ... heigho. Here we are again, back in the land of imponderables, the heartland of the horseman. If there was a horse that was always consistent, always ran the same way at the same speed, a warm-blooded pacing machine, then every trainer in the land would want him. A horse that is a known quantity against which all horses can be measured empirically would be the answer to a trainer's prayer ... but such a horse does not exist.

But the horses were Working their way to fitness, and as the racing season came upon us, some of them were fit enough to take their chance on the racetrack. These would all be better, fitter and sharper for the race: that is part of the point in running them. But things don't always go according to plan: on the fifth day of the season, and impossibly early by all Castle Stables traditions, Darley Knight won a race at Folkestone. It was the first score on the board for Dunlop's yard. Pat Eddery had the ride, and took the horse to the total of £684 in prize money. Castle Stables had won more than a million in the previous year, remember. But the horses were off and running and a winner is, yes, always a winner. The business is about winning and Castle Stables were back in business.

7

RACING PEOPLE ARE not great ones for nostalgia, on the whole. It is always the next race that matters, not the wonderful race this time last year. But as Castle Stables started the season with a modest little bang, it was impossible not to look back at the previous season and wonder if it was possible to equal it – or go beyond it.

For sometimes, even in racing, hard work will be rewarded, and the carefully laid plans will all work. But everyone in racing works hard and everyone in racing has plans, plans by the dozen, a bewildering, shifting succession of targets and intricately thought-out schemes. All you need to realize them, apart from all the hard work, is a lorry-load of luck.

But if John Dunlop had written his script for 1986, with sober ambitions and attainable goals – not asking to win all five Classics and the Arc and the Diamonds besides – then 1986 is more or less exactly what he would have asked for. It was a season of immense solidity. There was nothing stunningly spectacular or glamorous; it was a year that started slowly and built up into a record of unrelenting achievement.

Paul Coombes, one of the lads, summed it up: 'The governor, he's always slow to get going. But by heck, he comes on at the end.' Autumn is Dunlop's season of mellow fruitfulness, and he led a stirring charge in the later part of the '86 season to rattle past the hundred winners and the million quid in prize money. Moon Madness, winning the autumn Classic, was the perfectly arranged high point of the season. 'After the '85 season, when I had the most awful problem with the virus, I did rather need a good year,' Dunlop said. 'And fortunately we were more or less free of any virus problem.' Dunlop won more races and more prize money than ever before: you cannot really argue with a season like that.

'Historically, we always have had a good end to the year. This is because I don't bring the two-year-olds on fast early in the season. I follow a policy of bringing them on much more slowly than many stables.' And in they all pinged in the last third of the season: the luck and the hard work combining to perfection.

Overall, the year was a great achievement. But apart from splendid old Moon Madness, it was a year without stars. 'There were two two-year-olds which I thought might achieve something startling. But they didn't. They both won ... but I'm afraid neither of them could be described as startling.'

The horses were Love The Groom and Arabian Sheikh, now both thundering up the gallops and looking, perhaps, for startling achievements as three-year-olds. Both had a run in the Futurity, the big mile race that comes at the right end of the season for Castle Stables. But one was third and one was fifth, and no one was startled. The race was won by a promising looking thing called Reference Point. 'I was slightly disappointed that mine didn't do just a bit more. Both had run only twice before in their lives, and they were running against more experienced horses. So I must say that, as we stand, they are both possible Classic contenders.'

Sanam made an uncharacteristic early strike for the stable in the 1986 season. He was given an early chance because he was behaving so appallingly at home: 'I thought a race might give him something to think about.' He won a decent race in Ireland, and then won the only Italian Group One race for two-year-olds, and won it well. 'So he was champion two-year-old in

Italy – and just how that relates to the top two-year-olds in England is difficult to assess.'

A nice filly called Three Tails – rather a nice name, too – became Italy's top two-year-old filly, so Dunlop had the top colt and the top filly in Italy. 'But for England, we do not have an obvious Classic horse. The general feeling is that last year's was not a particularly good crop of two-year-olds. That is, of the ones that have run. In England, they were unexceptional; in Ireland, they seemed to be worse. Now, it is true that a moderate two-year-old *can* be an exceptional three-year-old . . . but I think if we do have something exceptional as a three-year-old, it will probably not have run at all, or if so, have been raced very lightly. But horses can always surprise you.'

'Do you have anything that might surprise, do you think?'

'I don't think I do, not that I can see right now. There is Wood Chanter, who is a full brother to Moon Madness. This time last year, Moon Madness had one run and finished fourth. But whether Wood Chanter is going to be as good as his brother – well, I rather doubt it.'

The end of every season is marked by a lot of coming and going: the yearlings come in, wide-eyed and snorting, and the older horses move on; the more glamorous colts go on to the pasha's life of a stallion at stud, many fillies become broodmares. The Horses in Training Sale is racing's annual used car auction. Some might be sold on to have another try at racing on the flat: there is scope here for picking up a real bargain. Also, the potential for disastrous speculation is enormous. Dunlop was particularly pleased to have sold on a horse called Final Try; it had won as a two-year-old and then had a very lean time as a three-year-old. He fetched 100,000 guineas, which was then the largest sum ever paid for a horse that was to go jumping. The horse went to Josh Gifford's yard, which, as it happens, is the one that overlooks Dunlop's second yard at Findon. Another horse went for 85,000 guineas, and was to go flat racing in Saudi.

Obviously, it is the owner and not the trainer who pockets these interesting sums. But the trainer picks up a little credit when a horse proves to have been a decent investment, and of course, the trainer is always hoping the owner will re-invest. Another horse, this one called Mister Wonderful, was sold back in August and went racing in California. This was one Dunlop was sad to see go: 'The thing is, we had a very good offer for him. He had won a Group race at Newmarket, perhaps a little fortunately, but he looked pretty good.

'But the thing is, it is very easy indeed *not* to sell a horse when you have a good offer. That happened with a horse called Efisio. He won stakes races at two, three and four. We had a good offer for him last July, and turned it down – and since then, the market has gradually declined. I think now that we made an error of judgement.' He gave a thinnish sort of smile. 'Happens now and again.'

Trainers give their advice to owners in varying amounts and degrees of warmth: it all depends on the owner's experience, depth of horsiness, financial constraints and general bloody-mindedness. 'Some owners are new to racing life, and need all the help they can get. Others have had horses for years. They know all the markets, and especially, they know all the pitfalls. You can devalue a horse so easily. Or you can increase its value dramatically if things go right. It all comes down to why the owner is in the game, and what his or her expectations are.'

A classic example of the selling dilemma came with Tommy Way. The horse won the Italian Derby, and then went on for a rather exotic coup in the Japan Cup, which is run in Tokyo. But he ran very disappointingly, and no one could understand why. When he got back to the stable, he was bleeding from the nose: it was obvious that he had burst a blood vessel. Some horses are prone to breaking blood vessels under the extreme stresses of racing: as you breed in speed, so you can breed in fragilities.

'We were left with three possibilities, and it was up to the owner to make the decision,' Dunlop said. 'We could sell him as best we could, over here. We could sell him to America, where he could race while being given the drug called Lasix, which is a coagulant. It is banned over here for racing, you see.

Or we could keep him in training, give him a winter's rest and hope the problem would sort itself out naturally.'

It is not hard to work out which is the biggest gamble. But that was the decision his owner, an Italian named Gezio Mazza, finally went for. Tommy Way remained in Dunlop's yard, and was now working up to a four-year-old campaign. He spent the winter at a stud, away from all the stresses of the training yard, and we would see in the coming season if he had grown out of the problem – or if keeping him in training was an expensive error.

There are some owners who always take the sporting option, always want to see their horses running, more than anything else in the world. Others cannot wait to maximize their investment. Robert Sangster, the mega-owner, acquired a bit of a reputation for whisking his horses out to stud with indecent haste. Golden Fleece, which won the Derby and never saw a racetrack again, is the most notorious example of profit-taking winning out over sporting instincts. Other owners, more romantic, less businesslike, have wanted to maximize not profit but glory. The Arab owners tend towards this view, and so, unquestionably, does Lavinia, Duchess of Norfolk. That is why Moon Madness was still out there blazing up the gallops.

But for Moon Madness, as for Love The Groom, Arabian Sheikh and Three Tails, and indeed, every horse in the yard, there really could be no clear fixed plans. Only hopes. The only certainty about any racing season is that it will not go in accordance with any fixed plans. If you read any trainer's pre-season predictions for his yard, and compare it with the actual results at the other end of the season, you find the most enormous divergence. Racing is, in fact, not amenable to prediction: which is, presumably, why there is a vast army of people professionally employed in trying to predict it. 'We'll have to see,' said Dunlop, when I pressed him further on his plans. 'We'll just have to see.'

8

W ITH ONE SUDDEN bound, spring was with us. It arrived just in time for the Craven Meeting at Newmarket: the meeting John Dunlop always sees as the real start to the season. He had prepared his two top three-year-old colts for the occasion: we would all have the chance to assess the Classic potential of Love The Groom and Arabian Sheikh. There was spring in the air and in everybody's step. Conditions were perfect for assessing Dunlop's horses against first division opposition.

Craven Stakes Day, 16 April, was the first bright and promising day of the season. All of racing seemed to be at Newmarket for the day, and to have left its coat in the car as well. The paddock was a mass of utterly boring grey suits topped by identical brown racing trilbies. The British passion for uniforms is a most curious thing. Only Henry Cecil, wearing a suit in the most painful shade of blue, seemed immune to it.

The lads have a different dress code. They wear a lucky suit, or a lucky, generally rather jolly pullover. Stable lads are, of course, on the small side: but for some reason their lucky suits are always smaller still. If you ever see a smallish person wearing a suit tightly buttoned across the chest, and with his wrists protruding in a businesslike fashion from the cuffs, you can be certain this is a stable lad on a racing day. Arabian Sheikh, led by Peter Sanderson, looked as nicely primed as a horse could be. Dunlop, his racing trilby worn over his eyebrows, gave Pat Eddery a leg up, and stalked off to watch the race from the trainers' eyrie. There were pretty decent things expected of Arabian Sheikh.

I had arranged to make contact with Dunlop after that race, but in the end I didn't make it. I didn't dare. In fact, I did the best I could to keep out of his way. For Arabian Sheikh ran an absolute stinker. Stone last. Tailed off. Never a factor in the race. The horse was a waste of time, a waste of space. It was a time for pinched expressions, pursed lips, and already, it was time to start re-thinking the plans for the coming season. The race was nothing less than a disaster.

I wondered about meeting Dunlop after Go Henri's race. It could not, I thought, be as much of a disaster as the last. And indeed, I was right – in so far as the race was not nearly as important, and Go Henri was not a horse from which anything spectacular was expected. All the same, Dunlop would have been happier had the horse not finished last. Two successive results like that are the sort of thing that starts rumours and prompts speculation: do you think there is something seriously amiss at Arundel then? Do you think he's got the virus again? I always said he was overstretched when he took on that second yard at Findon. If you ask me, he's made a balls of the pre-season work. Well, I think the real reason is that people just don't send him decent horses any more. . . .

Reputations go up and down like yoyos in racing: reputations of horses, reputations of people. In the space of a two-minute gallop, a jockey, a trainer, a horse can swing from 'brilliant' to 'useless'. Or go the other way. In a game full of intangibles, people will seize on anything that looks remotely like a fact. If enough people mutter that Dunlop isn't up to it any more, then owners will drift away, the best horses will get sent elsewhere, and only owners with third-rate horses will be left. And suddenly, all the results will be third rate. The trainer's skills, and his facilities, will be the same as ever, but just as the jockey can't go without the horse, nor can the trainer. In polo, the horses can turn on a sixpence. In racing, reputations can turn on a ha'porth of gossip.

After these two horrific last places, then, it follows that Dunlop was rather hoping that Love The Groom did not finish last. He was to turn out in the Craven Stakes, which is an important Classic trial for the emerging three-year-olds. The favourite was Ajdal, who was already a warm favourite for the 2,000 Guineas, and he was expected to enhance his reputation over the eight straight furlongs of Newmarket's perfect turf. I must say, Ajdal really did look a picture in the paddock: his price seemed to fall with every imperious stride around the parade ring. He was eventually sent out at 6–5, with Love The Groom 16–1. Love The Groom was not seriously expected to win, though it would be awfully pleasant if he did. But what Dunlop wanted, wanted very much indeed, was for the horse to put up a good show, for him to look the part of a Classic contender from a decent stable. The stalls banged open: Dunlop is not a man who goes in for heavy emotions, but he was certainly thinking pretty hard. Ajdal roared smoothly to the front: he cruised to victory looking a winner with every step of the race. But there was Love The Groom thundering along in his wake, outrun in a race that was too short for him anyway, and certainly not out-fought. He finished fast and fourth, and Dunlop finished a great deal easier in his mind.

For this was a good race by a horse that needed the race. It was a gutsy performance against the Newmarket horses, who were all noticeably more forward than the rest. It was a thoroughly decent run, and a giant-sized relief, too. Almaarad completed the day with a reasonable run in the fourth race, finishing eighth.

After that, I felt it was acceptable to make contact with Dunlop. We drank coffee – in fact, in the entire racing season, he did not once permit me to buy him a drink sort of drink at the races, refusing to live up to one's fantasies about champagne-guzzling trainers. With us was Paolo Benedetti, an Italian agent who acts for a number of Italian owners, including Gezio Mazza, owner of Tommy Way, and (take a breath here) Signora Veronica Gaucci del Bono, who owns Love The Groom. Signor Benedetti stood out in the crowd, he is even taller than Dunlop, and wore a suit that made the standard English racing suit look distinctly shabby – not actually the hardest thing in the world to do. He did not wear a racing trilby. Dunlop introduced him as‘ *Il maestro di Pisa*’, which betrayed his own excellent spirits. He wanted to talk about Love The Groom's race.

Dunlop, like most trainers, likes dealing with agents. Agents are less bound up than owners in their babe's progress, less blinded by love. It is important to try for cold realism in racing, even if few people ever actually achieve it. Agents are always fully understanding of a trainer's problems; the relationship is between two men of business. Benedetti and Dunlop clearly had an excellent working rapport.

Willie Carson had ridden Love The Groom in the race. He was cautiously impressed: 'On this showing he would have been fifth or sixth in the Guineas,' he said. 'Fifth or sixth doesn't win any prizes,' said Dunlop. And anyway, the point was that Love The Groom was not a mile horse: over a longer distance he would do a lot better. Like a mile and a half. In short, he looked like a Derby horse. 'I agree,' Benedetti said. 'Not the Guineas.'

But all the same, you could not say that this performance was going to send shivers of fear through every racing stable in the country. No one was going to make him an instant odds-on shot for the Derby. But the thought could not be ducked. When a horse is a Derby possibility, then every time the notion must be to give it a go. The rewards of winning the race are beyond belief: not just in the mountains of cash that are thrust upon the winner, but in joy and prestige and in future rewards at stud as well. The rewards for winning the Derby are beyond computation. When in doubt, kick on.

But nothing is ever clearcut. There were two possible plans for Love The Groom. The horse should have one more race before the Derby, that was agreed. He could run in England in one of the accepted Derby trial races – or he could go for the

Italian Derby. 'I know the owners would like that,' Benedetti said.

'But the thing is, this isn't ideal preparation for the Derby,' Dunlop said. The travelling and the competition involved in chasing Italy's top race would make for considerable stress, which could take away from the horse's performance on the much more important day at Epsom. 'On the one hand, he might very well win the Italian Derby. But on the other hand, that could put paid to his chances at Epsom.'

Racing always seems to be like this: this is a classic Classic argument, and it could go round and round forever. Dunlop had won the Italian Derby the previous year with Tommy Way. 'When the horse went past the post, Paolo almost threw me off the roof in delight,' Dunlop said. Benedetti roared with laughter at this splendid memory. He would certainly like to try throwing Dunlop off the roof again some time. Why not the roof at Epsom?

'I will talk to the del Bonos,' he said, as a parting shot.

I asked Dunlop for a post mortem on the afternoon's entertainment. 'Two horses I was happy about. Two I was very unhappy about. Arabian Sheikh has been good at home, but he has run decreasingly well, albeit in increasingly good company. That could mean that we have just overrated him. He ran a very disappointing race: stone cold dead from two out. Pat said he got very upset in the stalls and ran very free in the race. He was drawn nine out of eight, (there had been a withdrawal) and so he had enormous open spaces in front of him. Pat could not get him over and tucked in behind. And so he ran himself out.' In fact, the run was too bad to be true. Perhaps more money has been lost on that particular judgement than any other in racing.

'Almaarad, the last runner, is very lazy at home, and this was a race he needed. He should win a decent handicap – and he must do it sooner rather than later, because he doesn't care too much for hard ground. As for Love The Groom, I'll wait and see what the owner says. So there we are: two I was happy with, two I was unhappy with. That's racing.'

9

CHRIS BLYTH IS the lad who looks after Maksab, 'he's a full brother to Wassl', and a decent, reliable sort of filly called Bronzewing. Blyth was getting ready to take her to Sandown, to run in a £12,000 handicap. 'Do you fancy her?' I asked.

'Well, I do a bit.'

'Will you back her?'

'Well, we're not great gamblers. Not really. At least, I'm not. We have the odd flutter, that's about it. A lot of us have families, you know. People do sometimes put the week's wages on a horse, but I've never done it personally. I'll have a little on Bronzewing. A little, you know. She's got a good chance, I reckon.'

April had come, and brought a little bit of summer with it. Not a lot of winners for Castle Stables, mind: the 600 quid winner was still the only one as Blyth took Bronzewing off in the horse-box on 25 April. John Dunlop remarked: 'I had one win and two seconds from the first four runners. I thought at the time that it was too good to be true, and of course, it was. I had a good few runners on 11 April, a Saturday, and they were a very disappointing bunch. And I had my first foreign raider, War Brave, who was only third in the Italian 2,000 Guineas, which left me depressed for a couple of days. It has been an awkward start. It has been so wet, until the last few days. We were able to keep working, but it affected the pace of the Work. I wanted to put some real strong Work into some of them, but the ground was so bad, it wasn't possible.'

But the weather had turned bright – would we actually have a nice summer, for once? – and when the sun shines on a racing stable, everyone's mood is lifted, horses as well as lads, for the horses are beasts of summer. When the sun comes out their coats shine, they toss their heads and they meet life with a new verve. And the lads, they start looking for winners.

That is what their job is all about. Every day they work, every stride of exercise, every crumb of oats, every strand of hay, every stroke of the body brush, is to prepare a horse for winning a race. The vital part of job satisfaction in any job is seeing a task through to its conclusion: when a lad takes his horse to the races, leads him around the ring before the punters, surrenders him to the jockey, and watches the jockey take the horse to victory, then he knows what his job is all about. When the sun comes out every lad in the yard sniffs victory for the first time in the year. Victory: for they are racing men and racing women through and through. And with victory comes great pride, pleasure and satisfaction.

'It's not a good job for paying, you know,' said Blyth. 'But the rewards are rather high.' Blyth spoke slowly and methodically. He gave out an air of utter reliability. Any trainer would like a yard filled with Blyths. If Blyth were a soldier on sentry duty, and you told him to stop every car and inspect everyone's pass, he would do exactly as you asked. He would stop the general, he would stop the queen as well.

He seemed to have no ambition whatsoever for himself, only for his horses. He was 38, and had been in racing looking after horses since he was 15. 'If you're lucky enough to do a good job, you get a lot of satisfaction,' he said, without a trace of selfconsciousness. He accepted totally that it was his job to clean horses' feet, just as it was Dunlop's to control the operation and Carson's to hammer them home. Blyth has probably never had a rebellious thought in his life. 'I've been quite lucky. I started off here doing a horse for Sheikh Mohammed called Hatta, the first horse he ever had, and she won four times, she was a good filly. Then I did Jalmood, also for the Sheikh, and I did a horse called Wassl for Sheikh Ahmed, and he won the Irish 2,000 Guineas. So I've been lucky.'

'It must be the way you ride them at exercise,' I said.

'Well, it's got a lot to do with them, really,' Blyth said seriously. And I suppose it has. 'If it's not there, no one can put it there.'

'Obviously the worst part is winter, not just because it's cold, but also because it's boring. It's the quiet time of year. The horses are being let down' – given tickover exercise only – 'and you are doing exactly the same work every day. Whereas in the summer, Mr Dunlop could turn round to you any day and say: "Your horse is entered in Rome," and of course, you go with them. We all love to make the trips abroad.'

Blyth, like all real racing people, will of course start reciting pedigrees at the drop of the hat. If you are a stable lad, racing is the most interesting thing in the world, probably the only interesting thing in the world: 'And this here is by Danzig, who is a son of Northern Dancer, of course' – and everybody in the world knows about Northern Dancer, don't they? Ignorance on such a cosmic scale is beyond the imaginings of almost everybody in racing: surely they have heard about Northern Dancer on Mars.

The involvement is total. It has to be. There is not much time for anything else in a lad's life. The day starts at half past six: stables are early places. In theory every lad has two horses, hence every lad is 'doing his two'. Often, in fact, he will be doing his three. When a lad is off to the races with one of his charges, or when he goes on holiday (and even stable lads have holidays) someone must cover for him.

'First off, you muck them out, and you give a little bit of water to the one that's not going out first lot. Then we tack up our first horse, and when Mr Dunlop shouts "Ride away" we all pull out. We go to the cricket pitch and do the walking exercise. Then we trot them, and walk them again at the ring at the top. Mr Dunlop sorts out which horse is going to do one canter, and which are going to do two, and he will pick which horse is going to Work with which.

'Then we do the same for the second lot, and finish about twelve o'clock. Or a quarter to one, if you have a third horse to ride. Then you let them settle down for the afternoon, for, shall we say, a siesta. And at four o'clock we are back again, and we do exactly the same as we did in the morning bar ride them out. We make them all nice and comfortable, hay and water, and then we start what we call "strapping". You actually strap a horse with a body brush, which is the smooth one. You have a hard brush, a dandy brush, like a broom, for mane and tail, and to get the mud off their legs. Then we dress them over: every one has his own individual way of dressing a horse over.

'I normally wet mine down first, just very lightly – like, say, polishing your boots. The more you brush them, the drier it gets and the shinier it gets: it's the same with a horse's coat. A horse has got to look well in his coat. With them all being so nicely fed, it should show in the coat. All the oils come out in the coat with the brushing. His coat will show you that he's in perfect order.

'Horses' coats can be very different. A black horse is very difficult to look after, because he tends to get a dusty, dandruffy sort of thing in his coat. You can be there three-quarters of an hour with a black horse, and still find dust on him. To dress a horse over *should* take three-quarters of an hour. Some people take an hour. It depends on how many horses you've got to do. But you must spend 20 minutes on each side of a horse.

'When you've finished dressing them over, you've got to pick their feet out, and grease them, wash the eyes, muzzle and nostrils, and then with great care, you go behind and lift up the tail and clean out the dock. Then you're finished.'

Blyth is, in his unassuming way, a dedicated man. He has no particular pride in this: it is his nature to be loyal and straightforward and conscientious to an impossible degree. In his terribly prosy, terribly straightforward way, he has a great feel for horses, not that he would dream of making a thing about it. He happens to like his job a great deal: working with racehorses.

Racing would simply collapse without the Blyths of the profession. It is, in many ways, a terrible job he has, but it has fierce joys as well: like horses: like horses winning. So you can imagine, then, how pleased I was when Bronzewing came back from Sandown a winner: Dunlop's second of the season. At 8–1, Blyth would have got a decent return for his modest stake. 'The thing about this job,' Blyth said, 'is that you've got to like animals. No good at all if you don't.'

10

Bronzewing's victory was, as John Dunlop would say, 'pleasing', but it was not followed by a glut of wins. Dunlop's yard was finding it harder than usual to get in gear. 'They'll be coming good soon,' Tim Dunlop promised. He had left his merchant bank and was off to spend some time in a racing stable in France: a step on the way to fulfilling his ambitions, he hoped.

Castle Stables was stuttering a little, trying to get some momentum going. The 1,000 Guineas and the 2,000 Guineas both went by without a runner from Castle Stables. (Miesque won the first and Ajdal got beaten in the second, which was won by Don't Forget Me. This was, I boast shamelessly, tipped in my Sporting Diary column in *The Times*; my now legendary racing snout having passed me the good news. He had also given me the Grand National winner, Maori Venture, a few weeks previously, so I was pretty happy. I told him to transfer some of his magic to Castle Stables.) John Dunlop had another winner on the same day as Bronzewing, Billy Newnes picking up a £7,000 race at Leicester on a four-year-old called Flower Bowl. Then Graham Foster, who is an apprentice still doing his two at Dunlop's Findon yard, picked up a win in an apprentice race on

Almaarad. Willie Carson won a smallish race on Uptothehilt, and then Brian Rouse picked up an extremely small race on Piffle. Castle Stables was not doing everything wrong, but on the other hand, it was clear enough to everybody in racing that Castle Stables was not doing everything right.

'Trainers and jockeys are the most publicized people in any profession,' Dunlop said. 'Or at least, that is how it seems to us in the racing industry, anyway. The point is that every day, the people who follow racing read the results – and it is very obvious who is successful and who is not. Continued success, then, is terribly important in holding the operation together – particularly an operation of this size. There is an example of a senior trainer who, not so many years ago, was very much the leader. Then he had three or four moderate years, and suddenly you find you have slipped. It is very easy to slip very quickly. Often you can maintain the numbers, but the quality slips.'

Sport is quantifiable, that is why its issues are often so delightfully simple. You can argue all day about whether so-and-so is a good executive, and thingy a good politician, but there is no arguing with a hundred winners. Or with a hundred losers, for that matter.

The tyranny of results affects everyone in the sport, but it is jockeys and trainers who are at the sharp end. Newspapers and television make the most of jockeys: everyone else in the game is involved in the preparation of the horses for racing: jockeys are the only racing people ever seen in anything like action. Media people are always looking for what we are taught to call 'human interest'; the trouble with racing is that it is basically an equine interest story. But a human face is constantly sought: hence the somewhat obsessive attention the top jockeys get.

Presenting racing on a daily basis is, in fact, a very difficult job for media people. The problems of maintaining a level of equine and human interest simultaneously, both for the knowledgeably obsessed and the mildly interested, is a very difficult balancing act (this is exactly what Brough Scott does so well, as a matter of fact). The task is made more complicated by the fact that the jockeys themselves, always the most obvious subject for human interest, are not ideal people for making much of.

They are not wild, reckless, flamboyant, Errol Flynn types. They are about as wild and reckless as the men who cut diamonds for a living. And they all understand that being diplomatic about horses is part of the job. Jockeys are not, by necessity, frank people in public. They will not tell newspeople that 'the horse was useless' for fear of being accused of taking thousands off a horse's value. It was always the ground that beat him, or maybe the draw, or maybe bad luck in the running, or maybe, yes, the run was 'too bad to be true'. And several times a year, it seems, one jockey or another will tell us that such and such a horse 'is the best horse I have ever ridden'. All part of the job. Hard for the poor hack to get a story out of this.

Occasional punters like to follow jockeys, and find it hard to believe that a top jockey, leader of his profession, can be tailed off, stone last, when carrying their money. The trouble is that the public understanding of jockeyship is completely upside-down. People like to see jockeys as goal-scoring strikers, or as swashbuckling batsmen: as the person who has the responsibility to score; the person who, by his initiative and inspiration, conjures up the victory. This is not the case at all.

The fact is that a jockey has much more in common with a goalkeeper or a wicketkeeper. Certainly the jockey has a decisive influence over the horse's progress in any race he ever starts, but this is not in the main about the inspiration he puts in, but about the mistakes he does not make. Like a wicketkeeper or a goalkeeper whose primary responsibility is to not drop the ball, the jockey's primary contribution is a negative one: not making mistakes. In 100 per cent of races, a jockey has the power to lose it. In a tiny, tiny percentage of races, the jockey can put in something extra and win it for you. But most races are won by the combination of the horse's ability coupled with the jockey's avoidance of mistakes. If you think this sounds easy, try watching an apprentice in a race with grown-up jockeys: when he gets it wrong he can get it so horribly wrong that even a layman can see it. The jockey's prime skill is invisible as well as invaluable. A good jockey will scarcely ever lose a race that the horse should have won: that is why a good jockey is worth a great deal of money. But there is a further dimension to all this.

'How much difference does the jockey make?' I asked Dunlop, leaning against the Japanese Range Rover on the gallops one morning.

'He can have a very adverse effect, first off. If he makes a complete cock-up it can have a very ill effect. But given a clear run, it is all down to the horse – 90 per cent, more than that even, it is down to the horse. The difference between a very good jockey and the absolute top is that the very best will *sometimes* win you races you shouldn't have won. Pat Eddery can do this, Steve Cauthen can do it. And Lester Piggott, of course, was the man who could do this to a quite exceptional extent. Willie Carson at his best can do it too.'

Dunlop does not retain a jockey, which is most unusual for a top stable. He inherited Ron Hutchinson when he took over Castle Stables; Hutchinson was with the stable under Dunlop and before him, under Gordon Smyth, for a total of 13 years. 'But when he retired, after the 1977 season, there wasn't a top jockey – what I considered a top jockey – available. This has been the case ever since. I have not wanted to go out into the market place and buy out the contract of another retained jockey. My stable is made up of a combination of owners: there is not one person who dominates, and who would be prepared to pay a retainer.

'So I haven't been in the position to buy up a top jockey. And I do feel very strongly that if you retain a jockey, you must use him virtually 100 per cent of the time. There is no point in having a retained jockey if you are not prepared to have him ride your two-to-one-on favourite for the Derby. And if you can't get someone like that, then you are much better off not being tied down, and selecting the best rider available to ride your horses.'

Jockeys are the most visible men in the racing business. Because of this, they are subjected to more abuse than anyone in sport. Losing punters are always seeking for someone to blame, and the jockey is by far the easiest target. There is a kind of punter who really rather likes to feel cheated, who really rather enjoys blaming somebody for the failures of life, the universe and their pound-each-way investment. It is never the foot that got bruised when the horse hit an uneven stride, but that bugger Carson who didn't try a bloody yard. Such is jockeyship: you spend 90 per cent of your life getting blamed for defeat, and the remaining 10 per cent hearing the horse get praised for victory.

'Jockeys are a necessary evil,' I have heard people in racing declare. 'Brains in proportion to their bodies.' There is a whiff of an antique master-servant relationship in any trainer's dealings with any jockey, for all that, often enough, the jockey is a millionaire and the trainer frighteningly in debt. The most famous story illustrating this is, naturally, a Lester Piggott story: 'You'll never ride for me again, Piggott!' 'Well that's it then. I'll have to pack it in.' The relationship between jockey and trainer is based on ancient days when the rich man's groom rode the horse in races. There is an anatomical reason for the natural one-downness of jockeys as well: simply that people with six inches more legbone tend to feel morally one up straight away.

Jockeys cope with all this without getting ruffled. They know their value, they know they are an essential part of the machine. The sport starts with a stallion and a mare, and involves breeders and salespeople and lads and owners and stewards and trainers: but the whole act is not finished until a jockey has driven the horse past the winning post in front of the others. That is the consummation of the sport.

Dunlop has, for several seasons, used Willie Carson as his unofficial number one jockey. Carson is retained by Dick Hern, who has first call on his services. Hern is a great organization man, who likes to get his plans in good order at an early stage. This means that Carson knows his commitments a good way in advance, and this enables Dunlop to work his own plans around Carson's availability.

Carson has the gift of a naturally perky temperament, which may well be the result of his natural lightness: his official riding weight is a mere 7 st 10 lb. You can see from his moist and still boyish face – and he was born in 1942 – that he has not spent his life suffering the agonies of starvation and dehydration that is for so many jockeys part of life's inescapable rhythm. Piggott said: 'You get used to not eating'; Fred Archer, driven mad by incessant wasting, shot himself. But Carson makes jokes and struts about and roars with laughter at the slightest provocation.

'He is a great enthusiast, which I like,' Dunlop said. 'He is very strong, but also very light, which means he can ride far more horses than, say, Cauthen or even Eddery. He is a very good man abroad, and has had lots of international experience. He is tremendously experienced, but for all that he still looks like a boy. He is older than one thinks! He is not the sort to freeze at the sight of a load of wild Italian horses ridden by a load of wild Italian jockeys. He is consistently one of the top four jockeys in this country. He has his critics, but then every jockey does, even Cauthen. Even Lester at the height of his career.'

'But there must be disadvantages to your system,' I said.

'There are – and mostly at this time of year. Right now, everyone is trying out their Classic hopes, and the leading stables are naturally using their own jockeys in these trial races. It is a difficult time, because naturally I want a top man to ride my own leading hopes, and sometimes I miss out, and I have to rely on the many men who are useful jockeys without being absolute stars. And there is, clearly, not the sort of continuity one would like. But normally, by the time the Classics are being run, and if you have something that is a serious contender, you can pretty well always get a top man to ride it.'

'Willie Carson doesn't always ride for you when he is available, though, I see.'

'No. This is normally because I have used another jockey when Willie has been unavailable, and the replacement has struck up a useful relationship with the horse. So I stick with the relationship: Pat Eddery and Moon Madness, Richard Quinn with Patriach. But primarily, Willie rides for us, and he does awfully well.'

On 12 May Brian Rouse, who is a regular rider for Castle Stables, won a small race at Chepstow on Lagta. But Castle Stables had little joy in it. On 14 May Tim Dunlop was killed in a car crash in France.

11

THE NEWS OF Tim Dunlop's death was devastating for everyone at Castle Stables. Inevitably, John Dunlop was out on the gallops at first lot the following morning: the lads admired him greatly for that. He decided, however, not to go to the races, and Tony Couch, his number two, took on that duty.

But the vague misgivings about the season, the slight stuttering that had greeted the early months, seemed to resolve itself into a cloud of depression. Castle Stables seemed to settle down into a run of the most hideous luck imaginable: when sorrows come they come not as single spies but in battalions.

Arabian Sheikh's dismal showing, his airy abandonment of all the Classic hopes that had been invested in him, had been the first blow. Then came Fleet Lord, who suffered one of those freakish racetrack injuries that occasionally happen right out of the blue. Racing puts enormous stresses on a horse: on 21 April at Warwick, the stresses were too much for poor Fleet Lord. He broke a hind leg in the race, and was put down at once.

And the horses just didn't seem to be running well. Wherever you looked in the yard, you found problems. There was clearly something wrong with Arabian Sheikh after that disastrous race at Newmarket, when he was so dismally tailed off. The vets put him through every kind of test, and found nothing. This did not mean that the horse was well, far from it: just that whatever it was, it was undetectable. There was nothing for it but to give the horse great quantities of rest and see what Time could do. So the one-time Classic hope was left standing in his box, just one more dream down the plughole. Another horse, called Tiquegrean ran abysmally at Newmarket, returned injured and was put on the easy list. George James, after a rather encouraging run at Kempton, came back with problems: if a horse has any whisper of a problem, be sure that a race will find it out. This time the problem was diagnosed: and, the horse turned out to have damaged his back. So that was the end of his season, at the very least: the horse went to his owners to be turned out with plenty of rest.

There was nothing going right: just when the yard needed a few good things to cheer everybody up, the malign fortunes of racing piled one problem on another. It was all enough to remind everybody of the grim and depressing 1985 season: the season when the stable had been forced to close down because of an attack by the dreaded virus.

That had been, Dunlop said, 'disastrous'. This, remember, comes from a man much given to understatement. 'The virus' is one of racing's characteristic inexact terms. It is normally used to refer to a highly infectious viral complaint that affects the respiratory system. The effects are not permanent, but are bad enough to prevent a horse running, or, indeed, from taking any serious exercise. Another complaint, also called 'the virus', is the frightening one of contagious abortion. When it strikes at a stud, all the broodmares will miscarry.

The virus – either virus – is basically an act of God. All stables take elaborate precautions: the hygienic standards of racing stables make those at a normal yard seem desultory. There is constant screening and veterinary attention: vets are almost permanent residents at a stable with a large string. But the virus can arrive anywhere: a new horse can bring it in, a long-term resident can bring it back from the races. But once it has dug in, the stable is in real trouble, and when it struck Castle Stables in

1985, it was an unmitigated disaster. Everything stopped: the 15 million quid's worth were left standing idle, eating their heads off, while their owners paid the bills and champed at the bit with impatience: what is the point of having a racehorse if it doesn't race? The stable was not earning its usual share of prize money, and that affects the incomes of everybody in the yard. The owners were not getting their return of excitement and pleasure. Everyone was unhappy.

By 12 August of that year, Dunlop had managed the pathetic total of 12 winners. 'We started the season perfectly all right,' Dunlop recalled. 'But then quite suddenly everything started to go wrong. It was diagnosed that we had a virus.' The stable was forced to close down for two entire months. It came to a complete halt at the end of May. There was not so much as a single runner at the big Goodwood meeting, and Dunlop has always made something of a thing of cleaning up there, at his local track.

The thing ran its course, and Dunlop even managed to have something like his usual sparkling autumn. He finished the season with a just-about-respectable 64 winners. 'But it really was pretty grim. It had a very bad effect on the stable generally. It affected the stable's reputation, and therefore it had an economic effect.'

Dunlop had then but recently acquired his secondary yard at Findon: it was a bold, expansionist move. To get struck down by the virus so soon was the worst possible publicity. 'Bitten off more than he could chew,' people said wisely. However unfair it may seem, after such a disaster the names of everyone close to it stink a little. And racing is a game about reputations: a racing reputation is a more volatile thing than the most neurotic racehorse.

And there is a rational reason for thinking twice about sending your best horse to a stable that has had the virus: it very often happens that a stable will have it two seasons in a row. Sometimes even a third. 'The staff were marvellous,' Dunlop said. 'We weren't racing, everyone's income was reduced, and everybody's job was monotonous and dull, so job satisfaction was also dramatically reduced. It is not a year I want repeated.'

It happened that the numbers were not affected at all. As Dunlop has observed, it is often possible to keep up the numbers: it is the quality that counts. 'Who is to say,' Dunlop said, 'that we have not missed a very good owner who was on the verge of sending a top horse to us? The virus cannot help but have a bad effect. That is why it was such a double blessing to have had such a good year in 1986, with more winners than any other stable in England. We have certainly kept up the numbers – and they seem up to standard quality-wise as well.'

But in the current season, things were not quite right. Certainly a win or two would help things along. Three Tails ran a splendid race in an Oaks trial at Newbury on 15 May, going there very much in need of a race, and she finished a length behind Percy's Lass. Not a win, true, but she looked very good indeed. She was installed as one of the market leaders for the Oaks, so that made for something to look forward to, at any rate. A win would have been even nicer, however.

Then Moon Madness had his first outing for the season, running at one mile two furlongs, a race that was much too short for him, and a race he needed anyway. He finished a brisk fourth, which was cautiously rather pleasing – at least, it was to begin with. But afterwards, he was found to be lame. With one Classic hope standing in his box and the stable star hobbling about the place, it was not a time to inspire optimism. And this was a time, if ever there was one, that the stable needed something to be optimistic about.

Sergeyevich stuck his tongue out and won a maiden race at Newbury on 16 May. If all of us at Castle Stables had realized exactly what this win was to mean, we would have found the next month utterly unbearable. But as it was, a win was a win, and to be enjoyed.

12

MICHAEL ASHTON, ONE of the vets who works with Castle Stables, is a large, gloomy man, as befits someone who frequently has to hand out large, gloomy pieces of news. He has rather a gift for comic timing, with a kind of slow, merciless, pedantic pessimism. He and John Dunlop have the kind of working banter that you would expect between people who have worked together for years.

'Well, Michael, what about all these bloody lame horses then?'

'I don't know, really,' Ashton replied, with a facial shrug that doubted if any man had ever known anything about equine lameness.

'Let's have a session with them on Monday morning.'

Ashton allowed a Pinteresque pause before saying: 'Perhaps they'll all be better by then,' in which case he'd be scanning the sky for flocks of passing pigs.

'I'll probably have a few more bad ones,' Dunlop counter-proposed.

'I suppose all our old friends are back lame again. Love The Groom?'

'Moon Madness.'

'All our old friends.' Ashton turned to me: 'It would be better for these trainers if we could take a horse away from them the instant it went lame. If they didn't see it all the time, they'd get less frustrated.'

'That's one of the reasons why I have Findon,' said Dunlop.

'Lame horses annoy them, you see. If they keep seeing a lame horse, they are constantly aware of it, and it niggles them all the time.'

It is, of course, doubly niggling if the lame horse you keep seeing is your stable star. Moon Madness's box was right near the stable office, a sight that would give good cheer in racing's ordinarily difficult times. But in this hardest of hard times, Moon Madness peered gloomily out of his box on his sore feet, giving no comfort to anyone at all. It niggled everyone in the yard. He was 'lame as a cat', as stable people say; I never know why. Cats are especially surefooted creatures: lame as a racehorse seems a far apter simile.

Moon Madness had gone into the spring in terrific nick, but as soon as he began serious Work, he bruised a foot, and had to have his training schedule cut down straight away. He recovered, had that run at Sandown, and ran a race that was pleasing – not a Dunlop 'pleasing', as in 'out of this bloody world', but pleasing as the world understands it – and came back, as we know, lame as a cat once again. If you have a horse that goes lame every time you ask him to extend himself, then you have no chance at all of getting a proper training programme into him. It could even have been that Moon Madness's season was over before it started. Love The Groom was also having problems with sore feet: he had to go without a further preparation race before the Derby. The Italian Derby plans were scrubbed: no one had the chance of throwing anybody off the stands roof this time.

Racehorses seem to spend most of the time going lame. To own a horse is to spend your life receiving phone calls from your trainer: 'He's gone lame in that off-hind again, so obviously we can't run him tomorrow. . . .' A horse is an animal designed by God as a running machine. In the wild, a horse's life depended on its ability to find sudden exploding speed from a standstill, to outrun anything else in the world. A horse's reaction to trouble is to run; a horse's natural form of self-expression is running, as anyone who has seen a horse playing in a field knows.

So why, then, are horses so fragile? Robert Allpress, Ashton's partner in the veterinary practice, said: 'The horse may have been designed by God, but the thoroughbred was designed by man. We have selected from what God designed as effective beasts to suit our own requirements. And as a matter of fact, I don't believe they are fragile. I think they cope with the stresses we put on them extremely well. At least as well as human athletes. Human athletes are always breaking down, they always have sore shins and Achilles problems – lameness problems of every kind, which are caused by the stresses of training.'

Racehorses are athletes, and their racing years are full of stress. That is the point: to bring out the best in them: and you don't get the best out of any athlete, animal or human, by letting him take it easy and eat lots of Polos. There is also the point that racehorses in England are mostly very young animals. All the two-year-olds and a good many of the three-year-olds will still be growing and filling out and coming into their full strength in the course of their racing lives. Boon Point, a handsome chap in the main yard, proved this point by sprouting muscles like Rambo in the winter before the current season, which he was contesting as a four-year-old.

It follows logically that lameness will always be a problem among the serious athletes of every species. The bloke who runs round the block twice a week is always hot to trot, but Sebastian Coe and Steve Cram never stop breaking down. Racehorses are Formula One machines. A decent family runabout keeps going forever: a Formula One car needs to be taken apart completely every time it is raced, so great are the strains put upon it. A Formula One car is the result of years of research and unending hours of work from the finest mechanics in the world. And the damn things are always breaking down in the middle of races. If you want to achieve the maximum, you must push everything to the maximum: under these stresses things are likely to go wrong. That is life – certainly that is racing, anyway.

And it is those lovely slim racing legs that are the danger points in the mechanism. A racehorse will travel at speeds in excess of 30 mph: every ounce of its weight, which is to stay, about half a ton, is taken on the leading leg, absorbed, and then punched on again by that crucial cable of the main tendon. 'Imagine sitting in a car with the door open,' Allpress said. 'You could beat your foot along the road easily enough. But if you were to suddenly load that limb, what would happen? Something would go. This is what can happen with fracture cases, like Fleet Lord last month. The horse just hits an uneven stride, maybe a piece of false ground, and instead of travelling forward over that limb, it will load the limb momentarily.

'The Americans have done some gruesome experiments in their investigations into the strength of horses' limbs. They have held bones down in clamps, and calculated what pressure is necessary to fracture a cannon bone, or whatever. And the conclusion they have come up with is that *with every single stride it takes, the horse is at risk.* So long as he keeps that magnificent action, he is fine – but at the same time, every stride he takes is a potential disaster.'

This is the reason why racing people pay such intense attention to a horse's conformation. They want to see if the horse is put together as a racing machine should be. They look for a stride that does not deviate an inch from twin parallel lines: the sins of dishing, brushing, and turning the toes in signal potential disaster in a racing animal.

But the difficulties are compounded by the fact that most of the buying is done when the horses are yearlings, with a lot of growing and developing still to do. Unevenness can level out, or it can get worse, for that matter. A horse can also grow out of evenness and straightness: the sad tale of Snaafi Dancer says everything about that. 'The thing about a well-conformed horse is that he is meeting the ground evenly at every stride,' Allpress said. 'The weight is evenly distributed from the foot, through the joints and ligaments and tendons. So the risk of damage is reduced. If there is a slight bend or twist anywhere, then you know there are going to be problems somewhere along the line.'

But when you have problems, you automatically have still more problems. When a horse goes lame, it is not a simple matter of figuring out which leg the horse is favouring, and concentrating your treatment on it. No, there is the problem of secondary, or compensatory lameness. It happens in humans. You might have a nail in your shoe, ignore it because the discomfort is slight, and end up with a bad back. This happens because you have unconsciously been holding your body in an unnatural way to reduce the discomfort of the nail. The point is to be quick enough to notice the problem of the nail: this is pretty easy, if it is you, but harder when it is a horse: horses can't say: 'Oi, mate, I've got a bleedin' nail in my shoe.' Instead, they end up with a limp somewhere else, and that is the first you know of the original discomfort. With horses, knowing how to treat them is comparatively easy: it is knowing *what* to treat that drives you mad.

Added to all these other problems, the racing industry is always struggling under the pressure of time. Every owner and every trainer – every racing vet, for that matter – wants to see the horse out there running races, winning races, not spending its fast-vanishing racing career in its box, or walking round in the indoor school gingerly and reluctantly putting its feet on the floor.

Eye and experience are the greatest aids to trainers and vets in detecting the source of lameness. But there are plenty of fancy modern aids, as well. Radiography and ultrasonic scanning can detect injuries to tendons, and there is also a process called scintigraphy, which involves the injection of a radioactive substance into a horse. This is taken up selectively by damaged bones. After the injection the vet scans him with a geiger counter: yes, where it clicks loudest, there you will find your problem. At least, you will if the problem was skeletal, and in that particular limb, anyway.

The problem with Moon Madness was not complicated:

bruised feet. But the problem was that he seemed to bruise them every time he was asked to, as it were, put his foot down. A superstar with sore feet was not going to help anyone. May ended with Moon Madness still lame as a cat, and on 31 May it was 16 days since Dunlop had had a winner.

13

THE FIRST WEDNESDAY in June is always Derby Day, and it had come far too soon for Castle Stables. Still not a winner since Sergeyevich. Still a pall of depression hanging over the stable. Tony Couch was still deputizing for John Dunlop at the races. The stable was in a sad state, and badly needed things to go right on the track. And this was the Derby: no ordinary day.

The Derby is far more than merely special. It is one of the two horseraces that attract the attention of people outside the usual band of racing's followers. It is one of the races for the twice-a-year punter. The other is the Grand National, and of the two, the Grand National is slightly more popular with the uncommitted outsiders. It lasts longer, and it is packed with events which you do not need to be a racing person to understand: all that crashing and tumbling and flailing about, all those jockeys and horses flying through the air in all sorts of directions. It is far more prone to outrageous shifts of fortune, as the 28–1 winner in 1987 demonstrated. (What a fine piece of tipping that was!) The National is always something of a lottery, and it is treated as a lottery quite literally by every office in the country.

It takes rather more than luck to win the Derby. The horses

that win it tend to go on to become great stallions, syndicated for the kind of money that makes normal people go dizzy. The prize money on offer that season was £450,000, but that is just the start for a good Derby winner.

'I have the winner of the Italian Derby, the Scottish Derby and the Welsh Derby in my yard,' Dunlop once remarked as I accompanied him at evening stables, these being Tommy Way, Moon Madness and Highland Chieftain. 'I would swap the lot for the winner of the Derby at Epsom.' This sounds like exaggeration, but naturally, Dunlop was indulging in his usual practice of understatement. He would abandon 199 of the 200 horses in his care if the one horse remaining could win the Derby by half a nostril's width. Any trainer in the country would give all he had in exchange for a single Derby winner.

No one in racing talks of anything but the Derby for weeks before the race. The ante-post market zooms about all over the place as horses pick up a following, and others withdraw from the race. Vincent O'Brien caused consternation when he pulled the much-fancied Seattle Dancer out of the race with a week to go: hundreds of intrepid ante-post punts went straight down the drain, to the usual cries of anguish.

But as time went on, the proceedings were dominated more and more by a single horse: Reference Point. I was unwilling to believe, myself, that a horse with a dull name could win the Derby. His price got shorter and shorter, and the prices of his rivals got longer. My racing snout told me to tip Reference Point: 'But that's dreadfully boring!' I whined. 'He might be odds-on.' 'Yes. That's because he's going to win. You tip him.' So I did.

Reference Point had ground all his rivals into the turf in the Mecca Dante Stakes at York, a race often used as a Derby trial, and the effortless and relentless style of the win had given sighs of pleasure to all racing enthusiasts – unless they had connections with one of the other runners, of course. Dunlop's Derby hope, Love The Groom, was not getting much attention. In fact, no one wanted to know. *Racing Post* summed him up in the brutally unsentimental terms in which a serious racing person always tries to approach life and betting: 'Love The Groom has not raced since the Craven Stakes, when he was behind Ajdal and Most Welcome. Also held by Reference Point on juvenile form and looks to have something to find.' He was finally sent out at 33–1.

And the world stopped, as it does every year, to watch the race. To most of the watchers, the Derby is a bewildering televised two minutes of high-speed commentary, in which you watch a multi-legged magic carpet of silken colours hurtle around a wide green bend and then learn that you have not, after all, won the office sweep. To a few people, they are the most important two minutes of the year. To one or two people, they will be the most important two minutes of their lives.

Derby Day is traditionally unlike any other in racing. It was always a jolly, boozy democratic Londoners' day out, with half a million or so flocking to the acres of public downland. It was always a day of gypsies, fairgrounds, beer, health-hazard pies, good times and the Queen. In recent years the atmosphere out on the downs has soured: instead of families, there are roving bands of the dreaded Shirtless Lager-Drinker. The gypsy caravans carry warnings about guard dogs. It is not just those who have seen 50 Derbys who complain that things are not what they were.

The crowds are as enormous as ever, but nothing is as big as the expectation. The Derby is a great test of temperament: the horses' and, most particularly, the jockeys'. Epsom is the most fiendishly difficult course to ride, and it provides the most searching and exhaustive test of a horse. The Derby is not won by a galloping machine pure and simple; the horse needs the balance and poise to handle the maniacal switchback curves and slopes of this wild, weird and unconventional track. They say that Epsom is a freakish track, but it is never a freakish horse that wins there. Year after year, the race sorts out the best horses in the race and throws them to the front.

There was no real pretending that Love The Groom was in that sort of company, no *logical* hope whatsoever. But yet, as any friend of the Dunlop family could not fail to admit, there was a sneaking, treacherous, tiny little grain of hope creeping in from somewhere: a knowledge that miracles do sometimes happen in racing. Why else is racing so greatly loved? The horse, said the *Racing Post*, has a lot to find: but what if it found it? Stifle the hope, logical counsels said, have a fiver on Reference Point and enjoy the race for what it is. But that millionth of an ounce, that treacherous little grain of hope would not be denied. Perhaps a fairy tale would take place around that tortuous, undulating track. Perhaps the unpredictability of Epsom and of the gods of racing could provide the family with some tiny taste of comfort in a year of such sadness. Terrible to think such a thing, of a horserace of all things. But such thoughts would not be silenced.

Willie Carson had the ride on Love The Groom. Carson had won on that marvellous giant Troy in 1979, a horse that exploded into belligerent action a furlong and a half out and simply murdered the lot of them. Carson had also ridden Henbit the following year, Henbit who broke a bone in his foot in the final few yards of the race, but with unbelievable – courage, if you like, herd instinct, guts, fear, whatever it is that makes a horse run – held on to win.

The horses paraded, and Reference Point (horrid name) strode out before us with his jockey, Steve Cauthen, in the horrid colours of searing yellow with black spots: hangover colours. The horse itself looked wonderful. Those who had held off until then dived to the bookies clutching handfuls of fivers. He seemed a horse with a generous eye to me, but I held off. I couldn't bear to back anything, in truth.

The combination looked unbeatable: dapper Henry Cecil, Cauthen, the Henry James American, and this awesome looking horse. Cecil's second runner, Legal Bid, was second favourite for a while, but he was finally sent out at 8–1. There was a flood of late money for a French trained animal called Sadjiyd, which started at 11–2. Reference Point was 6–4, not quite odds-on, in the end, but a short enough price for all that. There was very little money for Love The Groom, but there were a few horses at even longer odds: 100–1 shots; and Love The Groom had a couple to keep him company at 33–1.

The horses filed their way across the middle of the course towards the start: the most nerve-racking walk in a horse's life. Their eyes out on stalks, they are led by their lads across the downs to the starting stalls. There the girths are checked, once or twice more than is strictly necessary, and then the horses are loaded into the stalls. It was then that Sadjiyd, the French horse, found the occasion somewhat overstimulating. To be pedantically exact, he sprouted the most enormous stallion's erection. Racing, not normally very hot on euphemisms, calls this 'becoming colty'. His jockey, Yves Saint-Martin, summed up later: 'Sadjiyd became sexually excited on the way to the start. He was slowly out of the stalls, and did not want to race. He has never done anything like it before.'

Then came the hush, as the hundreds of thousands of people out on the downs held their breaths, and all over the country, in shops and offices and betting shops and in front of television sets in the street, everyone else did the same. And then, with a bang and a clatter and a roar, the 208th Derby was off and running.

And within a dozen strides or so, the horrid yellow shirt of Steve Cauthen was glowing like a beacon at the front. Sadjiyd, dreaming of the hordes of gorgeous mares that a Derby winner must deal with every year, fell behind by about 100 yards. Love The Groom took a little finding in the bunch, but there he was, tucked in near the front, with Carson glowing somewhat more tastefully than Cauthen in red and yellow.

But already there was something relentless, something almost anticlimactic, about Cauthen and Reference Point. And what a beautiful race it was that Cauthen rode, as the horse swept around Tattenham Corner and into the straight. Cauthen rode with the utmost sensitivity, settling his horse in front, just far enough in front. Reference Point had a habit of 'changing legs' –adjusting his stride – and the trickery of Epsom can get any horse unbalanced. But Cauthen, riding with all his invisible skills, had the horse perfectly balanced and running truly, entering the straight and aiming him like an arrow at the line. The pack set off in pursuit, and in the tidal wave of silks that surged after him, poor Love The Groom got buried. But the more the field pursued, the more Reference Point ran.

Bellotto, in Dancing Brave's pink and green colours, made a startling late run but could not get there. Sadjiyd finally forgot about sex and started racing, and finished eighth, rather fast, to give his connections one of racing's standard might-have-been experiences. Most Welcome, a 33–1 shot like Love The Groom, startled his jockey Paul Eddery and his connections by finishing second. *Racing Post* had remarked that the horse 'has a tendency to hang and is not guaranteed to stay'.

It was Reference Point's day all right: a great victory for competence. Terrific training and terrific riding, but it was not a horse that stirred my blood. Perhaps this was because my heart was not in it for him, too involved with a 33–1 shot that was never a factor in the race. For Love The Groom it was, perhaps, an inevitable disappointment. Today's miracle did not take place.

Castle Stables was not asking for a miracle in the fillies' Classic in four days' time: Three Tails was warmly fancied for the Oaks, and if she showed all her ability that day, she would win. That would be the perfect answer to disappointment. It was now 19 days since Castle Stables had had a winner.

14

THE DISAPPOINTMENT OF the Derby was not followed by a sudden winner to compensate. Everyone at Castle Stables was wondering just what he was doing wrong or, if not, was wondering whom to blame. Willie Carson and Tony Couch were going to the races, saddling and riding losers. John Dunlop was riding his hack ('the hack') up and down the gallops wondering which of his vast string of horses – if any – was going to halt this heart-breaking run of losers. Time and again, he looked at the filly Three Tails, and thought that perhaps she would be the one. The vets were asking themselves question after question; what had they missed? What more could they do? Was there any piece of magic that would stand the stable's luck on its head and start the winners thundering in again?

Perhaps the horses were simply all running in the wrong races. When that thought crossed people's minds – and it did – people turned their eyes up to a small window above the stable offices and wondered what was going on in there. On the far side of the window, Marcus Hosgood was working unceasingly, and worrying the same amount. What arcane permutation of horse and race could conjure a winner out of nowhere and put a spring back into everybody's stride?

Hosgood is Dunlop's racing secretary, and it is his job to enter the horses in their races. This is not as straightforward a job as it might sound. It happens that there is a very easy formula for success in racing: the right horse in the right race at the right time. Making this formula work is the tricky bit. Hosgood has the job of hunting for the right race. It is a job of niggling accuracy, clear sight, realism, and an eye for seeing the diamond of an opportunity in all the mud of detail.

Hosgood works in an eyrie overlooking the yard in 'the boxroom', as the secretarial team from the ground floor call it. There he reads through the acres of small print that surround every single race in the calendar, waiting to pounce when the nature of the conditions, track, and going are right for a race-ready animal.

The entries must be made for most races two or three weeks in advance: the process is based on steam-age communications and will in fact be changed, if everything goes according to plan, in time for the 1989 season. For the major races, the Classics and the Group races, entries are required much further ahead – six months, and even longer in some overseas cases. Everything in the system is full of variables, just to keep things good and confusing.

The details of every race are listed in all their complexities and glory in the programme book. This tells you what horses are permitted to run in the race, the distance, and the amount of prize money. The conditions of the race are crucial: some require a certain amount of racing experience, others a certain lack of it. A maiden race is for horses that have not won a race at all; other races insist on horses that have not won more than a certain amount of prize money or a certain number of races. The conditions are often complex and convoluted: they can require that a horse be of a certain sex, or have a certain minimum or maximum handicap rating. There is plenty of room for embarrassing yourself here: the Racing Calendar is full of horses entered for races for which they are not qualified. In the course of the season, Henry Cecil entered a filly in a colts' race, which is the sort of thing that can easily happen with a large string. It gives everybody in racing a cheap laugh, and it gives people like Hosgood a slightly breathless there-but-for-the-grace-of-God feeling.

The handicap system is the cornerstone of racing life. All racing, once you are away from the lofty company of the stars, revolves around the handicap ratings. The weekly arrival of the Racing Calendar is a major event for those who must place horses to win races. As a horse races, so its handicap rating is altered. The rating is expressed as a figure: the higher the figure, the better the horse is thought to be. The figure relates directly to the amount of weight the horse will carry in his next handicap race.

The idea of a handicap race is, of course, to get horses of different abilities racing on equal terms. The theory is that the handicapping should be done so perfectly that the entire field of runners should finish in a line abreast. It never happens, of course, but a blanket finish never fails to make a handicapper feel pretty good about life.

The trainers, and the racing secretaries for that matter, are forever aiming to get one jump ahead of the handicapper: to come up with a horse that is improving faster than the handicapper can slow it down. A horse like that makes a trainer feel pretty good about life. But a horse that is doing badly, or which has been overrated by the handicapper, will start to lose races, and therefore will slide back down the handicap again. In the previous season, Patriach managed to outstrip the handicapper, and put together a series of wins that kept the lads in beer money and kept Hosgood cheerful up in the boxroom.

The boxroom is full of files: it is full of a sense of order and purpose. Hosgood is a great one for facts and for filing. (Throughout the course of writing this book, it was to Marcus I turned time and again to verify a fact. He had every single answer just an arm's stretch away. He also compiled the statistical appendix for this book.) He records the details of every race run by a Dunlop horse. The trainer's and jockey's post-race comments are always included: if Willie Carson says he needs an extra furlong or two, Hosgood will write this down and hunt through the programme book to find the right race.

'You have to take a lot of things into account. I am looking for a race for Silver Dragon at the moment: I know he is a long-striding animal who needs plenty of room, and not every course suits him. Haydock would be ideal, so I will try and place him there, if there is the right race for him. George James doesn't like undulating tracks, so obviously Epsom is out for a start.'

Hosgood works in close consultation with Dunlop, who naturally has the final say. The races close at noon every Wednesday: when the two of them have gone through the entries and agreed or disagreed on them all (Hosgood will often give Dunlop a choice of two races, and will perhaps recommend one of them) and when Hosgood has been agreed with or overruled or given his head or whatever, he takes the list downstairs. There Sue Crossland will bang off a telex to Weatherby's, racing's central information pool, and the process of entering a horse will be underway.

But needless to say, it doesn't end there. That would be much too simple. There are always far more entries than there are eventual runners in every race in the calendar. Dunlop might have four entries and pull the lot out: there might be lameness, sickness, poor showing on the gallops: as we know there are a million things that can get between a horse and his race. In a normal, everyday race, you have a chance to withdraw your horse four days in advance, and then a further chance to withdraw the day before. The longer the horse stands its ground, the greater the cost to the owner. There are more complexities and more forfeit stages in the bigger races, especially for the Classics.

The day before any horse from Castle Stables runs, Dunlop and Hosgood will talk it through. Hosgood will have looked up the form of every horse still entered in the race. If there are two or three who will clearly have the beating of the Dunlop horse on form, Hosgood will ring up the relevant stables and ask if their horses will run or not. 'Trainers are very frank with each other, on the whole,' he said. 'Sometimes they won't have made their minds up, but there is no problem about asking for this information. Then at quarter to ten, I will have a talk with Mr Dunlop. I will say what I think, and he will agree, or perhaps he will not. The point is to see where we stand. There is absolutely no point in running a horse that has no chance whatsoever. So it is up to me to look for options: to say, Mr Dunlop there are three horses here that should all beat us. Why don't we wait for Kempton in four days' time? It is all part of the art of trying to place your horses to win. Any fool can enter and run them. The point is to place them where you know they have a chance.

'The good horses look after themselves. Mr Dunlop will make the decisions on these, but they are pretty logical and inevitable. The horses like Love The Groom and Three Tails don't pose the same kind of problems. Mr Dunlop knows where they will go next: we've got Three Tails in the Oaks tomorrow, and Love The Groom – he came back from Epsom all right, and we will run him, if all goes well, in the King Edward VII at Royal Ascot later in the month. You would like to have 200 horses all as good as that, but of course, that will never happen. You are happy if you have 15 good ones and the rest pretty average. And there are thousands, literally thousands of pretty average horses in training, and every trainer in the country is trying to place them in a race they will win. So I have a job on my hands as I try to find the right race for the lesser horses.

'I have noticed that it gets more competitive every year. It gets harder and harder to find an easy race. In fact, I don't think there is such a thing any more. A few years ago, a big southern trainer like Mr Dunlop could go to places like Carlisle and Thirsk, take the northern trainers on and be pretty confident he was going to win – even without looking up the form of the other horses! That is no longer the case. You get valuable horses running at places like these, for very little prize money. Every year racing gets more competitive. This year is more competitive than last year, even.'

Entering horses in races is a minefield, and the vital skill in picking your way through is an ability to read the handicap ratings. It is your dream to see a horse rated lower than you believe it is worth. If you know that a horse is Working well beside other high-rated horses, then you can see a good cheap win ahead . . . unless, of course, some progressive type from another stable tries to work the same surprise on the same day. Sometimes a horse will seem to be greatly overrated by the handicapper: there is little choice but to enter it in races it will probably lose. Horses can always surprise, as we know, but the likely result is defeat and consequently a lower rating. And perhaps in the end it will find its level. And win – ah, if only it was all as simple as that. 'You can hunt through the programme book, and you might just discover a race that you think will suit a horse that has been overrated,' Hosgood said. 'They do exist. But there is an art to finding them!'

Hosgood was a racing journalist before he joined Dunlop. He was ten years with the *Evening Standard* and four more with the *Daily Star*. He worked as a tipster, which is the archetypal job of being on the outside looking in. But he sought a midlife career change, and wrote to Dunlop. Much to his surprise, Dunlop gave him an interview. 'I didn't think there was much chance of anything coming from it, but when he explained what he wanted, I was very interested indeed.' So Hosgood became Dunlop's racing secretary: doing the entries is a fulltime job for him, with so large a string of horses to find races for. It is normal practice for a trainer to do the entries himself, but with the size of his string and the number of race meetings he must attend, there are simply not enough hours in the day for Dunlop to give the job the niggling attention it demands. Delegation is the way Dunlop operates: and that is why Hosgood lurks among his files in the boxroom.

'I think Mr Dunlop will agree that in the past he has entered horses in races where, looking back, they had no conceivable chance. This is a complete and utter waste of time for everybody. So he gave me this job – and I tell you what, it is fascinating. I was on the outside looking in before, but now I'm inside. I'm a small cog, I can't emphasize that enough. Mr Dunlop has forgotten more about racing than I will ever learn. I'm not even from a racing background – unless you count my grandfather, who lost his pub through gambling.

— 79 —

'Sometimes you get it right, sometimes you get it wrong. When you get it right, it is marvellous. But it's never plain sailing. Everyone involved can do his job absolutely right, and something can happen that will spoil everything. It can pour down in the night, for example, and if your horse happens to be unable to act on the soft going, then all the planning, all the work has gone out the window. It is a game of chance, this, in so many ways.'

Hosgood returned to his form books, seeking that elusive winner. What was wrong? Was it him? Or what? When was the next winner going to arrive? Was it ever going to arrive? Bronzewing, the horse that had given Chris Blyth such pleasure back in April, seemed to have a great chance for the following day. And the same day was Oaks Day: Three Tails was going to start high up in the market, carrying a lot of stable money with her. And a great deal more in stable hopes. She was cast as the one to dispel the gloom at Castle Stables. It was time to win. It had been long enough. It was now 22 days since Dunlop last had a winner.

15

IF YOU THINK that colts are temperamental, then try spending
time with fillies. There is a certain kind of thoroughbred filly
whose incomprehensible quirkiness, whose baffling caprices are
enough to drive the sanest of people batty. Fillies won't do this,
or maybe they won't do that except on alternate Tuesdays.
When you think you have got the hang of her, she will invent
some other unusual way of facing life. You need patience and
gentleness with all racehorses: you need a double share with
fillies. The terrific filly Triptych was so good that she was paid
the 'compliment' of being considered more of a gelding than a
mare. You will recall that Shirley Heights, Dunlop's Derby
winner, had so many irritating habits that the lads said he had a
'fillyish' temperament.

The Oaks is the major fillies' Classic. It is run over a mile and
a half, on exactly the same course as the Derby, and three days
after the Derby itself. Oaks Day is a little strange: the vast crowds
are all gone. The Derby meeting lasts until Saturday, but after
the Wednesday of Derby Day it is like a ghost meeting. The
uncommitted public have wandered away, leaving racing to
itself once again. And on the Saturday, the twitchy, skittery
fillies assembled to race for £190,000. One of the best fancied,

Balabina, brought a goat along with her. The goat was her friend and adviser, and was brought along to keep her feeling calm and secure in the stables before the race. Three Tails, also greatly fancied, was goatless herself. But her lad, Eileen McGuffie, was pretty confident she would win, and had made a serious and sober investment in that belief. John Dunlop also thought she would win. He doesn't bet, but he had invested a great deal of his reputation in the filly. It was time for a win, and she was the horse to do it.

There comes a point when the disinterested observer comes out of the closet, abandoning every pretence of objectivity and impartiality. That was the way it was for me on Saturday 6 June. My first thought on waking was of the Oaks: of Three Tails. I knew the pleasure, the comfort, that a victory would bring. Life goes on, and the lifeblood of racing is winning.

The *Racing Post* was in the same tough mood as it had been on Derby Day. 'Three Tails has the best form, and is certain to stay, being by Blakeney out of Musidora winner Triple First, and thus a half-sister to Oaks third Maysoon. The doubt with her is the current form of the Dunlop stable (last winner 16 May), although yesterday's racing shows that things are looking up.'

This was a reference to Batallion, who finished second to the favourite in the fifth at Epsom on the Friday. A further pointer to the stable's form was, I hoped, to be shown by Bronzewing, Chris Blyth's charge. She looked a very good bet for the race before the Oaks.

Willie Carson had the ride, and before the race even got underway, he had one of the more unpleasant experiences of the season. Bronzewing rather inconsiderately unseated him on the way down to the stalls, and as Carson came out of the saddle, his foot got caught up in the stirrup. This is one of the nastiest things that can happen to anyone who rides horses. If the horse gets frightened and gallops off, you are helpless, dangling head down among the hooves. You could well be killed. John Francome, the jump jockey, once had a horrific moment when suspended upside-down from a horse called The Reject: it was, he said, one of the few times he has ever been truly terrified on a horse, and it was a major contribution to his decision to retire while the going was good.

Bronzewing couldn't decide whether to gallop or not. She stood there thinking about it while Willie stood there on one leg, one foot on the ground and the other up past his ears in the stirrup iron. Bronzewing looked jumpy and shifty. But before she could make up her mind, one of the stalls handlers managed to get a hand on her bridle: the horse jumped about a bit, regretting she had not galloped off earlier, but by then things were under control. Carson was legged back into the saddle, and Bronzewing accepted being led into the stalls with a reasonable show of dignity. It was a nasty moment for everyone, and not the most propitious omen for the day.

It cannot be said that Bronzewing ran badly. But she didn't win, and that was bad enough. She finished fast, but third place is not the thing that makes racing people smile. In truth, the horse didn't get a decent run. When things are not running for you, one small item of bad luck follows another with desperate urgency. The sport is a jagged graph of stratospheric peaks and subterranean troughs. Every half hour of a racing afternoon is a peak or a trough for legions of racing people, owners, trainers, jockeys, lads, punters. When the bad luck builds up, there is no choice but, as cricketers put it, to keep buggering on.

For there is always another race, and in every unraced race, there is hope. The desperate gambler always believes the next race will see him win it all back; the beleaguered trainer knows that every horse that runs *could* come back a winner. 'Horses never cease to surprise.'

The favourite for the Oaks was Scimitarra, trained by Henry Cecil, the man for whom everything was going right. Steve Cauthen naturally had the ride, and they were sent out at 5–2. Three Tails was 3–1, with Balabina also attracting a healthy following. Balabina had been third behind Three Tails in Three Tails's only run of the season, when she had finished a pretty impressive second: *Racing Post* commented that she had 'had

none too clear a run and shaped with a deal of promise. . . .'
Three Tails had two wins as a two-year-old under her belt, and
really was a first class prospect for the race.

Off the horses went, and the 1987 Oaks, which was to be one of
the most peculiar races of the season, was underway. Fully committed, I watched with consuming interest. But to my horror, Three
Tails showed no interest in the proceedings at all. She didn't want
to know. The race is over a mile and a half: with a mile still left to
run, Carson had his whip out in a desperate attempt to make the
filly realize that this was serious. Carson is renowned for his
bobbing and weaving all-action style in a finish: but with a mile to
go he was practically turning somersaults on her back. It was
incredible thumping, pushing, driving, all-out riding, and it had
no effect on the horse whatsoever. The sight of the Carson elbows
beginning to flap so far out was enough to make anyone tear up his
betting ticket. To watch the rest of the race was a long two
minutes of purgatory for anyone who knew the Dunlops.

And then, with a couple of furlongs to go, Three Tails
suddenly noticed that she was in the middle of a horserace. How
splendid, she thought, and kicked up her heels and flew like a
bird. She ran with immense style and verve through the final
furlong: it was all far too late to do any good at all, of course,
and just enough to show that if she had put her mind to it, she
would certainly have been there or thereabouts. She was third:
third in a Classic is jolly good. Third in a Classic you thought
you were going to win is bloody awful.

Racing luck is as fickle as any filly. Dunlop's stable had been
under a cloud, where Cecil's had been lit with great shafts of
sunlight. The Derby/Oaks double had seemed to be his for the
taking as Scimitarra cruised into the lead with two furlongs to
race. But with alarming suddenness she veered away from the
pack and out of the race. Cauthen pulled her up in a couple of
strides. The vet rushed out to her: she had broken her off-fore
cannon bone. For a while it looked as if she would have to be
put down there and then, but the vet was able to splint and
bandage the leg, and she was taken back to Newmarket. It was
later discovered that a three-inch piece of bone had chipped off.

This was attached to the main bone with three screws in a surgical operation: there is every likelihood that she will recover and make a broodmare: rather a good one with any luck.

The horse was owned by Sheikh Mohammed, who also owned not only Three Tails but Unite as well – and this was the filly that went through to win the race. Michael Stoute trained her and Walter Swinburn had the ride: 'I would have beaten Steve,' Swinburn said afterwards, which is the sort of thing jockeys are supposed to say.

Dunlop had watched the race on television, still preferring not to go to the races. Tony Couch was there instead, and a weary journey home it was for him: he had set out from Arundel with two potential winners, and came home with two shattering defeats. 'It was an awful, awful day,' said Eileen, Three Tails's lad. Most awful perhaps for Couch, who had not only to look after the losers, but to field questions from the fascinated press. 'There is no question of there being a bug at Castle Stables,' he said. But even the thought of the possibility was depressing enough. 1985 all over again? God forbid. But it was now 23 days since Dunlop had last trained a winner.

16

I T WAS 12 JUNE, the day after the general election, and six days after the disaster of the Oaks. The Conservatives had won the election by a huge majority, so naturally there was a bit of talking politics to be done out on the gallops that morning. Most of racing's top people were pretty pleased with that result. The Conservatives had abolished on-course betting tax, and a Conservative government is always more likely, at least in theory, to leave the rich more spending money with which to buy racehorses. Racing survives on spare cash: people bet with it, and pay training fees with it. Racing's survival depends on the rich being rich: the top racing people voted for Maggie in their droves.

This was also the last week before Royal Ascot, which is the biggest meeting of the year. It is not a meeting with one big race: the point about Royal Ascot is that they are all big races. One race of enormous quality is followed by another, and a winner here is a real prize for any trainer in the land. Mind you, for Dunlop's stable a winner in a selling plate at Thirsk or Carlisle would have been a great leap forward.

After Three Tails had disgraced herself in the Oaks, nothing had run very badly. The only problem was that they did not go past the post in front of the others. The cloud of depression still hung over the stable. Every paper you picked up seem to imply in its smallest print that you would have to be an idiot to back a Dunlop horse.

At Castle Stables, the depression expressed itself as bustle. Everyone was charging about, shouting instructions at each other and getting on with things at a great pace: it was all terribly workmanlike and terribly forced. Everyone was putting a Brave Face on things. Because no winners meant that there was something very badly wrong; no winners meant no bonuses; no winners meant that the stable was not doing its job. Where is the job satisfaction in that? And so there was much whistling and bustling and banging of brooms about the yard: well, things must change soon, mustn't they? Well, they couldn't get any worse. Could they?

John Dunlop had still not been to the races since Tim's death. Who can blame him? English people know neither how to give nor how to receive sympathy. He decided to start racing again after Ascot: 'Ascot is such a social meeting, with all those lunches you have to have with people. If I went, I know everyone would be so embarrassed.' Instead, Tony Couch, bustling and sounding more Yorkshire than ever, was flying the flag at the races. His own bustling straightforwardness during these difficult times had set the tone for the rest of the yard. Someone had to look cheerful, after all.

The weather was doing its best. It was a beautiful sunlit morning, and it was a joy to be out on the gallops, to lean against the Japanese Range Rover and wait for the horses to come past. 'What about a nice big Ascot winner to put a spring back into everybody's step?' I said.

'Yes,' Dunlop said. 'That would be the thing. I thought the Oaks would be the race to cheer us all up, in fact. Ah well. It's either feast or famine.' The two-year-olds began to canter past in their tight groups of six. 'The Oaks filly was a total enigma,' Dunlop continued. 'Halfway through the race, I started to tear my hair out. I thought there must be something desperately wrong, the way she was running. I really thought she was going to be tailed off. It was quite remarkable that she managed to finish third in the end. I can't believe that was right. She came back totally sound – and I am totally puzzled.

'She very much slouches at home, she does her Work in a very relaxed way. But she has always runs her races perfectly normally. But she reverted to that sloppy, disinterested approach to life in the Oaks . . . which was not quite the day to do it. It could have been the course, I suppose, but she was in as much trouble going uphill as she was going down. Yet before the race she looked marvellous, very relaxed, and I thought she really was in tophole condition.'

In one way, Love The Groom's Derby run was less of a disappointment, since less was expected of him. In some ways it was more of one because, for a moment, it looked as if he might have been capable of doing something fairly useful. 'He ran an interesting race,' Dunlop said. You will notice that his habit of pared understatement remained unimpaired. 'I thought for a moment he was going to make it into the first four, which would have been more than pleasing. My feeling at the time was that he didn't get the trip, and Willie felt very much the same. But the thing was, he got baulked, and once that had happened he just couldn't pick up again. In a race run at that sort of pace, once you have been stopped, you can't get going again.'

The two-year-olds were sorted out in their pairs for Work, this being a Friday, and of course by now all the younger horses were expected to Work for their living. Two by two, they thundered past, each with a lad curled over the withers. Dunlop's Work is done on a six-furlong uphill stretch: horsemen love to see a horse do his preparation uphill. You can put a great deal of work into a much smaller amount of space and time, and therefore put the horse under less stress for the same amount of Work. And more importantly, you can get the horses to work at the same quality at less speed: and it is speed that causes most training injuries.

The two-year-olds were beginning to come to themselves, and it was a heartwarming sight to see them burning up the gallop with such enthusiasm. They did not look the products of a beaten yard. There were two in particular that caught the eye. The first was a very handsome colt, the white-faced Nureyev, who had acquired enough individuality to be referred to by his name, which was Alwuhush. The second was the delightfully made Lomond filly: 'Can you remember her name this time?' I asked.

'Yes. Ashayer.'

'She does look good.'

'I think she might be quite nice. And I like the way the Nureyev colt covers such a lot of ground. Alwuhush. Even though you can see that he's not properly organized yet.' These young horses tend to crash about on the gallops with great enthusiasm but their galloping action tends to be a little sprawly and babyish, and it fails to convert all their new-found power into speed. But it comes, it comes. And Ashayer had a precocious poise and balance that had Dunlop purring beside me. 'You can tell from the balance and action that she really might be quite nice.'

'Nice? As good as that?'

'Nice. Special.'

'Special means what?'

'Special means proper. Serious.' Dunlop was teasing, but he was also being serious himself. A possible Classic horse, though it would be ridiculously rash and downright improper to say so right now. Simply that here we have a filly that looks tremendous. Here, perhaps, was the great disappointment of the autumn, or of the following season – but perhaps the horse to rescue the season. Or to recall Dunlop's words of a few months back, it was possible that she might be the greatest racehorse ever to set foot on a track. There was still no knowing, but what we did know for certain was that, well, Ashayer was looking gorgeous. That was enough to be going on with.

Earlier that morning, Dunlop had whisked his entire Ascot contingent down to Findon. The idea was to give the horses a change that would put some ginger into them: and it seemed to have worked, at least that morning. They had been on their toes, sharp, excited, and ready to show what they were capable of. Richard Baerlein had startled and pleased me that morning by writing a piece in *The Guardian* that flew in the face of the accepted wisdom of the pundits and the obvious non-form of Castle Stables. Strong Dunlop Challenge for Royal Ascot, said the heading.

'John Dunlop, whose horses appear to be on the brink of finding their form, will be saddling nine horses at Ascot next week,' Baerlein wrote. 'Our old friend Patriach will be trying for the double in the Royal Hunt Cup, but the stable's chief moneyspinner, the St Leger winner Moon Madness, will be up against Henry Cecil's Yorkshire Cup winner, Verd-Antique, in the Hardwicke Stakes. . . . It will be the highlight of Friday's card.'

'So how strong is the hand for Ascot?' I asked.

'It could be stronger. But if I get a few to run well, I will be pleased.' So would I, so would everybody in the yard.

The weather remained marvellous until the horses had returned from second lot. What with the sun and the horses beginning to look so good at home, Dunlop was finding himself in a more cheerful mood than of late. Moon Madness had gone particularly well, and Love The Groom had also Worked impressively. 'He doesn't seem to have taken too much out of himself in the Derby,' Dunlop said. He had come back from the Derby very sore in front, but he soon recovered, and had Worked like a 100 percenter that morning. Unless he had hurt himself in the gallop, he was all set to run on the first day of Royal Ascot, on the following Tuesday. A trainer on a losing streak must nail his colours to the mast again and again before the eyes of the cynical public. The only way of squashing the rumours and restoring public confidence is by producing winners: every blank day added more pressures.

'It has,' I said, choosing my words like a man picking his steps through a minefield, 'been, er, a fairly leanish sort of spell. . . .'

'Bloody awful spell.'

'Can you see the light at the end of the tunnel?'

'I hope so. This week, the horses have all been running well, though without winning. A couple of seconds, that sort of thing.

I think it is possible, in retrospect, that we have had a little infection rumbling. We've taken tests, we're always taking tests, every kind of test, but nothing has shown up. It is possible that there has been some kind of low key thing that makes all the horses a little off-colour without making them really ill . . . on the other hand, it is possible that they're just not a terribly good lot. We're short of stars, that's for sure.' Moon Madness would doubtless be giving us hurt looks from his box had we been within earshot. 'But it's been a pretty bleak month, really. Things can only get better.'

'I suppose so,' I said. 'But you can't rely on those bloody four-legged things over there.'

'No,' said Dunlop. 'That you cannot.' The horses were now helping themselves to a quiet pick of grass, a customary relaxing treat for them after they have done their bit for the day. It was 28 days since Dunlop had last trained a winner.

17

A GREAT SWATHE of rain swept across the country and announced that summer was here. With it came just one more blow for John Dunlop. At the time there was an energetic campaign to bring down the price of Ladbrokes shares through the process of discredit by rumour. Whispers of improper conduct flooded the City – the source was later discovered and Ladbrokes ended up holding their own in reasonable comfort, but they had a few nasty moments on the way. Ladbrokes basically played a straight bat, offering blanket denials and an injunction. But they later added to their formal denial of everything by stating that there was no improper connection between Ladbrokes and John Dunlop.

Dunlop was outraged. This sort of thing has roughly the same soothing effect as an announcement on an aeroplane that 'there is absolutely no cause for alarm'. The story was only really taken up by *The Independent*, and Dunlop wondered about sueing. But of course, he could not: he had not been defamed at all. The point was the *denial* of any race-fixing. *Private Eye* operates the denial principle to great effect as a matter of policy, telling the world such things as: 'Obviously there is no truth in the rumours that the archdeacon and the bishop's wife are at it like knives.'

The Dunlop part of the Ladbrokes injunction was later withdrawn, but Dunlop was still deeply angry. He had rung around his many City contacts: all of them had heard plenty of Ladbrokes rumours, but none that connected Ladbrokes with Dunlop. Why, then, was it necessary to deny a Dunlop connection? Dunlop has the cleanest reputation in racing. He doesn't have an account with Ladbrokes, or with anybody else, for that matter: he doesn't bet. The idea of Ladbrokes having an improper relationship with Dunlop was, to anybody in racing, quite laughable.

Ron Pollard, a Ladbrokes director, was very frank when I spoke to him. 'We were trying to turn the whole thing into a laugh,' he said. 'Every ten minutes there was a different rumour. There was supposed to be a big exposé in the *Daily Mail*, but that never happened. The Dunlop thing was so ludicrous – no one would ever say anything against John Dunlop, he is the last man in England you would suspect of anything improper.'

'Did you stress the Dunlop line to emphasize how ludicrous the rumours were?'

'I would imagine that was so, yes.'

So there it is: if you are honest you have to carry an extra heavy burden. 'It was all very unsettling,' Dunlop said. 'What with Tim, and the bloody horses running badly. . . .'

Never was the small comfort of a winner so badly needed. Royal Ascot began on 16 June, the weather was awful, Tony Couch took the horses down to Ascot, Dunlop stayed in Arundel, and it was now 31 days since he had last run a winner. The racing world was full of sympathy and was conscientiously putting its money elsewhere.

Royal Ascot is the best race meeting of the year, only it is not. Every year it brings together the best horses in the country, and a band of champions from abroad. Hot prospect does battle with hot prospect: promise lines up alongside achievement, hope gallops beside disappointment. Ascot is one of the great proving grounds of racing.

And of course, Royal Ascot is also a social nonsense. Many of the people there would be as happy with a bunch of selling platers as they are with the finest horses in Europe. Indeed, they would not notice the difference. Their concern is not with the equine aristocrats that parade and race before them: it is the human aristocrats who count.

At no other sporting event save Henley does the actual sport play such a small part. It has the Scrooges of the racing world muttering 'Bah! Humbug!' but when the stalls clang open there is a treat every time for those who want it. The rain fell on the massed hats of Ascot, and the wind got up and tried to whisk the sillier confections across the heath, and it became the Ascot of the designer umbrella. Rain fell in torrents, but everyone tried to ignore it and to get on with the business of being jolly.

At the stable end of Royal Ascot, everything is quite deadly serious. The Royal Enclosure and the pre-parade ring: two more different atmospheres could not be imagined. One is all froth and nonsense and jollity, the other is all grim purpose. That is professional sport for you: sport is basically frivolous and jolly, and its purpose is to give us all pleasant times. But to achieve this, the pursuit of victory must be performed with consummate seriousness. If there is no jollity on one side and no seriousness on the other, then the sport has lost its way. It is just that at Ascot the contrasts are more marked than they are elsewhere.

Down came the rain, and off went Dunlop's first challenge at Ascot. He sent out Siyah Kalem and Flower Bowl in the first race of the meeting. It was yet another race that Dunlop failed to win. The race was won by the favourite, and the crowds cheered while the Dunlop contingent backstage glumly got on with the routine they had grown used to: losing.

The next horse from Castle Stables was Love The Groom, he who had met such ill-luck in the running in the Derby. He was to have a crack at the King Edward VII Stakes, and the punters were not over-excited by him, and he finally started at 7–1. They liked Legal Bid a great deal more; the horse had won that season already. He set off at 6–4.

It is conventional racing wisdom to keep Derby runners away from Ascot. It is too soon after. In particular, it is considered unwise to run your Derby failure at Ascot: all he will do is lower his reputation still further in a race that everyone is watching. Dunlop decided to ignore conventional wisdom and give Love The Groom his chance.

Willie Carson was suspended at the time, so Pat Eddery had the ride. Legal Bid sailed off, attempting to do a Reference Point and make all. He had won the Derby Trial at Lingfield using those tactics. So off he went with the field in pursuit, but this time, as the winning post came into view, the field started to surge back. A couple of horses briefly sparkled and gave their backers a start of delight that was soon squashed. For suddenly the race was won. Decisively, strongly, inevitably, with one and a half furlongs to go, Love The Groom made his run and, with Eddery poised and compact, kneeling on the withers and urging the horse on and on, he slammed the field of equine aristocrats and hammered past the post. The drought was over.

And it was done with some style, in a Group race at Ascot worth £50,000. The crowds laughed and got on with the routines of jollity. For the Dunlop team it was joy unalloyed, the relief of Mafeking, a restoration of order. After 31 days, it was time to look the world in the face again and to talk about the business of winning. Castle Stables was flooded with good wishes: it was almost as if the Derby had been won, though this was not pure triumph but relief. All Dunlop's friends were aching with delight for him and for everyone in the stable. Thank God, went the thought, and quite without blasphemy, thank God that's over.

'Dunlop Back In Groove' said the *Racing Post*, and continued in its sober way: 'Love The Groom, who cost $325,000 as a yearling, had run third to Reference Point in the Futurity last back end and on that showing was entitled to do much better than he did at Epsom. The Dunlop horses got very behind in the spring, and now that Love The Groom has found form there could be more good things to come from him.'

Love The Groom looked a very good horse indeed, and suddenly it was time to think of the Classics again. The Irish Derby, the St Leger? Couch, standing in for Dunlop still, told the world: 'Pat was very impressed with him, and said he got the trip well. He's in the Irish Derby and the Gordon Stakes at Goodwood.' This, then, was a better horse than he had looked, running for a stable whose form over the past few weeks had been, as they say, too bad to be true.

Dunlop had three more runners the following day. He had won the Royal Hunt Cup the previous year with Patriach, who went for it again, but with 25 lbs more to carry. It was too much for him: he finished eighth, 'far from disgraced' as they say, but this was a bit of a ho–hum result. Almaarad managed sixth in the Bessborough. Earlier Sergeyevich, the horse that gave Castle Stables the last win before the drought set in, ran a blinding race in the Queen's Vase. Arden, from the all–conquering Cecil stable, took the lead, and Sergeyevich, he of the lolling tongue, set off in pursuit, storming after him, and the two fought the most stirring battle along the final furlong. They drew ten lengths clear of the rest as they gave us a heart-lifting struggle for the line. Arden it was that won it on the nod: a disappointment, but as disappointments go, a pretty exhilarating one. No one could say that the Dunlop horses were running badly. And that was triumph enough to be getting on with.

Back at Castle Stables, the change in atmosphere was startling. The lads were whistling as they swept the yards, the banter with the girls had lost its routine quality, the jokes were flying about: the lads were all singing and the horses were all up on their toes. 'It's cheered us all up, you wouldn't believe how much,' said Mark Campion, one of the pupil assistants. 'We're ready to go now.'

Paolo Benedetti, the Italian agent, had turned up to talk plans, and he was fizzing with good humour and apparently half an inch off the ground into the bargain. 'Fantastic, eh?' he greeted me. 'This is a good horse. Fantastic.' Signor Benedetti is not one of life's pessimists, nor has he caught the habit of Dunlopian understatement.

Couch came into the office at that moment, and heard the word 'fantastic'. He gave one of his sly smiles: 'The press said the owner's representative had developed a craving for Guinness.

He needs to go to Dublin to sample traditional Irish spaghetti.' And Signor Benedetti roared with laughter: it was that sort of day. The Irish Derby, then? He looked good enough on Tuesday. Fairly fantastic, at the very least.

And then there was Moon Madness, who had run so nicely at Sandown before the drought, and who seemed to have recovered from his sore feet. He looked capable of great things on the last day of the Royal meeting: 'Oh yes, we've got to show these Cecil horses a thing or two sometime,' said James Burns, another pupil assistant and, like everyone else in the yard, in great heart. Lads and horses and all: everyone had a spring in his step, and everyone was convinced that things really were looking up.

On Thursday, Dunlop had no runners. On Friday, Moon Madness went out to run in the Hardwicke, and Dunlop was pretty sure he would win it.

Throughout the week, the rain fell without mercy. Every open space in the country had pools of standing water. At Ascot, the going got worse and worse, and by Friday it was officially Heavy. Moon Madness had never shown any quirky preference about what sort of ground he liked to run in: a good, solid workmanlike horse who took everything in his stride. But he found he simply could not do the business that day. He got stuck in the mud. He was tailed off, and he looked like a horse running way out of his class. Suddenly all the questions that had been asked about Castle Stables had to be asked again. A new bout of depression was exactly what Dunlop's yard could do without.

In the end then, it was not quite a fairly fantastic Ascot. 'Fairly satisfactory except for one débâcle,' Dunlop said. 'A good high and a very bad low. Love The Groom was very pleasing, he won it and won it well. Moon Madness was a complete disaster, when I thought he was – not a certainty, but he ought to have won it. All was well at Ascot apart from him. Sergeyevich ran a good race, the others ran more or less as expected.

'I now believe that the problem has been a low grade infection, and I think it has affected some horses more than others – Three Tails in the Oaks being a case in point. One must just be grateful when a horse does come back to form.' Or when 200 of them do.

18

MOON MADNESS WAS not in disgrace. Conditions were so extreme in that race, it could only be that the ground had beaten him. As horses grow, horses change, and for whatever reason, it was obvious that Moon Madness was no longer capable of handling such appalling conditions.

Certainly his owner, though disappointed, bore him no grudge. Lavinia, Duchess of Norfolk, continued her morning ritual of going to the gallops to see the horses. And his rider Tom Hamill was as used to it as the horse: the horse would see the Duchess and immediately stop, so that she could pat him and make much of him. A few caresses, a few words of horsy drivel, and Moon Madness got on with the job again.

The Duchess does not live in the castle, but in a house in Arundel Park. The view is beautiful, and made lovelier still by the daily passage of 150 thoroughbred horses. The Duchess is a horsewoman through and through, and she has known a few animals over the years. But Moon Madness is her favourite horse ever. 'Oh yes, the best I have ever had. A wonderful constitution, a wonderful character. He has given me more pleasure than any racehorse I have ever known. His character just shines out of his face. He's quite lovely. One of those horses that always seems to know exactly what's happening.'

There are some owners who know nothing, and others who know everything. The Duchess is in the latter category. She has run a training yard herself, and she rode in point to points before she was married: 'I can't remember how many I won. Not very many, I shouldn't think. I married when I was 19, and my husband stopped me. I told him it was much safer than hunting, because at least you knew what was on the other side of the fence in point to pointing. But he wouldn't let me risk it. I used to race in Mickey Mouse colours. I rode in black with a white cap, like Lord Derby's colours, except that I had a big Mickey Mouse on the front and the back.'

Her husband Bernard, the 15th Duke of Norfolk, was a racing man every bit as much as he was a cricket man. He was the Queen's representative at Royal Ascot for years, as well as being a great owner and supporter of the game. 'When my husband was alive one had great fun,' the Duchess continued. 'I had a great deal more to do with the stables and when and where the horses ran. When he died, I didn't go racing so much. One didn't have terribly good horses. And I was terribly busy with all my work in the county as Lord Lieutenant – so I had really rather given up going racing, apart from when I had something exciting running.

'But Moon Madness revived my interest. All the same, I don't think I'd go any more unless I had a horse that was running. In the old days I went to the races a lot. But all my great racecourse friends have died: Jack Clayton, Peter Hastings, Gerry Fielden . . . about eight people I used to see all the time at the races have died. So the racing world has changed for me. I go when I have a runner. I really am so busy these days that if I have a runner at Goodwood, I might go just for that race.'

Most of us owe a special debt to one person, and generally a quite unpayable debt at that. John Dunlop knows that he owes an immense amount to the Duchess; that is why he was so pleased to win the St Leger for her with Moon Madness last year. It was the Duchess and her late husband who gave Dunlop, as a young nobody, the job of trainer at Castle Stables. The debt goes further than that: had it not been for the Duchess there would be no racing stable in Arundel.

Arundel has not been a training centre for hundreds of years, like Newmarket: it just feels that way. Arundel Castle and the surrounding park is simply the seat of the Norfolk family, which is the most prominent lay Catholic family in England. The town is dominated not just by the castle, but also by a monstrous cathedral, one which looks enough for a sizeable French town, not just a little spot in Sussex. In fact, the cathedral looks as if it had been uprooted from France and dumped incongruously in England: it is a 19th-century job, and was designed by Joseph Hansom, the man who gave the world the eponymous cab. The cathedral contains the remains of the Norfolks' own family saint, St Philip Howard, who died in prison during Elizabeth i's reign, possibly poisoned.

But Arundel had never been a racing centre. Cricket, yes, in that lovely arena: they started the cricket at Arundel in the 19th century. It was not until the Second World War that they brought in the racehorses. There had always been stables there, obviously, but they were for transport and for hunters. The Norfolks kept their racehorses further from home, at Mitchel-grove.

Mitchelgrove was requisitioned during the Second World War, and it gradually became impossible to train horses there. The bangs of the rifle ranges were problem enough, but when they started to use the gallops as tank tracks the end was in sight. The Duchess then had her inspiration: bring the lot over to Arundel Park.

'Oh, it was such hard work. We had no gallops, so they had to be made. We had to take up a lot of trees – not trees that mattered, of course, but a great number of them all the same. Our trainer, Victor Gilpin, had gone off to the war, and his head lad, Fred Bancroft, held the licence. So he and I trained the horses together. We started with a very few horses.

'My daughter trains a few horses herself these days, not far from here. That means I can go down and interfere, which I thoroughly enjoy – that's what I really like doing best. One can't do it with a big string such as John has now, of course. I used to ride out every day – but now I prefer to see them working.'

The Duchess owns a stud, which is managed by Dunlop, yet another string to his bow. Most people would have found training 200 racehorses enough, but he likes to be involved with such things as the European Pattern Race Committee, a Jockey Club committee involved in research into the virus, and running the stud as well. The Duchess bought a share in a stallion called Vitiges, who turned out to be such a disaster that people wouldn't send him the mares to submit to his embraces. He ended up being packed off to Japan, to stand at stud there.

The Duchess said: 'I had a mare called Castle Moon, which was quite well bred, but really rather small, and not very good either. So I put her to Vitiges – and the result was Moon Madness. The mare has also given us Wood Chanter, who is a full brother to Moon Madness, and quite promising, and Sheriff's Star, a good horse by Posse – and Posse was a failure at stud. So it is not the sire I have to thank, but the mare. She has a two-year-old in training by Mummy's Pet called Moon Mystery, and a yearling by Touching Wood, and she is in foal again.

'I have ten mares at the stud. The whole fun of that is seeing the foals and the yearlings, and keeping them in training. I haven't actually bought a horse for ages, I can't remember the last time. But I owe so much to Moon Madness. Thanks to the generosity of Moon Madness, I can afford to have ten horses in training. If it wasn't for all the money he has won, I shouldn't think I would have one. Training is so expensive, you see. It used to be so different. When I used to do the accounts, it cost £4/10 a week to train a horse.'

'And what is racing all about, for you?' I asked. 'Is it the winning?'

'Oh no. No. I think it's the horses. The thing is that you can't afford to keep horses nowadays unless they do win. Racing is so commercial. It is always a question of trying to find the money to pay for the horses you have in training. I can't afford it – but

Moon Madness manages to pay for it. I have had such fun racing all my life, and I have done so much of it – but I think now that I would only go racing so long as I had decent horses.'

Not long after Royal Ascot, the Duchess fell ill. Moon Madness looked for her in vain on the gallops. Her trainer, and everyone else at Arundel, began to get worried about her.

19

I T WOULD BE nice to write that Love The Groom opened the floodgates, and from that moment on, John Dunlop could do nothing to prevent himself from training winners. But racing does not go like that, as Moon Madness had already shown. Naturally, the sport will not always live up to its own rules: Henry Cecil was having a season of impossible, unimaginable success. Apart from his own débâcle in the Oaks, in which his filly broke her leg, everything seemed to go according to plan: stars won big races, middle rankers won their tasty handicaps, the plodders won their small races. It was a year in defiance of everything that everyone in racing is accustomed to: and it went on and on happening.

But at Castle Stables, at least the dark times were over, and the winners had started arriving again, even if they could have done so more rapidly for everybody's taste. Nine days after Love The Groom, Castle Stables won a small race with Sea Island, and the day after, picked up another with Betty Jane. It wasn't feast, but it was a lot better than famine. Most of the people at Castle Stables had been accustomed from the cradle to the rhythms of winning and losing, and after that dreadful period was over, they were content to remember that winners would come in their own good time.

So many racing people are surprised when you ask them how they came into racing. They don't really understand how anyone can *not* be in racing: racing is life, the universe and everything: another way of life simply cannot exist. So many of them have mothers or fathers in racing: racing is the natural business of man, and there is an end to it. People who frowst in bed till seven of a morning and who have two days off and as much as £150 a week: such people are weirdies, abnormal people to the average stable lad. Racing is life, and there is no more to be said on the matter.

In a couple of sentences, most lads will make you feel dizzy and wonder which century you are in: my father was with Mr This – not old Mr This, of course, but young Mr This, a great governor, but he moved on when Mr That took over. Later on I joined Mr Thing . . . it is not just the pedigrees of horses that are effortlessly recalled: half the trainers, lads, assistants and owners seem to have connections with racing that go back through generations.

The sport seems to be quite literally self-perpetuating. Racing people are brought up surrounded by horse-talk and the names of winners. No one had had to learn the jargon about rigs and crypt-orchids and good doers: they have all known it more or less from conception.

Almost all racing people are born horsy. But a few of them achieve horsiness. Such a one is Jeremy Noseda, who had joined Dunlop five years previously as a pupil assistant, and had since been promoted to assistant trainer, which made him number three in the yard. He is fluent, intelligent, and has a natural eye for a horse: you would have thought him a racing man from generations back. But no, he entered racing not in deference to family traditions, but in defiance of them. 'I applied for university when I was at school, and I had a choice of places to take up. This was what my parents wanted me to do. But I said no: I wanted to go into racing.'

It must have been slightly appalling for them: wealthy people in property, who naturally looked for their son to move into the fine business that was waiting for him. It is not only racing that values continuity. But racing, rackety, louche and financially precarious: this was neither a safe nor a respectable calling. Racing has never been much of a sport for the middle classes: it is traditionally a joy for 'the nobs and the slobs', with the virtuous folk in the middle cheerfully squeezed out, unable to understand the point of it all.

Noseda saw the point of it all right. In fact, he was irredeemably hooked. 'I had wanted to go into racing since the age of ten. And I had been fascinated by racing from much younger than that – all from the television. I can remember watching the ITV-7 every Saturday until I went to boarding school, watching it when I was five or six, fascinated. By the time I was seven, the first thing I would do every day was to read the racing results. By the time I was at boarding school, I was always in touch with racing, I always knew all the results.

'I remember skiving off to watch Empery win the Derby in 1976, and I got caught. I was sent to the headmaster, and I got six ferrulas – this was a Jesuit school, and the ferrula was a whalebone covered in leather. You got six of these on the hand, and you would see all the blood vessels come to the surface, and where they had broken.'

But Noseda's early attempt to rival the blood-vessel breaking performances of Tommy Way still failed to put him off racing. His life seems to have featured a series of determined attempts from a succession of people to put him off racing, all of whom have failed. 'I still didn't regret the ferrulas, because Lester Piggott was riding Empery, and he was a hero of mine, so I was just delighted. And I still wanted to go into racing. I have never wanted to do anything else, in fact.

'But I never wanted to be a jockey. I always wanted to be a trainer. Lester Piggott was a hero, but the real one for me was Vincent O'Brien. He was the man I wanted to be. The only trouble was that I had still never sat on a horse in my life. The nearest I had been to one was on Horse Guards Parade. I was 15 before I started riding. I told my parents that I wanted to go into racing, and I wanted to learn to ride.' Doubtless they thought he would grow out of it. But as kind parents do, they gave him their genuine, even while patently bewildered, support, and tried to do their best by him. They sent him to learn with David and Marion Mould. This was a good choice. There he learned not to sit on a horse but to ride, and there is a lot of difference.

And Noseda was not put off by the reality of horses. He confessed to David Mould that he had set his heart on going into racing. Mould instantly and kindly told him he was mad. As a matter of fact, there is a great wariness between all the different sects of horsy people, rather as there is between various denominations of Christianity. All horsy people are brothers under the skin, but they tend to concentrate on their differences rather than on their similarities. Rather like the church, in fact, or if you prefer, like factions of the Labour party. A showjumper will think that eventing people are too hard on their horses; a steeplechaser will think a showjumper is a cissy; and carriage drivers will scarcely be able to comprehend racing people. And because of its rackety reputation, much exaggerated as it is, flat racing always seems the most peculiar and most foreign discipline for the average horseperson to accept. Most ordinary horsy people are sublimely uninterested in racing, which is, of course, their own loss.

Mould had a good and kindly notion: he said he would send Noseda down to work for a couple of months with Brian Swift, 'and if after that you still want to work in racing, we'll know you must be serious.' Brian Swift trained at Epsom before his death, and he had Noseda with him for two months, doing horses, riding out, and working all the hours that God sent. After two months, Noseda returned to school and the real world with nothing but reluctance. He was more determined than ever to go into racing. By this time, there was not a lot anybody could do about it.

In the summer before his A-level year, he went to work with Jeremy Tree, and there seemed to be no further question of his having second thoughts or getting put off. As expected, he loved his time with Tree, too. He returned to school, and did his A-levels, in politics, English and history, and was offered university places to read politics and history. But by this stage, there was no danger whatsoever of his coming to his senses. Instead he started writing to racehorse trainers. He was given an interview by J. L. Dunlop, and joined him as a pupil assistant. A pupil assistant is expected to work his brains out, learn and absorb everything, and slowly acquire responsibilities, becoming 'less and less pupil and more and more assistant – at least, that's the idea', as Dunlop himself explained it. And Noseda might have been born to the job.

The current season was his fifth at Arundel, and when the correct next move opens up before him, he will take it. Dunlop will always be the man he owes his biggest debt to, for all that Dunlop may think he has repaid it pretty well. But it was Dunlop who set him on the road his heart wanted, and it is hard to do more for anybody than that. 'I love it here, and Mr Dunlop is a great man to work for. I have had the chances to work in other yards – but the thing about working here is that there are so many opportunities to do so much. In a smaller yard it just wouldn't happen, I wouldn't be given the same sort of responsibility. But Mr Dunlop works by delegation, so I get so many really important jobs to do.'

Naturally, Noseda's long-term ambition is to train himself, to have a crack at being Vincent O'Brien, or J. L. Dunlop, or something. To be a racehorse trainer, you need luck, contacts, an understanding or better still a demented bank manager, or simply money. (To be a successful trainer requires a little more than that, but I am talking about starting.) Noseda's family may not be horsy, but they have been very successful, and they have that commodity that is so useful in racing, money. And that will give Noseda the most perfect kickstart to his training career: the family have already bought a training yard in Newmarket. It is a profit-making venture, and was leased to Pip Payne. There are 24 boxes there, planning permission for 30 more, and long-term ambitions of increasing the capacity still further. It is a sound investment for a property business: it is a dream come true for an aspiring trainer. It is unbelievable, and in a way, terrifying. It would be so easy to go off at half-cock.

'I want to train one day, and I will have a go at it. I don't say I can do the job properly as yet. But I am well on the way to saying that in three years' time, perhaps, I will be ready. When the time comes, I'll know if I'm ready or not.

'But I am not planning to go into training to hang around for 20 years or so. I'll either make it, or I won't. I won't have people saying, oh, Jeremy Noseda, yes, he's all right, trains 20 winners a year, but he'll never train a really *good* horse. No. I'll stop before that happens. But I'll have a go!

'I could go into the family business, and make a lot more money than I do now. But I have an ambition to do something. And even if I fail, I will have tried. I won't be looking back and saying, well, I thought about it, but in the end I didn't bother.' He will probably end up a great success, and siring a great dynasty of racing people. In years to come, people may be saying: 'I was with Mr Noseda – not old Mr Noseda what trained Whizzbang to win the Derby in 2001, but young Mr Noseda . . .'

20

'Look at him,' said Mike Huntley-Robertson. 'Isn't he a glorious horse? Aren't you boy? A glorious horse, eh?' And getting the better of his diffidence, he leaned over and gave the glossy black neck half a dozen wary pats. His son Oliver and his girlfriend Ulle watched with even more wariness.

Huntley-Robertson was full of delight and pride, but he didn't quite know what to do. He didn't know what sort of etiquette horses expect. He was very happy, but also completely out of place, and that is not a usual thing for a rich man. He owned half a share in that muscly four-year old, Boon Point, and he found everything to do with horses baffling. He had worked out which end to feed the Polo mints, and which bits a man might pat without giving offence, but that was about the extent of it. His ignorance was boundless: but then so was his pleasure. He was like a domestic chicken that had somehow reared a bird of paradise. He was delighted but somewhat bemused.

He is involved in the oil business, and is very successful in it, too. Nobody's fool on his own ground. His best friend and partner is man called Nathan Avery, and Avery has been involved in racing for years, and has owned several horses.

Outside of work, it is his big thing. 'Nathan is so keen on it,' Huntley-Robertson said. 'He is two feet off the ground when he is looking at his horses.'

Like all men with a passion, Avery is convinced that all men's lives would be richer for sharing it. Naturally he had taken his friend and partner to the races and to share other horsy treats, and Huntley-Robertson seemed to understand and to be infected by the joys of it. And so it was natural that the two of them went to the Highflyer Yearling Sales in Newmarket in 1984.

The Highflyer Sales are bewildering to an outsider, but no one was as bewildered as Huntley-Robertson when he was approached by his friend's trainer, a chap called John Dunlop. Dunlop shook his hand and congratulated him on being the new owner of 50 per cent of a chunky black yearling colt. 'I didn't know what was going on,' Huntley-Robertson said, roaring with laughter at the memory. 'Mr Dunlop said to me: "You are about to be hooked."' He laughed again, full of delight. 'And here I am!'

Boon Point is a son of Shirley Heights, the colt with the 'fillyish' temperament who Dunlop trained to win the Derby, and who is now such a terrific stallion. Nothing fillyish about him these days, ask the mares. Shirley Heights is a son of Mill Reef: Mill Reef is the name of a real reef that lies off Antigua. Shirley Heights is the highest point on the island. After the chunky black son of Shirley Heights had been bought, the Avery family turned to Antigua in the atlas, and his wife found that the name for the northernmost point on the island was Boon Point. A pretty good name.

And as it turned out, a pretty good horse, if not quite as swift as his dad. He won three times as a three-year-old: you really could not ask any more from your first horse, or any horse for that matter. It is no wonder that Huntley-Robertson is so proud of him. 'And how is he going?' he asked the lad who was riding him, Mick Gettins – Boon Point's usual lad, Steven Brain, was on holiday.

'Very well, sir,' Gettins answered.

Huntley-Robertson couldn't think of another question. He didn't know the sort of things you say to lads or horses, but all the same, he was delighted to be there. He lives in Lucerne, and works supplying drilling tools for oil exploration. Neither Arundel nor the great racecourses of England are exactly next door, but he and Avery have managed to get to a fair number of Boon Point's races. 'Once I missed him win when Swissair, of all people, broke down. But we received a wonderful telex that said he had won.' Sad, indeed, to have a horse that wins over the telex, but all wins must be savoured and revelled in: Huntley-Robertson had learned that all right.

'John Dunlop is so kind, he lets us take up so much of his time,' he continued, with a businessman's instinctive understanding of the problems of another. A trainer is a public man, and is also a public relations man. A major part of his business is coping with people, and being constantly available to people: in a way, a racehorse trainer is rather like a vicar: always in a good humour, always prepared to give time and trouble to his flock. The hardest part of training is training the owners: many a trainer will tell you that. If they all trained on as well as Huntley-Robertson, a trainer's life would be a great deal easier. You couldn't wish for a more easy-going fellow, freely admitting his own ignorance, and eager to learn and enjoy more.

We all bounced across the grass in the Japanese Range Rover, Dunlop to see the string and Huntley-Robertson to see his boy. His son Oliver was looking eager with a tremendously fancy camera. And Huntley-Robertson was able to recognize his own horse: not at all an easy thing to do, as a matter of fact, especially for a novice owner. Many more experienced owners would have trouble picking out their own beasts from a string of 70-odd horses: many don't even recognize their own horse in the parade ring at the races. Acquiring an eye for a horse takes a bit of doing: Dunlop always very tactfully tells his owners which horse to feel a gush of pride for: 'Here's your boy, with the black jacket and the red cap.' (The clothes will actually be worn by the lad.)

Gettins thundered past, stirrup leathers a sensibly conservative length. 'Here he comes, tongue hanging out as usual,' Huntley-Robertson said.

'His dad always did the same thing,' Dunlop added.

The horses cantered past us, and we moved on. 'It is not a business,' Huntley-Robertson said. 'It is only for pleasure. He has paid for his feed, though. But I am just happy to have had something to do with this glorious horse. I don't bet much – I spent three days at Ascot, had a wonderful time, and didn't have a single bet. But when my horse runs, I like to have fifty or a hundred on him. Just for loyalty.'

At the end of the exercise, the horses were let out on to a long rein, so that they could crop the grass as usual. 'It relaxes them,' Dunlop said. 'They soon learn that this means the day's work is over.' It is not always the most relaxing time for the lads: racehorses can get the twitches and leap about at anything: the lads are particularly vulnerable with the reins let out so long, and the heads down so low. The chances of staying on board at a sudden alarum are drastically reduced.

Huntley-Robertson approached Gettins and Boon Point with a packet of Polos. Boon Point ate the lot. Then something startled him, and he whirled away through 180 degrees, in one of those frantic Torvill and Dean spins that the thoroughbred specializes in. Gettins sat beautifully tight and reeled the horse back in, persuading him that a frantic gallop into the middle distance was not strictly necessary. Dunlop is very hot on lads who go effing and blinding in front of owners, so Gettins contented himself with a brief and pungent mutter.

There was another kerfuffle at the far end, where the fillies were standing, and this time one of the riders was unshipped, and a filly was revelling in the freedom of Arundel Park. Dunlop's loose horse catcher, Denis Hartigan, who drives behind the string in a van, set off in pursuit; Shona Crombie stood up ruefully. Mostly these spills are a good laugh to everyone else, but horrible accidents are always a possibility where horses are concerned. But Shona was all right. Not happy, but all right.

The string meandered back to the stables. Gettins hopped off, and led Boon Point back to his box and untacked him. 'Beautiful mover, isn't he?' Gettins said, 'Big bugger, too, isn't he? I reckon he grew over the winter, even bigger than before. He's got some shoulder on him, hasn't he? Great ride too – but he gets the old heart going sometimes. Eh, you old bugger?'

Gettins knows the horse one hundred times better than his co-owner, likes him, gets on with him, has a rapport with him. And Boon Point isn't even the horse that he 'does'. Boon Point has given Huntley-Robertson a great deal of unblemished joy. But there must be the odd moment when he envies Gettins. Horses can give some people the kind of riches that you can't put in a bank.

21

O N 30 JUNE, Willie Carson booted Angel City over the line for a nice little win at Newbury. During the Great Drought, Angel City had got turned over when starting at even money favourite, so this win, at 9–4, did a little towards paying people back. Angel City looked a promising horse that day, one to keep an eye on.

The lad doing Angel City was Ken Bedford, but he is always called Scobie. Even the governor calls him Scobie. He had ridden in races as an apprentice, and had once attracted the comment that he rode like Scobie Breasley. 'I've had my chance in races, and I've ridden alongside the best,' he said. 'It didn't work out for me as a jockey, but well, I've had my chance, I've been there, and I've got no regrets.'

Another of the lads, Stuart Johnston, always called Angus, had been through the same disappointment, with the same start-lingly cheerful acceptance: 'At least I've had a go. I remember one time trying to ride a finish, and I was absolutely knackered a long way before we reached the post. You read reports on races, they say "horse blew up". Mine should have said "jockey blew up".'

Many lads go into the business wanting to be jockeys, but

few make it. As Steve Coppell, the former England footballer, now manager of Crystal Palace, said of apprentice footballers: 'It's like turtles and the sea: thousands are hatched but very few ever make it.' A lot of small townees come into racing not knowing how to ride, with careers masters naturally wanting to shove every five-footer into an obvious niche like a racing stable. They can learn on the job, or better at the apprentice school at Newmarket, as did Shona Crombie, who had involuntarily dismounted the day Mike Huntley-Robertson had been up to see his glorious horse. Dunlop will often have a school report on his desk: schoolteachers tend to a certain kind of frankness. '"It is hard to make a comment on a pupil I have seen so rarely",' Dunlop read. 'His mother says: "I know the report is not marvellous". Ha. Still, he seemed a very jolly chap, I think we'll give him a month's trial.'

The door to ladship is always open; the door to jockeyship is barred to all but a few. You need a rare combination of talent and luck to burst through apprentice jockeyship to the real thing. Your governor may well give you rides – an apprentice is allowed to ride with seven pounds less weight, and so a good one is a very useful thing to have about the place – but breaking through into real jockeyship, that is another matter entirely.

'If I told you my ambition, you'd laugh,' said Paul Coombes, another lad. We spoke just after second lot, which meant that the day was over the hump, and that Coombes was disposed to be chatty. Intelligent, articulate and sharp, it wasn't quite clear to me whether he was ideally suited to the job of being a stable lad, or whether it was a constant frustration to him.

'I promise I won't laugh,' I said.

'Ever since I was a little kid, I've had a thing about the Grand National. And I've always wanted to ride in it. Even just to fall at the first fence. I was born within spitting distance of the Grand National course – literally. You know there are three houses you can see on the television where the horses pull up? I was born in the one on the left. But I know I'll never fulfil the ambition. I'm much too light for it.'

Coombes seems to know everything about racing; any pub

dispute in the land could be settled by asking Coombes the longest priced horse to win the Derby or who won the Guineas in 1974. And of course, like every true racing man, the blood-lines of the great horses run through his conversation unceas-ingly. He knows every pedigree as a matter of course, and at the drop of a hat will tell you every race Jalmood won and the sort of distance at which you can expect the progeny of King's Lake to succeed.

For the average punter, flat racing is an endless succession of change: a new and bewildering cavalcade of two-year-olds to learn every spring. But the racing person sees nothing but con-tinuity: a lad at Dunlop's yard will probably have seen Mill Reef, known Shirley Heights and now Boon Point, and the vari-ous other Shirley Heights offspring at Castle Stables, Kalia Crest, Piffle, Height of Folly, Hi Lass, Sergeant At Arms: it all fits together, and it is all of utterly absorbing interest to the real racing person: sons, grandsons, granddaughters, half-brothers, the thousands of fillies who go on to become broodmares and who mother champions, the overachievers who become stal-lions: this is, quite literally, the lifeblood of the business.

Coombes was 30, and had been riding for all but seven of those years. He had been in racing for 13 years, and at Castle Stables for the last seven. 'I had been given the run around by one trainer, and I was thinking of getting out of the game. But I got this job with Mr Dunlop.'

But horses are what Coombes does, and what he knows a frightening amount about. He doesn't even think that the low levels of pay are the worst part about being a stable lad. 'No, the worst part is getting hurt. Touch wood, I've never broken a bone, but I've had a bruised tailbone, and dislocated shoulders.

'I remember one time I did that, with my old governor. I had this horse, he was a dirty animal. Even when he was gelded, it never changed him. He was like it since he was a yearling. He was the worst horse I've ever had. Out on the gallops one morning, he stuck his toes in and whipped right round. I stuck my hand out and grabbed his neck to save myself, and I pulled my shoulder right out.

The industry in full swing. *Above*: cantering in Arundel Park. There must be worse ways to start a day. *Below*: the front office at Castle stables. Tony Couch, Dunlop's assistant, and Sue Crossland sort out an owner's problems on the phone, Claire Wayland at the filing tray, Eddie Watt summoning the lads on the Tannoy and Jane Martindale trying to butt in.

Hands on leadership: John Dunlop, the governor, on the unnamed hack, off to supervise the gallops.

John Dunlop, with his team right behind him. From left to right: Ken Bedford (Scobie), Tim Taylor, Gerry Germon, Glen Jump. Second row: Peter Button, Ken Carey, Sean Masters, Sue Crossland, Eddie Watt. Third row: Tom Hamill, Alison Reading, Ian Semple, Gary Hatfield, Russell Boult, Claire Wayland, Vera Burgess, Dave O'Donnell. Fourth row: Jane Martindale, Sean Kenny, David Kitcher, Brian Grove, Tony Couch, Mark Campion. Back row: Martin Boult, Martin Littler, Kevin Brown. Behind: Jeremy Noseda with Alquoz.

Away the lads. *Above*: Ken Bedford, or Scobie, pays his mortgage by running a disco. Chris Blyth (right) is one of the seniors. *Below*: Eileen McGuffie is the yard's shop steward; Graham Foster, apprentice jockey, had a crash course in the ups and downs of race-riding.

The thrills and spills of racing: Mandy Bryan determined to get it all finished by twelve.

Eddie Watt is head lad or senior NCO. *Below*: Watt is caught leading from the front. Lads seem to spend almost as much time sweeping as riding.

An eye to the future. *Left*: Jeremy Noseda is Dunlop's ambitious second assistant. *Below*: Stuart Johnston, or Angus, with a sweet-natured Shirley Heights yearling – just reward after the departure of the eccentric Efisio at the end of the season.

Work, *above*: the heart of the training process; Jessie Smith (leading) and Lee Hill on top, demonstrating the latest in riding fashion. *Below*: Chris Blyth takes a yearling for an educational stroll in the park.

'I was meant to be riding Work, and this other horse was meant to come up and join me on the gallops. Well, he never got near me. I was fuming so much at him for what he'd done, that I kicked the shit out of him. And he went. I couldn't feel my shoulder at the time, I was just fuming at the horse, and I knocked him for five furlongs.

'But when I got off the horse, my shoulder dropped, and the governor said, are you all right? So I said no, I'm getting a bit of stick off this shoulder. Well, he's a big bloke. He took hold of my arm and told me, trot round in a circle. Don't look at me, just trot. So I did, and he did something – bloody hell! He pulled it back into place. Christ, never again!

'He was a hard bloke all right. I remember one time when he left the yard to go to the races to have a touch on a horse. He was driving a six litre Jag. Our horse got well turned over: we stuck faithful to him, and backed him, and lost the lot. Then the governor came back. He was driving a six litre Bentley.'

'Do you bet much yourself?' I asked.

'Only when I feel good. I'm married now, with a kid, so I've got to be careful these days. I married a Dutch girl, she comes from a horse family, so she knows all about it.'

The popular image of the stable lad is of the betting-mad midget, never good enough to be a jockey, working for peanuts, for the sake of his frustrated dreams of being Steve Cauthen and for the unending opportunity to throw his wages away on one wild punt after another. But like most laymen's racing clichés, this one takes no account of the horses. Coombes could no more live without horses than a sailor could without boats. The rhythms of his life are caught up in horses, in the rising and falling of the racing season: spring and the Guineas, autumn and the Leger. The great bloodlines of the racing thoroughbred course through his life. There really could not be a way of life for him that does not mean a personal involvement in this world, intimate daily knowledge of the horses themselves. He knows just about everything about every horse in the yard.

'Oh, he's cantering beautiful now. A bit lazy walking and trotting, but once you get him cantering he's beautiful. Two months ago, he was all backward and out of proportion, but his shoulders are coming. He's not got the prettiest of legs, but he's a great old stick, eats all his food, never leaves a thing. My missus likes him – but then everything that's grey she backs.'

Ah, the eternal quest for winners. Coombes, intelligent, knowledgeable, the right weight, and an accomplished rider – he seems the ideal stable lad. But the grinding routine and the poor money – how long could such a man be expected to stick it?

22

THE GOOD NEWS was that Moon Madness was sound and in great shape. His sore feet problem seemed a thing of the past. The bad news was the Duchess: she was still ill, in fact she was worse. Yet being the sort of lady she is, she was insisting on going to France to see her beloved Moon Madness do his stuff in the Grand Prix de Saint-Cloud. John Dunlop was concerned about the horse, but most especially he was worried about his owner.

Moon Madness's disaster in the Hardwicke at Royal Ascot was perhaps the disaster of the season so far, though the performance of Three Tails in the Oaks ran it very close. Both horses ran again on the same weekend: on Saturday, 4 July Three Tails ran in the Lancashire Oaks at Haydock – a much less significant race than the real Oaks, of course, but worth nearly £30,000 and worth picking up.

She raced all right, but she was ducking and diving all over the place. Tony Ives, the jockey, spent half the race trying to get her straightened out, and when he did, she ducked in behind the leaders and seemed happy to stay there. But Ives kept at her, and she whipped ahead with 50 yards to go, and in the end 'won cleverly' in Dunlop's opinion. He felt this was more or less an honest run, and a nice win, too. The same day, Gilberto won a small race at Nottingham, and at 14–1 on, so he should have done.

On Sunday, the Moon Madness contingent set out for Saint-Cloud, with the Duchess still looking frighteningly poorly. But there were good hopes for her horse. The one good thing about Moon Madness's previous disastrous race had been the fact that he came back from it sound. Though the result was a shattering disappointment, there was, when you sat down to consider it, really pretty good news in that the horse had got over his problem. And surely at Ascot it was the ground that beat him? Surely he had a decent win inside him waiting to get out?

The more you thought about it, the more obvious it was that Moon Madness would have had trouble with the truly bottomless going at Ascot that day. He had had a very nasty accident as a two-year-old – yet another example of the racehorse's talent for finding ingenious ways of damaging himself. Moon Madness had made a creditable attempt at disembowelling himself on a railing. He got a little het up about something: some horrific sight like a paper bag blowing across the path is enough to send vast waves of atavistic terror coursing through a horse and stir his age-old instinct of flight. This is the kind of accident that every trainer and every lad dreads: the strains and stresses of normal training are an inevitable part of life, but such freakish accidents are acts of God. Moon Madness tore his chest quite dreadfully, and needed 60 stitches. And all one could do was to give thanks that it was not a great deal worse. The spike came within an inch of the nerve that leads to the near fore: had that been damaged, he would have lost all movement in that limb and, instead of having stitches, he would have been put down.

There was, inevitably, a great deal of muscle damage, but that repaired itself in time. The muscles affected were those that pick the feet up: after that awful performance on the soft, it seemed that Moon Madness lacked strength when performing that movement. Bowling along on the firm, he was quite fine, but he lacked the strength to wrench his feet up from the bog. On the good-to-firm, he was your boy: on the soft, forget it.

So there was a logical explanation for the disaster: and the fact that his bruising problem had been eliminated was a further bonus. No one was more pleased about it than Jeremy Noseda, Dunlop's pupil-assistant-turned-number-three. He had taken to spending his annual holiday working in a racing yard in California, pupil-assisting, dogsbodying, acquiring experience and learning American ways of doing things, some of which were radically different to those he had learned in England. 'The ground they race and train on is a lot firmer,' he said. 'So foot problems are something they have to deal with all the time. The tracks don't give – the feet do. To make up for this, they have become a lot more adventurous in their shoeing techniques than we are. Their blacksmiths are the best in the world, and their ideas are the most advanced. I had seen a fair bit of the sort of thing they do to horses with bruised feet, so I said, why not put Moon Madness in eggbar shoes?'

The problem with Moon Madness's feet is both simple and comic: flat feet. He had dropped heels: from the moment he came into the yard, this was clear to those who can read a horse's stride. He wasn't getting his feet up, and nothing in the world was going to make him change. On the other hand, he was bloody quick, and that is something that helps a trainer to cope with a horse's peculiarities.

But over the winter, between the ages of three and four, the horse had thickened up and butched out a good deal, and was a lot heavier over the shoulder. All this meant that he was now giving a great whack to the soles of his feet when he did his Work. This led inevitably to bruised feet and bouts of lameness, and his increased weight made it still tougher for him to cope with soft going.

Dunlop was interested in the possibilities of Noseda's suggestion, and called down a shoeing specialist from Newmarket to have a look at the problem. And the expert agreed: eggbar shoes seemed to be the ideal thing. These are shoes that go all the way round a hoof: a bar at the back protects the heel as the conventional shoe protects all the rest of the foot. The eggbar spreads the weight around more.

Moon Madness was still racing in conventional racing plates, those wafer thin knives that are designed to give a horse the smallest possible load on his feet. Anyone who has walked through a ploughed field knows that the worst place in the world to carry extra weight is on your foot.

But Moon Madness trained on eggbar shoes, and was able to get a decent backlog of Work behind him. Love The Groom then started to suffer from bruised feet as well, and that meant that he had to miss the Irish Derby. He was tried in eggbar shoes, and they worked for him, too, and so he was aimed at the Goodwood meeting instead.

Three weeks after Moon Madness's disaster at Ascot, he got his chance to redeem himself. Some typically canny opportunism had paved the way for him: Dunlop rather specializes in raids on European races, and is adept at spotting opportunities. A weak race and a strong horse is the ideal combination for any trainer. The Grand Prix de Saint-Cloud was worth £120,000, had Group One status, and would be, to say the least of it, a neat one to win.

There was no persuading the Duchess to miss the treat, ill as she was. There were five runners in the race, and the punters read Moon Madness's recent form, read Dunlop's recent form, shrugged their shoulders, and placed their francs elsewhere. They sent Moon Madness out at 11–2 and it was probably the nicest 11–2 of the racing season.

Moon Madness was third as they turned for home, and Pat Eddery always looked poised. They straightened out with three furlongs to go, and Moon Madness needed just one of them to take the lead. He idled in front, rather, but then he had every excuse to: nothing was getting near him. He won by one and a half lengths, and Eddery said afterwards he had been utterly sure of victory some way out. It was a race won without a sliver of anxiety.

It was a triumph, but as with all the Castle Stables wins of late, triumph was mixed with relief. For the Duchess it was pure joy: the elixir of life. The opposition was not up to much, but Moon Madness casually set a new track record as he hammered them. It was a brilliant, tricksy placement from Dunlop, and getting the horse back to winning form after the bruised feet and the Ascot disaster was a top-rate training achievement.

The Duchess proceeded to shrug off her illness, and thereafter, as Dunlop said, 'was improving about two stone a day'. The stable, with a Group One race well won, was clearly a place where the business of winning was being conducted: in short, this was one of those rare, fragile, treasured racing days in which for once it seemed quite clear that God's in his heaven, all's right with the world.

23

'T HE OWNER OF one mediocre horse can give you more trouble than someone who owns 25 champions,' John Dunlop once remarked. This was not a bitter remark, in fact, though it looks like one written down. It was said with great good humour, with cheery acceptance of a trainer's lot. Every owner who pays his training bills is a vital part of Castle Stables. But as you would expect, some of them are easier to deal with than others.

And Dunlop was in great good humour: Moon Madness's win in France was the first racing moment that year to give him real, unmixed pleasure. And there he was, going to the races again, and winning a big race, and winning it for his number one owner, the Duchess. Castle Stables was firing again: Bronzewing, Chris Blyth's mare, made up for her disappointment on Oaks Day, when poor Willie Carson had got tangled up in the stirrup leathers, by winning a very nice handicap at Newmarket, and Chilibang and Almaarad also picked up valuable races: training racehorses was suddenly a satisfactory way to live again.

'My owners are a remarkable cross-section,' Dunlop said, 'though fewer and fewer of them are British, because fewer and fewer British people seem to be able to afford to keep horses in training. Undoubtedly my most important owner is Lavinia, Duchess of Norfolk. It is totally thanks to her that I am here training at Arundel. And so you can imagine how delighted I was with Moon Madness the other day.'

Racing is paid for by the rich: the sport could not exist without people who can afford to toss rather a lot of money away. Trainers exist by keeping owners happy. The principle of any business is the same, and very simple it is too: give the customers what they want. What Dunlop's customers want is winners.

Dunlop's customers range from the Duchess and the major Arab owners down to syndicates in which 10 people share the cost of running a single moderate animal. All have but one thing in common: a readiness to lose money in pursuit of the dream of victory; in exchange for the sweet involvement with a wonderful animal, a 'glorious horse'. Some look at racing in a tough and businesslike way, others are quite unabashedly sentimental, and there are a million shades in between.

But no one with serious pretensions to a businesslike approach would have put Promise Kept into training. The first time I saw him was at evening stables, when the horses have their daily inspection. Promise Kept, clad in just a headcollar, was there to be seen 'in all his glory' as Dunlop sardonically put it. For the poor fellow had a deformity of the spine, which gave him a startling dip in the middle of his back. It looked quite impossible to get a saddle on to him. What is more, it looked impossible to get a win out of him.

Promise Kept was owned by Windflower Overseas Holdings Inc., and was represented at the stables primarily by an overseas lady of considerable charm who preferred to keep anonymous. Let us call her the Señora. Her interest in racing was certainly not based on the ruthless pursuit of profit.

She had become an owner-breeder, and Promise Kept was the first horse she had bred herself. It was a start that would have dismayed many, but the Señora wanted very much to go ahead. She called the horse Promise Kept, because Dunlop had promised her that he would train the first horse she bred. Dunlop remained a man of his word, though there was a pretty reasonable case for saying that the horse had no right to be in training. There are few owners who would wish to race such an oddity: after all, it costs as much to keep Promise Kept in training as it does Moon Madness. Duffers eat just as much as champions. But there is no accounting for owners: despite Dunlop's warnings of the likely problems involved in trying to train such a freak, the Señora still wanted to go ahead. And so the promise was kept.

The point is that the Señora is in the game for fun. So, indeed, are the Arabs: it is just that their fun is on a slightly different scale. One of the greatest empires in racing is run by the Maktoum brothers from Dubai: and it all began only a few years ago when they sent a horse or two to Castle Stables.

Sheikh Mohammed Al-Maktoum paid a visit to the sales at Newmarket, to think about buying a colt. But 15 lots before the end of the day, he decided that he wanted a filly. There were just four of them left, and the Maktoums were not the enormous spenders they became. One of the fillies was by Habitat and clearly too much. Finally they bought a filly for a very reasonable price, mainly because it had a slight deformity – nothing on Promise Kept's scale, but there was something a little amiss with one of the forelegs. This filly was Hatta and, as luck would have it, she grew into a distinctly useful horse. Dunlop trained her, and she won the Group Three Molecomb Stakes at Goodwood. By this time, the Maktoums owned three racehorses. But as I write, they own more than a thousand: racing and the joys of winning are among the most potent addictions in the universe.

Other Arabs became involved in British racing, and as their vast strings grew ever longer, they sensibly spread the load around a number of leading trainers. 'Like everyone, they want to be on a winning team,' Dunlop said. 'If you are winning races, people all want to send their horses to you, and their best horses at that. That is obviously the best publicity in the world, and it is a question of them coming to you – though I know of a couple of trainers who have promoted themselves, and have actually made videos about their yards and mailed them to various people in America and the Gulf States.'

Dunlop is delighted to train horses for his Arab owners. For a start their horses are likely to be very good indeed. For some reason, none of the Arab-owned three-year-olds was terribly exciting that year, but the two-year-olds really did offer something to think about. There was Ashayer, the pretty Lomond filly, there was Alwuhush, the white-blazed Nureyev colt, and there was a promising colt by Caerleon, the one with the white star, called Alquoz, all owned by Hamdan Al-Maktoum: a trio any trainer would adore to train. Indeed, the only objection anyone could have to the Arab presence in British racing is the confusing names they give their horses: at Castle Stables we had Ashayer and Ashshama as well as Almaarad and Ali Mourad. But if the horse goes fast, a weird name is something everyone can live with.

'On the whole the Arabs are incredibly good,' Dunlop said. 'Both as winners and as extremely good losers. They are understanding, sympathetic to their trainers and to their staff when you have a disaster. They understand that a loss is felt as much if not more by the people here.' Dunlop said this with some feeling: it would take a while for the memory of Three Tails's performance in the Oaks to fade: Three Tails is owned, you will remember, by Sheikh Mohammed.

'The best owners know the ups and downs of racing. They know that good periods are always followed by bad periods, and vice versa. They know that you are always going to train a lot more losers than you do winners. You do have gloomy times, even if, on the whole, one has been successful. You have understanding and knowledgeable owners . . . and then again, you have some who understand nothing, people who are totally lacking in all knowledge of how racing works. You get some owners who really ought to know better, and from some you get pressures that people simply would not tolerate in another line of business.

'But most of my owners are very good. I mean, really very

good. They understand that most of the time, your job is to do all you can with the shortcomings of their horses. Others don't look at it in that way at all. If anything goes wrong, it's your fault.'

There is no respite for a trainer, especially for one who has as many horses as Dunlop, and a consequently huge number of owners. Availability is part of the job: a trainer is, by profession, perpetually available to owners, press and anyone else. There is no other sport that lists the office and home telephone numbers of its stars in its annual, but in the *Directory of the Turf* you can look them all up and call Dunlop at two in the morning to ask him to explain why his horse failed on the fourth leg of your 10p Yankee. No other sporting people are as exposed as that.

'People don't treat you as they would a stockbroker,' Dunlop said. 'No one would dream of calling his stockbroker at home. But an owner might come in from the office, have a couple of drinks, feel in a good mood, and decide to phone his trainer. Without considering that you have been working since oh-six hundred hours that day. . . .'

But that is the penalty Dunlop pays for his effortless knack of amiability. Talking to owners is one of the vital training skills, and Dunlop has this gift in abundance. He is a virtuoso performer on the telephone: every time it rings he is able to give the impression that it is this horse, and none other, that has been constantly on his mind for weeks. Flushed with Moon Madness's triumph, he will immediately be able to lead a learned discussion on the latest state of Promise Kept and his chances of ever running in a race.

'He is such a nice man!' the Señora confided to me. 'This is a lovely yard, a lovely atmosphere. I have had horses trained elsewhere, but I will never do so again.' We were on the gallops, standing by the Japanese Range Rover, and waiting to see if Promise Kept could gallop.

The horse didn't look quite as peculiar out on the gallops as he did in his box. Once you had placed a vast quantity of foam rubber underneath the saddle, he looked more or less like a proper racehorse. 'There goes your boy,' Dunlop said, as the horse did his Work with touching eagerness alongside his partner. 'Actually, he is going rather well.' The pair came by, and went on past, their lads gradually easing them up. 'His action is improving the faster he is working. And that is rather encouraging.' To get a win into that horse would have to count as the training feat of the season.

Then came the Lomond filly, Ashayer: you did not need to be a genius to tell the difference between her and Promise Kept. Nice: proper: serious.

The horses were walked cool, and then went to take their customary pick of grass, and the Señora went to discuss her horse. It was ridden by Eileen McGuffie, who looks after the splendid and infuriating Three Tails. 'He seemed to be going quite well,' she said, sounding particularly Scottish in her attempt to school total amazement out of her voice. 'He really is a lot better than you'd expect from his looks.'

The Señora returned to the Japanese Range Rover, but I lingered an extra moment. 'What is it like sitting on a horse like that?' I asked.

She smiled. 'Let's just say a better horse for a woman than a man.'

For every star there are dozens of Promise Kepts, horses for which a single win would be a triumph. For every Sheikh or Duchess there are plenty of Señoras, people whose expectations are modest and whose hopes are forever soaring. A racing stable needs them all; indeed, racing itself could not exist without the lot of them.

24

A SHAYER CRUISED PAST at a cool, balanced clip: poised, pur-
poseful and such a looker. 'I always think of her as workmanlike,' said Jane Martindale, who does Ashayer. But to me
she seemed the embodiment of everything a racing filly should
be, and she seemed to look better every time I saw her. 'That's
the Lomond filly, I think she'll be quite nice,' Dunlop said, as
he had said just about every day since the spring. Beside him
was Peter Vela, who owned a horse called Nebula Way. Vela is
a New Zealander with his business interests in fish and his heart
in horse racing. He banged a pair of serious binoculars to his
face to watch Ashayer: 'Very nice. Very nice indeed.'

'Are you still purring about her as much as you were last
week?' I asked Dunlop.

'I'm not sure that I'm purring quite as deeply. She's a nice
filly. But I had a feeling that she was going to be something
quite out of the ordinary. We'll give her a run at Ascot next
week and see how she goes.' Whether this was a more realistic
assessment of the filly, or just pre-race nerves on the part of the
trainer, it was hard to tell, not least for the trainer. We would
have to see at Ascot.

But at least a win would not be a shattering world-shaking

event, as it was when Love The Groom won his race at the Royal meeting to end the drought. 'After Ascot the horses really did start to improve,' Dunlop said. Things were continuing to be good without setting the River Arun on fire. We were not at lush waterside pastures, but certainly we were a long way out of the desert.

Dunlop's decision to miss the Eclipse looked better and better in hindsight. The following day, Moon Madness had made his splendid strike in France. 'It was a weak Group One race, to be honest,' Dunlop said. 'But there we are, thank you very much.' The race was worth £14,000 more than the hotly contested Eclipse, too. Here the mighty Reference Point was beaten by Mtoto in a stirring and brilliant battle. Both horses were entered in the Diamonds, or to be formal, the King George VI and Queen Elizabeth Diamond Stakes, one of the most valuable races of the English season.

Moon Madness was also lined up for the race. Reference Point looked an extremely tough nut to crack, especially as Moon Madness, being a year older, would have to carry thirteen pounds more, and the race would be over the very ground where he had disappointed so dreadfully on the heavy going in the Hardwicke. It was time to start wishing that we were going to have a summer, and that the rain would keep away.

'On form, Moon Madness shouldn't win the Diamonds,' Marcus Hosgood said. 'But there is plenty in his favour all the same. The race should be run at a good pace, which should suit him with his turn of foot. I expect Tony Ives will keep him tucked in, begin to try and make his move around the turn and then try for a run from two out.'

'Well,' Dunlop said. 'There comes a time when you've got to give it a go.'

After that, there was Goodwood, or Glorious Goodwood, as it is always rather vulgarly known, the splendid race meeting that is second only to Royal Ascot in sparkling racing and glittering racegoers. Goodwood is just a few miles from Arundel, and Dunlop always likes to make a bit of a splash there. And a properly glorious Goodwood to give notice, in the loudest way possible, that Castle Stables was in the business of winning: that would be ideal.

Vela's two-year-old, Nebula Way, was lined up for a race on the first day: he looked a good colt and promised to get a win behind him that season. And indeed, it was the time of year when Dunlop's two-year-olds began making their delayed entrance into racing. Ashayer at Ascot; Alwuhush of the white blaze at Newbury in a couple of days: the season was gathering pace, and there was no longer a question of Castle Stables getting trampled in the rush. When there are 200 horses and nearly as many owners, this is just as well.

'Why do you insist on such a quantity of horses?' I asked. 'Why not simply go for quality?'

'Well, I have had experiences of both extremes, of working in a very small yard and running the operation I do now. And I have a strong feeling that racing, successful racing, is very much a percentage business. Say I wanted a yard of 50 good horses. The thing is, it is very easy indeed to have 50 bad horses. It is fairly easy to end up with 200 bad horses for that matter, but having 200 increases your chances of having one good one. Secondly, I *enjoy* running a big operation. There is no doubt about it, it would be very pleasant and convenient to train 50 very good horses, all owned by one very reasonable and understanding person. Preferably oneself! It would be ideal. But it isn't very practicable. Vincent O'Brien is unique in running a small but very high class stable. And after he had made the decision to cut down on numbers and concentrate on quality, he had his great years of success before the Arabs came into racing. So he and Robert Sangster had pretty much of a free hand when it came to buying the top yearlings, particularly at the American sales in Keeneland. But things change: he is still a marvellous trainer, but now that Sangster no longer completely dominates the top end of the market, he isn't able to have quite the same uninterrupted success.'

Dunlop is a man with a restless mind, a mind that needs problems as a stomach craves food. If he had gone into the retail trade, he would not have run a nice little corner shop, he would have run a supermarket, or better still, a chain of them. The problems of looking after a single horse are considerable: with 200 you are guaranteed a dozen or more problems every day, all of which require a solution. Dunlop occasionally gets weary of the incessantly baying telephone, but for all that, he basically loves it when the telephone rings and there is something else for him to make a decision about. There are some people who love a quiet life: and Dunlop had a cosy little niche all ready for him, when he got the job of private trainer to the Duke of Norfolk. But no, he insisted on expanding the corner grocery into a massive supermarket, with a lavish range of luxury goods and customers from all kinds of backgrounds. Dunlop's decision to expand indicates a basic love of problems: problems he can then solve. And a win in a race is, in the end, the final and most positive proof that a problem has been solved

25

CASTLE STABLES PICKED up three winners on 17 July. Angel City got up for the second time, Ranyah became the stable's first two-year-old winner, and Domino Fire won an apprentice race, with Graham Foster, John Dunlop's Findon-based apprentice, bringing the filly home. The race was worth £1,820.

Well, not a great race, obviously. Not so much a bread-and-butter as a bread-and-marge race. The filly was obviously no world-beater. But it was still a pleasant enough win for the stable, and especially for Foster, and it was a win that gave more pleasure than most. For Domino Fire has not one but ten owners. The filly is owned by a syndicate, one organized by Sue Abbott, who runs several syndicates, and has a decisive voice in the affairs of three horses in the yard: certainly a customer John Dunlop is happy to keep happy.

Syndication is a way of democratizing ownership. It costs a fortune, quite literally a small fortune, to own a racehorse. Mrs Abbott reckoned that anyone who goes into ownership must be prepared to lose £50,000. You might, of course, do better, you might end up coming close to breaking even, but you need that margin of error.

There are not all that many people around who can toss away

fifty grand with a jolly laugh. But if you divide this problem by ten, ownership will look a great deal more attractive to a great many more people. Blowing £5,000 in pursuit of a dream looks, compared to solo ownership, almost like sanity. And that is what Mrs Abbott's syndicates supply: the affordable dream.

'I try to get people committed before I buy the horses,' she said. 'Then I divide the horse into tenths: people I know, people the trainers know, friends of friends. We've never advertised yet.' She is involved in six partnerships, and keeps the fillies with Dunlop, and the colts with Guy Harwood, who trains just down the road at Pulborough. 'I was one of Guy's first owners, and he is a great friend. But I am not sure that he is best at training fillies – he prefers colts, let's put it that way.'

Mrs Abbott runs the syndicates in a crisp and businesslike fashion. But the business she is involved with is pleasure: it is pleasure that keeps the racing industry in motion. 'Does owning ten per cent mean you get ten per cent of the pleasure?' I asked.

'Not a bit! I think you get 100 per cent of the pleasure.'

'One hundred per cent of the pleasure at ten per cent of the price?'

'Absolutely. I mean, everyone in every syndicate believes that the horse is his and his alone. No one feels like a small cog at all – at least, I hope they don't. They are all very much involved.'

Involvement is also very much what racing is about. A bet is an admission ticket to racing: it gives you involvement, it buys you a horse. 'My horse got tailed off,' 'My horse was beaten on the nod,' anyone can own a racehorse for half an hour for 50 pence. Ownership gives you infinitely greater involvement, at a massively increased cost. My own involvement with Castle Stables doubled and trebled the pleasures and excitements of the racing year: I wanted 'our' horses to win, not to make good copy for this book but simply for the joy of it. I was yearning to see Ashayer, the darling of the gallops, do her stuff in public and win her race. The more the involvement, the greater the joys.

Mrs Abbott's syndicates make such enhanced joys a possibility for a fair number of people. The cheapest horse in the Abbott string is Restless Wave, who cost £10,000. The most expensive cost £30,000, and that is very much the top limit. For this sort of money, you will, with enough luck, have a horse that will 'win its race' and – yes – you might have a flyer. 'Oh yes, we have had one or two,' Mrs Abbott said. 'Ulterior Motive would be about the best we have had, and she was smashing. She won the Galtres at York and a Group Three in Ireland, and she cost us £13,000. We had Battle Hymn that won the Wokingham. Pactolus won three times last year. It really has been very successful.'

She has used Castle Stables for the fillies partly because the Sussex location is good for so many of her owners, and partly because Dunlop makes all his visitors so welcome. Anyone who owns a tenth part of a horse can go down to Castle Stables to see the horses at exercise any time he wants to: a telephone call is all that is required. 'He is such a relaxed trainer, and so knowledgeable – he is an old friend, actually, he is godfather to one of my children, and I am godmother to one of his.'

One might think that the largest string in Britain is just about the worst place in the world for an average horse owned by ten people. One might think the treatment given to the horse and to visiting ten percenters would be equally impersonal. But that is reckoning without the Dunlop factor: Dunlop's unforced charm and retentive mind for detail make the deal a good one for both part-owner and horse. 'I have never once felt like a second-class citizen at Castle Stables,' Mrs Abbott said. 'Nor, I am sure, have any of my owners. Nor any of the horses – of that I'm certain.'

If you own 100 or so horses, you tend to take a broad approach. But if you own one horse, and even more so if you own one-tenth of a horse, you want to know about every single training niggle, every yard of any piece of Work that smells of promise. You want to taste every pleasure and every disappointment to the full. More than anything, you want to know the running plans: the racing days are the great landmarks of the horse's years, and of his owners'. 'I am always on the telephone,' Mrs Abbott said. 'Always copying letters. People want to be in touch. I charge £11 a month for all the stuff I do to make sure that everything is running smoothly, and that everybody knows about everything. It is a business as well as a pleasure to me: there is a lot of work involved.

'It is very important to do the best that I can to make sure the whole thing works out as well as possible financially. This means that I try not to hold on to a horse that isn't any good. In the old days, I would often keep a horse for the extra year, just for the fun of the thing. But that is just too expensive these days.

'I don't actually make the final decision myself. It is all done by a vote. The trainer will advise: if I say that John advises us to sell, then most of us will go along with that. But it is not always an easy decision. I had trouble with Pactolus; in fact, he had just won his third race on the trot when we got a very good offer for him. The thing is that he was winning every time he came out, and everybody was so thrilled with him. But I said, this is a really fantastic offer, and in the end, we accepted it. He went on to win his next race, and started joint-second favourite for the Caesarewitch – but Guy was absolutely right. That was the time to sell him. He was a cheap horse, and we got a lot of money for him, money that we could all reinvest.

'It is so hard to make any money at all from owning horses. You can't balance the books on prize money, you see – not unless you are at the very top of the tree. And we are pretty close to the bottom. Domino Fire, the little filly that won at Warwick the other day, she won a maiden at Goodwood first time out last year. She beat one of Khaled Abdullah's horses to do it. The prize was £869. The handicapper saw that she had won a race at Goodwood, and he simply murdered her for all he was worth. And she just couldn't win with the weight he gave her to carry. She's not very good, but she tries so hard – and she should have been better rewarded for winning her maiden.'

In the United States, an owner has a 50 per cent chance of breaking even; in England his chances are more like ten per cent. James Underwood wrote, in thundering style, in the *British and Irish Breeding Update*: 'Bookmakers have become so rich they are having to search all over the world for schemes to invest in. Yet racecourses are still semi-slums, prize money is far below that in many countries that race the runt of the thoroughbred breed, owners are quitting the sport at a snowballing rate and the small breeder, in spite of often producing an animal that in blood and type is superior to that produced in most parts of the world, is being driven out of existence.'

Mrs Abbott will sing the same song without needing a prompt. 'The money for winning at Warwick the other day was better – but by the time you have taken out the money for travelling and the entry fees and the jockey fees out of all that, you are still not left with very much. You won't make money racing. Selling them on is what you hope to do, and you hope to get your money back – by that, I mean the purchase price. You'd have to be more than lucky to get the running costs back as well. We have done it, actually – but it is very unusual. Most horses are sold at a loss.

'The £5,000 you must be prepared to lose: that will cover buying the horse, keeping it for a couple of years, and it breaking down so completely that you cannot get a penny back. And that happens, too. There is no point in going into racing with the idea that you will make money. That is not what it's *for*. You do it for fun. But it's certainly *nice* to get something back.'

'And then you can buy another horse?' I asked.

'Absolutely. Ulterior Motive is still paying for some of our horses. But the one we got as a direct replacement for her – well, he isn't nearly as good.'

'So if you could make one change in racing at the wave of a hand, what would it be?'

'Oh, prize money without a doubt. So that you don't have to go struggling round the country for £2,000. I mean, you go to Folkestone, you finish third, and they give you 60 quid. God, it takes a good horse to win a race – any race. Fifty per cent of them never win anything. When you do win a race, no matter how moderate, no matter how unfashionable the racecourse – then you really have got a good horse.'

'So many problems – why come into the game at all?'

'Oh, fun. If you enjoy racing, then the more closely you are involved the more fun it becomes.'

'Prestige? Snobbery?'

Mrs Abbott gave a roar of laughter at this impertinence. 'Anyone who comes into one of my syndicates has to learn to love Leicester evening meetings! It is about horses and seeing them run. Not about rubbing shoulders with the mighty at Ascot.'

'What is the worst thing about owning a horse?'

'Having it stand in its box. If they can come out and run, at least you have the excitement and the despair of racing. But if they don't run, if they are standing in their boxes, that's dreadful. You have to be philosophical. But standing in their boxes – that's the worst thing there is.'

'And the joys are –'

'Winning. Winning is the thing. That is marvellous. You get so terribly chuffed when they win. Because they don't do it very often, do they?'

26

'When most apprentices have their first race, they turn up in their best suit and a tie. But not old Elvis – he turned up in his Blitz Kids bomber jacket.' So said one of the lads, roaring with laughter at this classic piece of young thruster's impertinence.

Elvis is Graham Foster, who rode Domino Fire to victory for the Sue Abbott syndicate, and it was his third win of the season. He was delighted with it. He is called Elvis because he likes to look cool and to wear natty clothes, and he wears his hair swept back off his forehead. He does not take part in the lads' daily scruffiness competition: he is quite clearly aware that he is not as other lads are. He is based at Findon; when he comes over to ride at Castle Stables, he wears things like a bright, crisp nylon windcheater that you could almost mistake for a jockey's silks. His boots are always particularly beautiful, and they enclose calves as slim as a couple of HB pencils.

Foster, you can tell, is doing all he can to become one of those few turtles that reach the sea. But the odds against him, as against all apprentice jockeys, are immense. It is a classic catch-22. In order to get good enough, you need not just talent, but experience. If a trainer and an owner want to win races, they want a jockey who has talent and experience. So no one is going to put an apprentice up on any of his horses. Not without good reason, anyway.

There are races only open to apprentices, which gives some of them a chance. And of course, an apprentice gets his seven pounds weight allowance, which does not go down to five pounds until he has won ten races against grown-up jockeys. Putting up an apprentice takes weight off a horse's back, but the apprentice's own inexperience generally more than cancels out this advantage. It is a hard job for any apprentice to persuade a trainer and an owner to put him up.

Foster had his first ride (bomber jacket hanging in the weighing room) in October 1985, so this was his third season. And he was finding it as hard as ever to get people to give him horses to ride. An apprentice can lose 20 lengths in one second of indecision or over-enthusiasm. Let's have Willie as usual, an owner will tend to say, after having considered an apprentice for a moment. At least you know where you are with Willie.

'Of course the thing to do would be to have a nice, moderate handicapper of four or five, owned by myself,' John Dunlop said. 'That would give an apprentice the experience he needs so badly, without my needing to persuade any owners that they must put up with a boy. But unfortunately, I haven't got a horse like that at the moment.'

Despite the bomber jacket, Foster confesses without shame that he was a bundle of terror before his first ride at Chepstow. 'The worst part of it was the waiting. I was waiting four hours in the weighing room. I had walked the track before anyone else was there, to work out where the best ground was; you should always do that. The other jockeys' – note the quiet pride of 'other jockeys' – 'they were quite good. I'd seen Brian Rouse before, and he came up to me, he was quite helpful. You ask them a question, they'll answer as best they can.'

But Foster was now into his third season, and the terrors were less, and the ambition sharper. After his win on Domino Fire, he had had three wins and two seconds from ten rides. He had even had the joy of riding two winners in two days: the first of these was Almaarad, and he had the advantage of a quiet and helpful word from Pat Eddery before he set out. 'Pat told me they'd go at a fast pace, so get him to settle in behind. Well, he was right, they set off so fast I didn't have any option but to get in behind, though no, I didn't miss the break. I was happy to tuck him in at the back. There were six in the first group, and five lengths back, there were four more, and I was at the back of them as we turned for home.

'I was still pretty confident, because, you see, I knew how good he was. Turning for home, I just pulled him out, and we went past the back group, caught up with the leading group and went straight through.'

'That sounds like a slick race,' I said.

'Well, I do Almaarad myself, you see. I know what he's like.' And that is an advantage that no full-time jockey has.

'Anyway, the following morning, I got a call from Mrs Dina Smith, another trainer. Would I ride for her at Kempton that day? I said yes. I got there, and they told me, he don't like being bumped and he don't like being hustled along. Just bring him up quietly on the outside. It was a mile race, and that's just what I did. I came down the straight and put him on the rail, on the stand side. He won two lengths. Next time Brian Rouse rode him, and he won again.'

There is all the difference in the world between riding Work at home and riding in a race. So many lads are capable of riding the smoothest and most balanced of gallops at home, but when they get into the hurlyburly of a race, their brains turn into porridge. Racing requires the coolest possible head: jockeys do not set out to be excitable, volatile creatures. Leave that side of things to the horse: a good jockey works at being cool, precise and almost objectionably calm. That is what it takes when it comes to solving the traffic problems and judging time, speed and distance in the tumult and shouting of a race. But when an apprentice is sitting on someone else's horse that is worth God knows how many thousands of pounds, knowing that every rare race is a chance in a lifetime to prove himself, and that if he makes a public ass of himself he is highly unlikely to be given a second chance – then coolness is not the easiest thing to come by. Even if you are nicknamed Elvis.

But all apprentices will agree that there is only one thing harder than winning a race, and that is getting the chance to ride one in the first place. Foster admits, and again without any shame, that he uses the technique that schoolboys call 'greasing': the gentle art of ingratiation. Looking fearfully keen, making a jolly good impression; me sir, let *me* do it sir. Of course, everybody in the world can see through the act, but no one can mistake the genuine keenness behind it. 'You've got to show dedication and keenness, you've got to show you are willing to learn. Show that you want to get somewhere. It's no good standing around doing nothing. If there's something going on, I always try to be there. If I'm at the races, doing a horse or whatever, I always show I'm willing. If my horse is a late runner, I am still there early, helping to wash down the earlier runners. I always show willing, I am always handy.'

I do not suppose that there is anyone who is remotely connected with Dunlop's stable who believes anything other than that Foster is quite immensely keen. That is as it should be. Foster has other methods for getting rides, better than standing about looking hopeful. There is direct action. 'Every day coming off first lot, I have a look at the racing papers, to see what is going on. I keep in touch with the trainers I have ridden for, and the people I ride Work for. Just hoping. Some of them say they'll ring you back – but it's you that's got to keep ringing them. You've got to keep ringing people, and keeping your fingers crossed.

'I don't think there is any other lad at Arundel or at Findon riding in races at the moment,' Foster continued. 'I'm not being nasty, but I think that is because they don't have the determination. I never go out at nights. I never go drinking. I've got to watch my weight, you see. The sort of rides an apprentice can go for are normally at around the seven stone seven mark, so I've got to keep my bodyweight down to around seven stone. They are unlikely to put you up on a horse with a heavier weight, because that is likely to be a good horse with a decent chance.

'But it's getting known that is the thing. And that is the hard part. Recently I've been riding Work for Lady Anne Herries [the training daughter of the Duchess], and I've also ridden Work for Mr Harwood. So it's a matter of keeping hoping, keeping looking for rides. Even if they don't win, you can look good, you can make an impression with your riding.

'So I don't go to the pub. I stay in and study the racing papers, see what's going on, look ahead to next week. Mark the paper, and when the race gets closer, see if the horse you marked is still down to run. If it is, ring up. Keep going like that. Just hope.'

27

By the end of July I had come to the conclusion that Michael Fish was engaged in a passionate personal vendetta against John Dunlop. Michael Fish is, of course, the BBC weatherman, the man who controls the weather for us. It seemed that all through the alleged summer, Michael Fish had waited to see when a Dunlop horse needed goodish conditions underfoot, and then had whisked in his biggest and blackest clouds and turned the racetrack into a bog. And as we came up to the King George VI and Queen Elizabeth Diamond Stakes, Mr Fish threw 0.2 inches of rain on the course on Tuesday night knowing that the ground was already marshy. By Tuesday morning, it seemed that a walk across the course would have you disappearing up to your waist. The going was already heavy, with Mr Fish promising more rain as a probability, and no sun as a certainty.

Moon Madness was entered in the Diamonds, to have his chance against the Classic horses of that year. The Diamonds is always a splendid race, in which the Derby winner seeks to fend off those who have hard luck tales from the Derby and who want a second try at him, and to prove a point against the crack older horses. After the Diamonds you can make a fairly realistic assessment of the quality of the season's three-year-olds.

It had long been the plan to give Moon Madness his chance against the current season's champs. But the more the rain fell, the more the plan looked like a bad one.

As the weather stayed awful, the pre-race speculation was all about who would run and who would drop out. Chris Goulding, a colleague of mine on *The Times*, told me he had rung Castle Stables to ask about Moon Madness. 'But it's only Tuesday!' Dunlop had protested. Everyone wanted to know the answer. Moon Madness had made such a pig's ear of things at Royal Ascot, loathing every yard of the squishy track. Running him round the same track over the same going against better horses looked in theory an absolutely idiotic idea, contrary to every logical idea in racing. But then, how many logical ideas are there in racing? That was the flaw in the argument. And what was best for the horse? What was best for the owner? How would another disaster affect Moon Madness's future career at stud?

The Duchess mused over the various questions, and found the issue to be totally lacking in any complication whatsoever. 'I don't suppose I shall ever have another horse good enough to run in the Diamonds,' she said. 'So he shall run whatever the going.' Dunlop is a sportsman, who believes in taking on people and horses. If you don't enter horses, you don't win races. But I have a suspicion that even he was slightly taken aback by this gungho sportsmanship.

'Up and at 'em' is not an attitude shared by everybody in racing. Mtoto, who beat Reference Point in the Eclipse the day before Moon Madness won in France, was yanked out of the proceedings on Thursday. Mtoto's trainer, Alec Stewart, said: 'I just cannot believe that the going at Ascot is soft for two meetings in the summer. Are we going to have no summer at all?'

An excellent German horse called Acatenango was flown in for the race, showing every appetite for taking 'em on. An intrepid German punter called Henner Berke came over as well, determined to have a good bet on the beast. But no one would take his money, not the kind of money he wanted to bet. 'British bookmakers have no courage!' he said. He wanted to place a modest £20,000 at the price advertised in the papers – 25–1. But none of the big bookmakers would take the bet. The biggest bet he was offered was £2,000 a win and £1,000 a place. So he placed this bet at all of the Big Four bookmakers, and had £1,500 on the Tote as well. Wally Pyrah spoke for Coral's: 'If a total stranger comes in wanting to put £8,000 on a horse at 25–1, we think twice, because otherwise there would be no 25–1 left for our regular customers. We try to give everyone a slice of the cake.' There were you thinking that bookmakers are a bunch of greedy grasping little monsters, and all the time they are philanthropy itself.

The Diamonds meeting started the day before the big race, on the Friday, and that was a day I had no intention of missing. Dunlop had chosen the Virginia Water Maiden Stakes to give Ashayer her first run in public. The gorgeous filly had touched my heart on the gallops back in the spring, and she'd had Dunlop purring for months. Now for fulfilment, or disillusionment. She looked as lovely as you would expect in the parade ring, walking out calmly and athletically (workmanlike, indeed!) as if she had come to her rightful place at last. Willie Carson walked out with a stride just as jauntily athletic, though a trifle shorter, to take the ride: 'Now then, William,' Dunlop said, and the two went into their pre-race ritual of low buzzing instructions.

Ashayer cantered down the course without giving any sign of alarm, and entered the stalls calmly. Though this was the first time she had been on a racecourse, she knew all about starting stalls: Dunlop keeps a set at Castle Stables, and all the horses are taught that stalls don't bite, and that the idea is not to get out of them until the gates are open, and then to do so rather quickly. Ashayer broke cleanly, and Carson tucked her in behind, and then nudged her into second place behind Madam de Seul. By this time, they were about half way, or three furlongs into the race. With a furlong left to go, Carson asked Ashayer, in the nicest possible way, if she would like, please, to win the race, and, showing great charm and good manners, she did so. She cruised past the other runners with a slight air of disdain, and Carson didn't have to perform any spectacular gymnastics, didn't even have to hit her. Just point, nudge and win: she quickened when asked as if the whole business of racing were the easiest thing in the world to her.

Carson is not primarily noted for his gentleness of approach, but he rode Ashayer with nothing less than tenderness. And the world was impressed. The newspapermen gathered around Dunlop afterwards, scenting a story. Dunlop made the following statement: 'She's a nice filly.' Well, thanks a bunch, JD. The papers had to do the hyping themselves: 'Dunlop Juvenile Has Great Future', the *Racing Post* said. Strange to think that by the time these words are being read, Ashayer may have won a Classic – or been another racing disappointment. As I write this, in late December 1987, I recall being in her box last week, stroking her elegant nose and talking to her lad, Jane Martindale, who wanted to see her develop more muscle, particularly round the backside. Ashayer looked that day at Ascot, as she had looked every day that year, like a filly to get you buzzing, a filly full of racing hopes, and all the possible disappointments that every Great Bay Hope has written into the contracts in small print. Last week she was a dream, but there were perhaps a dozen of her all over the country, and a few more in Europe. Was Ashayer going to be the princess, or just one of the ugly sisters – well, no, never that. But by the time this is read, Ashayer may be a great, great winner. Or not.

The *Post* was less happy about Moon Madness for the Diamonds. 'He could not be supported with full confidence,' said Graham Dench guardedly. He went for the Derby winner, Reference Point, and he was not alone in that. So did just about everybody else: Reference Point was going to start odds-on. Moon Madness, if anyone was interested, was on offer at 25–1. My racing snout went for Reference Point, rather apologetically.

Diamonds Day begins with a race for lady jockeys, and Princess Anne delighted the crowd by booting home Ten No Trumps. When it looked as if the Princess Royal was going to do the job, the crowd shouted themselves hoarse. After she had done it, they packed around the winner's enclosure in thousands. I suppose that when you have been European three day event champion, galloping round corners is a fairly straightforward business.

The big race was just about as straightforward a race as you could wish for. Reference Point jumped off into the lead, and ran a race all by himself. The rest of the field conducted a tightly fought battle for second place. There was no thought of anybody passing the yellow and black hangover colours. It was a great deal more impressive than his Derby win and, Lord knows, that was impressive enough – but somehow I found it rather unsatisfying. I had seen Dancing Brave scorch to victory in the race the previous year, producing a magical turn of foot like a conjurer producing a rabbit, electrifying in its surprise. Reference Point seemed to me, in comparison, nothing more than brilliantly – well, brilliantly workmanlike. I felt rather so-whattish about the horse. (My remarks about him in *The Times* won me the rare double of making *Private Eye's* Pseuds' Corner, and a disapproving mention in *Sporting Life*. To annoy both publications simultaneously must be a unique achievement.)

But where, I hear you ask, was Moon Madness through all this? Well, Moon Madness was absolutely great. He put up a performance of immense courage and character on ground that did not suit him at all. He made a rattling good run at the end, and charged into fourth position: far better than anyone had a right to expect. The Duchess was delighted, and Dunlop was surprised and immensely cheery. Fourth place in this, the best race of the year, was worth £14,000. There are in theory only two things you can do in a race, win it or lose it, but just for once, fourth place was something to shout about in a quiet way.

Tony Ives had the ride, and said afterwards: 'Moon Madness doesn't move as freely on soft ground. But he still ran a very game race to get back at them and finish fourth.' Acatenango was sixth, so the bookies had their chance and they blew it. 'The going was too soft for him and they found him out,' his jockey, Cash Asmussen, reported.

But that Reference Point, and that Henry Cecil – when it is your time, you can do no wrong. A sure magic seemed to have taken over his yard that year. Cecil was handling everything with an assurance of touch that seemed nothing less than supernatural. It happens sometimes, in racing: and then the magic goes, and the trainer keeps on doing exactly the same thing as he did before, but somehow the horses finish second. The almost mystical control just disappears. It happened to Michael Dickinson in jump racing. He was the greatest trainer the winter game has ever known – for a season. When he turned to the flat, the magic had gone.

Dunlop has known times when winning seems almost a routine – God, how dreary, another winner – when it seems easier to place a horse to win than to lose. But at the stable, every victory is celebrated in the knowledge that losing will soon be your lot again. As Cecil continued his *annus mirabilis*, and as Dunlop pursued his own wins and looked ahead to his annual assault on the glittering prizes of Goodwood, both knew that, after death and taxes, the surest thing in the world is losing.

28

ON THE TUESDAY after Diamonds Day, the big Goodwood meeting began with its usual muted splendour. Royal Ascot is morning suits and top hats, Goodwood is panamas and Prince of Wales check. The racing is almost as good, and a lot more of the people who go there quite like horse racing. John Dunlop was ready for a serious raid on the meeting, as he has been every year apart from the horror year of 1985. Never mind what horrid trick Michael Fish was planning: Dunlop's way is to give it the gun at Goodwood.

However, he started off with a misfire. Goodwood began warm and muggy, and Strathblane was the first runner from Castle Stables. For a moment her white face loomed promisingly out of the bunch, but then she disappeared out of the back door with a couple of furlongs to go.

At five minutes past four, it was time for Love The Groom in the Gordon Stakes to try and put his topsyturvy season into perspective. After his splendid win at Royal Ascot, there seemed to be a case for maintaining that he really was rather a good horse. He might well have done better in the Derby − surely if he hadn't been chopped almost to his knees, he would have got in amongst them at the finish. The ifs and maybes of racing can stretch to eternity. But if Love The Groom ran as well as he did at Royal Ascot then maybe it would be worth sticking your mortgage on him. He was finally sent out favourite at 6–4.

The race was worth £23,000, and it is often seen as a St Leger trial. It is run over a mile and a half, and Love The Groom was top weight, with 6 lbs more than any other runner. Considering that Naheez, second in the Irish Derby, was also in the race, it certainly wasn't a pushover.

But all the same, Love The Groom made it seem like one. He looked boxed in for one nasty moment, but Willie Carson possessed his soul in patience: a gap appeared for him and Love The Groom bolted through it like a good 'un. The rest of the race was an academic argument about second place. 'A good performance in a strongly run race,' Dunlop commented amiably afterwards.

'What's the plan?' Racing reporters always want to know what the plan is. I remember one trainer being surrounded in victory by racing reporters asking: 'What's the plan?' The trainer smiled urbanely and said: 'That *was* the plan.'

'But what about the St Leger, Mr Dunlop?'

'I haven't really thought about Doncaster yet. He's in all sorts of races, some of them in America, including the Arlington Million. I was thinking of running him in the Voltigeur, but in view of the fact that Reference Point looks like running there, I'm not so sure.'

You want plans, we got 'em. But we are not quite sure what the plans are. We'll have to see. But this was a good win by a good horse, and that is quite enough to be going on with.

Two of the horses expected to do pretty decent things in the season had done so, two more had disappointed. There was Three Tails in the Oaks as a serious disappointment, who had made only partial amends for that by winning at Haydock. She was to have another chance to make amends the coming Saturday at Goodwood. And there was Tommy Way, the Italian Derby winner who had later broken a blood vessel in a race. His owners had taken the punt of keeping him on in training, in the hope that a winter's rest would help him get over the problem. He had run without distinction in a Group Two race at Newmarket, and was aimed at a race in France in August.

This had been an up-and-down season so far, or to be more accurate, a down-and-up season. Love The Groom won and won well, but then Nasr Moon lost and lost badly in the last race of the day. He finished last, in fact. Well, there is always another race, and tomorrow, Angel City surely had a great chance.

Angel City was, in the jargon, a progressive type and trainers and punters love them. He had won his last two races and, at 15–8, looked a good thing. If you wanted to seek omens, then you only had to look at Ken Bedford (Scobie), Angel City's lad, who won a five pound salmon for producing the best turned-out horse in the race. Angel City turned out to be the fastest horse in the race, as well. He went clear a furlong out, and never gave his backers an instant's worry. If only it were always like that! There are moments when racing looks so easy. He simply trotted up, and gave great pleasure to his legion of backers and to the stable that had trained him. How could anyone fail to clean up in racing, when it is all so simple and straightforward?

And talking of simple and straightforward, Harlestone Lake looked a damn good bet in the 3.30. With Dunlop's horses going distinctly well, 3–1 looked extremely good value. And indeed, the horse ran to the front with a furlong to go, and charged towards the winning post with every possible sign of gameness. It was a thousand pities, then, that Actinium was a shade faster, and caught her on the line. Efisio, Castle Stables' eccentric, completed a day of downs and ups by finishing sixth of seven in the Sussex Stakes.

On the third day of the meeting, Dunlop's challenge began with Chilibang, who had won last time out and started favourite this time. The horse finished last. True Gent then got comprehensively buried: and it looked as though we were in for a good, solid day of teeth-gritting. Sergeyevich started out even money favourite in the Goodwood Cup, which was run over the marathon distance of two miles five furlongs.

Sergeyevich always gallops with his tongue hanging out like a dog, and seems to try hard to look as ridiculous as possible. He was the only three-year-old in the race, and there was an awfully long way to run. But Sergeyevich, with his tongue hanging down practically to his knees, simply hammered everything into the ground. Two miles five furlongs seemed no trouble at all to him; another couple of times around and he would simply have won more easily.

Dunlop was uncharacteristically caustic afterwards. 'This was simply too far,' he said. 'All Cup races should be reduced to two miles. It is important that we do not lose the horses' stamina, and we do not just want all speed, but races over this distance are too much. If you reduce them to two miles, you would get much better and more competitive racing – but traditionalists do not agree with me.' Among Dunlop's many responsibilities is his membership of the European Pattern Racing Committee, which decides on the nature of the major Group races. This is a matter he has given a lot of thought to, and because his outspokenness was so unusual – and had the virtue of following a rather good win – his views were listened to with respect and seriousness.

Willie Carson rode Sergeyevich, and the horse won, yes, like a good thing – but that, however, was when the good things dried up. Four runners on the fourth day could not produce a winner between them. Three Tails, the filly with a little of the devil in her, was to go for a Group Two race on Saturday. She was to go in blinkers, and was under orders to behave herself.

Boon Point, Mike Huntley-Robertson's glorious horse, had a race that day, and finished fifth. Tony Ives had the ride on Three Tails, with Willie Carson claimed by Dick Hern to ride Dusty Dollar. The punters liked the idea of Three Tails in her blinkers, and sent her out favourite, and she zoomed into the lead with a furlong and a half to race. But Nom de Plume also did a bit of zooming, and stole the race. What happened, Mr Dunlop? 'Nom de Plume was faster,' Dunlop explained kindly. Thanks, JD.

'I thought she'd win with a furlong to go, but she didn't find a great deal,' he continued. And so to the plan: the Yorkshire Oaks at the big York meeting seemed to be the thing. The blinkers would stay. Ives said she went better with them. Not quite better enough.

Dunlop's Goodwood, then, was Fairly Glorious. Enough winners to make it a real success, enough losers to leave a taste of disappointment. I remember a footballer once saying to me: 'Ah well – some you lose, some you draw.' This time, however, there was a decent number of ups among the downs. And every victory tastes sweet enough.

29

RACING, AS WE have seen, needs owners to survive, owners who are prepared to lose £50,000 with every horse. And that, of course, is the minimum. Racing lives on the rich, the people happy to toss their thousands away in pursuit of a dream. But that is not all that racing needs in order to survive: it also needs a legion of people prepared to work long and hard and for a pittance. Racing needs its stable lads every bit as much as it needs its owners. John Dunlop pays his lads a basic of £105 a week, which is about average.

I am reminded of the line in 'All things bright and beautiful', the verse that is always omitted these days:

> The rich man in his castle,
> The poor man at his gate,
> God made them high or lowly
> And ordered their estate.

'Strangely enough, this is not something that people here tend to get hot under the collar about – but I do!' said Eileen McGuffie, the Scottish lad who does Three Tails, and who is also representative for the Stable Lads' Association at Castle Stables. 'Sometimes I get furious when I see the Rolls Royces in the yard, while I'm getting £105 a week. But it really doesn't seem to bother most of them. They're happy to see the rich people flourish, because it's good for racing in general, and good for them in particular. But I feel we settle for too little. We're a bit too humble.'

One former head lad told me: 'Racing needs owners, that's obvious. But if all the jockeys gave up tomorrow, there would be plenty of people who could ride the horses. If all the trainers dropped dead, the head lads could take over. But if all the lads walked out, racing would die tomorrow.'

All of racing gets just a little bit twitchy when talking about the stable lads. Racing needs lads with an antique attitude to their jobs: people genuinely grateful to be employed, totally secure in the governor/servant role, unquestioningly loyal. Racing depends for its quality on the work the lads put in: the endless grooming, which is for muscle tone and circulation, not just to make them look pretty, and the tough, exhilarating riding out on the gallops twice a day, six days of the week, riding which is intended not just to make the horses fit but to improve them.

Racing is dependent not just on the lads, but on their earning what is pretty poor money by anybody's standards. The fragile economy of the industry is based on how much the rich are prepared to pay for their pleasures. And the rich are not a desperately flourishing breed in England: racing owes an increasing amount to foreign owners who fall in love with the special zing that English racing can provide. But outside the mighty Arabs, there is a limit to what people are prepared to pay for what is basically a jolly amusement, and a cheery way of throwing money down the drain. All trainers fear that a hike in training fees will mean fewer owners and fewer horses in training. And it happens that it is the lads who get squeezed. To keep a horse in training costs about £150 a week (there are a lot of variables in this, shoeing bills, veterinary treatment and so on). The lads take home about £85 each. Dunlop has cottages in the castle grounds, 28 of them, which go rent-free to married lads. He has no hostel for the unmarried lads, so they must find bedsits, or board with the married staff. Some of the younger lads put up at their parents'.

There is a tang of feudalism about the set-up. Old style lads like Chris Blyth are happy to serve their governor and the rich. Others, in keeping with changing times, have different aspirations. This reached a head in 1975, with an approximate equivalent of Wat Tyler's Peasants' Revolt. Lads from all over the country banded together under the banner of the Transport and General Workers' Union. They went on strike and attempted to disrupt the Guineas meeting at Newmarket.

It was, perhaps, the ugliest few days in the history of the sport, and it horrified everybody involved. On the first day of the meeting, the lads staged a sit-down protest across the course; Willie Carson was dragged from his horse and struck. On the early morning of 2,000 Guineas day, a dozen craters were dug from the Rowley Mile course with a bulldozer. The damage was made good in time for the meeting, so the lads staged a sitdown protest in front of the starting stalls, and they were removed by the police.

There was no racing shown on television for three months, although Lord Wigg did manage to use his influence to get the Derby shown. Finally, a solution was reached by ACAS, under which the lads were to receive a new minimum of £37 a week.

But following the troubles there was a recoiling in horror on both sides. The TGWU lost a lot of support among the lads, and in the wake of the victory, the Stable Lads' Association was formed with a declared non-militant policy. Eileen has recruited to a high of 80 in Dunlop's yard, but with the comings and goings of the lads – as much a part of stable routine as the comings and goings of horses – this has fallen to around 60. 'It's time I had another membership drive,' she said.

'But has it done any good?' I asked her.

'I think it has helped. I think things have got very slightly better. I think it's been a success. If you ask any of the lads, I'm sure they'd tell you, ahh, it's bloody useless. But given the apathy you're up against, I think it's done quite well.'

In strictly Arundel terms, Eileen is cautiously pleased with the way things have gone. It must be a fairly intimidating prospect, to confront someone as sharp-minded, and with so powerful a memory for facts, as Dunlop. 'It is all right negotiating with him if you come to the table with a well-thought-out case,' she said cautiously. 'But if you come in and just go off half-cocked, he's very difficult indeed. You're dead before you start.'

'He's the sort of man who can be persuaded by argument,' I suggested.

'Yes, but it's got to be a bloody good argument! You practically need to hire a lawyer sometimes. . . . But no, I do think he's fair.' The two of them had a set-to about the undignified matter of staff lavatories, which Eileen argued were below the standards required. 'I was able to present that quite well, with material spelling out the legal requirements, and he has agreed to put more in. He is apparently waiting for planning permission.'

'Presumably it is money that is the biggest problem with the job?' I asked.

'Well, what I'd most like to see is a wage structure,' Eileen said. 'At the moment, every stable lad gets the same. I think a lad who has been in racing for six or ten years should be getting a hell of a lot more than a kid who has just started. You get no credit whatsoever for the time you have spent in the industry.

'We have already approached the Trainers' Federation on this, but there hasn't been much progress. The representatives we meet from the Federation seem to be a pretty mixed bunch. Ian Balding, for instance, has been very good. But then you have some other people who just seem to veto everything – no, we're not doing this, no, we're not paying for that. Presumably this is the attitude that the Trainers' Federation wants to put forward. After all, they choose the representatives.'

The problem with stable work is the same as the problem with all kinds of animal husbandry. To do the job well requires immense skill, a great feeling for the job. But there is nothing of that that can go down on paper, and the skills cannot be moved to another area. A good stable lad is immensely skilled at riding racehorses and in caring for them. But what other industry values such skills? A Newmarket lad said to me over a pint: 'A trainer once told me, "You lot are two a penny."' And that is how a lot of people feel about us. But I love my job, and

I am good at it. I break in the yearlings; it's a difficult job, and I love doing it. I don't want to do anything else – but the wages are a joke. You can manage on them. But you can't *live* on them.' He had been in racing for 20 years and, like Eileen, resented the way his skills were rewarded at the same rate as those of a kid wet behind the ears. The lads get upset at the way their skills do not seem to be valued.

Like all racing stables, Castle Stables depends on its core of loyal, skilled lads. The stable routine would collapse without them. The point about the work for many of the lads is not that they could not get another job, but that they do not want to. The intense satisfaction of doing a winner is wonderful and, to many, utterly addictive. Virtually all stable lads bet: for most, though, this is simply extra mustard. The addiction is to winning, not to gambling.

Racing is a closed world, with a freemasonry of its own, with a secret language for the initiates. Racing sharply defines the difference between insiders and outsiders: the thought of being an outsider is impossible for most stable lads.

But I do not wish to romanticize them. 'There are as many bad lads as good,' said Bill Adams, national secretary of the Stable Lads' Association. The job attracts a number of drifters, who spend two months in one yard, two in another. Stables attract a few disastrous gamblers, and like everywhere else, have their share of skivers, drinkers and idiots. But stable routine depends on the core of the best lads, and it is stable routine that produces winners.

'Trainers seem to hold all the cards,' I said. 'What weapons do you have?'

'Well, a strike is obviously always a possibility as a last resort,' Eileen said. 'But it isn't really practical. A less drastic tactic would be a boycott of race meetings, especially if we staged it during Ascot week. But none of us want to do that. I think if it came down to it, we would, but it's not what we want.

'Racing allowances are one of the things we would like to see improved. We get a tax-free allowance of seven quid when we go racing. If we're going to somewhere like Haydock, we'll be travelling up on, say, Sunday night, racing all day Monday and getting back home in the middle of Monday night. For that we get twenty quid. I'd like to see a proper system of overtime payments for going racing. Along with a consideration of the quality of our work in a wage scale.'

The prospect of Sunday racing has brought a startling novelty in the stable lads' outlook: unanimity. There is probably not a lad in the country who favours the idea of Sunday racing, and the British racing industry is continuing, as I write, in its moves in that direction. The SLA sees Sunday racing as something of a last frontier: not something it is prepared to cross for a couple of quid. 'The question of Sunday racing brings everything to a head,' Adams said. 'To this issue, we have attached all our demands – the need for a wage structure, the need for accident benefits, the questions of racing allowances.'

The basic pay of £105 a week gets bumped up by a few other things. There is the £7 racing allowance, which is not much help, of course, if both your horses are lame. It is far from unusual for a horse to go a season, or even a lifetime without racing. There is also the point that lads have to eat when they go away racing, and food at the lads' canteen will be more expensive than food at home. The benefits from racing are all a matter of luck in the horse the lad is allotted: you stick with a horse from the moment it comes into the yard right through its racing career.

Then there is prize money. A percentage of every chunk of prize money is divided up among the staff at the trainer's discretion: each trainer will have his own system of doing this. Everyone feels the benefit of a winner where it does most good, in the pocket, which is why the disappointment of Three Tails in the Oaks was felt with especial keenness, not just by Eileen, but by everybody in the yard. 'I'd like to see the head lads get a bit less, and the lads a bit more,' Eileen said. 'The way prize money is divided, the head lads do get so much more than us. It should be up to the trainer to pay them a little more in basic wages, and that is the sort of thing that is very much the concern of the SLA.'

Overtime is paid at the standard rate of £2 an hour, and if you do an extra horse, as you often do to cover for illnesses, holidays, and those absent racing, you get an extra pound a day. 'What keeps you all in the job, then?' I asked. 'Since it is obviously not money.'

'Well – the life. The open air. And to be a part of the excitement of racing. You get to travel, and many stable lads are people who haven't seen much of the world. And I suppose there is the spice of the gambling. Most of us have a bet, and there are some who are really only in it for the gambling. Sometimes we know a horse is going well, and yet there is a good price for him – it's pretty rare, but it can happen!'

To be happy and to afford a little jam on the bread, stable lads need winners: prize money filters down into their pay packets, there are presents from happy owners – and it is winning that makes owners happy, remember – and there are the little bonuses from sensible investments. When the winners do not come, the quality of life goes down with a bang. There are no treats, no extra beer, no job satisfaction. If you do not love the life to distraction, it will not hold you for long. Paul Coombes, the lad with the Dutch wife who likes to bet on greys, had left – but in his case, it was the chance to ride races in Holland that claimed him.

'There has always been a high turnover of lads,' Eileen said. 'Less here than at Newmarket, where it is so easy to go from one stable to another. We are isolated here, there isn't a big yard next door to take you on. But some lads drop out of racing altogether, we have a few every season. There is the money, and there is also the point that this can be a pretty boring job.'

'I can see it has compensations,' I said. 'But winners don't come every day.'

'They don't! Some lads go for years without doing a winner.'

'Winning makes it worthwhile?'

'That's what it's about. But with the conditions of the job, you can feel a bit undervalued sometimes. It's a difficult job to do. And you don't get much thanks.'

30

ANGEL CITY'S WIN at Goodwood was the perfect example of racing all going to plan. It looked as if every aspect of chance and fate had been weeded out of it; racing had been reduced to an exact science. On the rare occasions when the plan actually works, there is the most glorious illusion of being totally in control. The punter feels it when his double comes off, which is rare enough: how much more delicious and intense are the satisfactions for the trainer?

And for the owner, of course, and Angel City is half-owned by Castle Stables' most understanding owner, J. L. Dunlop. Angel City came back from Goodwood fit and still raring to go: so where to send him next? Marcus Hosgood, up in the boxroom with the *Racing Calendar*, had one idea, and John Dunlop had another. 'I think he's right for this race at Newmarket on Friday,' Hosgood was saying.

'Do you think this is quite sound, Marcus? What is the penalty for his win at Goodwood?'

'Four pounds.'

'Four pounds! And you want to run him at Newmarket.'

'Well, I think if we wait for the handicapper, it will be worse. I think the handicapper will put him up five pounds –

at least five pounds – for Goodwood. So if he goes for the Newmarket race, we will be effectively taking weight off his back.'

'You think that, do you?'

'Well, it looks very much like it. He's been doing nothing but improve, and that really was a very good win at Goodwood.'

'Hm. It will be a big weight for a three-year-old. And the race looks as if it will be rather a hot one.'

'But he'll have even less chance if he goes up five pounds. And he might go up seven.'

Marcus was adamant that running him on Friday would be the equivalent of taking three pounds off his back. It was the dangerous game of second-guessing the handicapper: keeping one jump ahead of that implacable, faceless foe. To race the horse before the handicapper had taken his latest win into account was a considered gamble: the race conditions imposed their own penalty for the win. But Hosgood was convinced that the handicapper's penalty would be more severe than the one given under the terms of the race.

'Very well, Marcus, we'll let him take his chance. But it goes against my better instincts.'

It is the sort of decision that gives you the horrors. Hosgood instantly wanted to say, no, no, I've just changed my mind, let's not run him after all. But he was stuck with it. He felt appalled at what he had done.

Angel City had been giving everyone in the yard a special buzz all year, and particular pleasure to Hosgood, whose job it was to find races for him. Being the classic progressive type, Angel City was managing to outstrip the handicapper all by himself, by the simple process of improving with every race. His win at Goodwood was his third in succession, or his third win 'off the reel' in the jargon. Each time he had run a pound or two better than the handicapper's assessment.

He started off the season racing off a very lenient mark, and then ran a couple of races principally intended to get him race fit, 'though horses never stop surprising you,' as Hosgood was quick to add. Naturally, the handicapper took note of these unsuccessful runs, and reduced his rating still further. And then, according to theory, the horse gets fully fit – 'And bang!' said Hosgood. 'He goes in.'

Angel City began the season a satisfactory fourth on ground that didn't suit him. He had another run at Bath, when Dunlop and Hosgood had pondered and wondered about running him, and he was beaten again, though not disgraced. He had got trapped on the rail, and since he is a horse that needs a fair distance to get up a decent head of steam, he lost his chance. He was more the type of horse to wear them down, rather than one like Moon Madness that can produce a sudden burst of acceleration, a 'turn of foot'. By the time Carson was able to take him out of the pocket, it was too late to inflict any damage on the opposition, and Carson was full of self-criticism afterwards.

So the horse went to Newbury, and this time the ground was good-to-soft, but the distance was one mile three furlongs. The handicapper kept him on the same mark. It looked like a pretty good race for him: on paper there was only one horse that could beat him. However, the one they feared got up and beat him pretty easily: so much for clever thinking. But taking a sensible look at the race, it was clear that one mile three was just not enough for him. It looked as if the horse could do one thing, and do that well: stay. So Hosgood and Dunlop decided to try him out over a longer trip.

And bang, as Hosgood would say, he went in. This time the best laid plan failed to go agley. And after that, Angel City was off and rolling. As the ghastly weather of the ghastly summer got into its stride, so did Angel City. The horrible conditions underfoot may have scuppered Moon Madness, but Angel City revelled in them. He was a horse purpose-built, it seemed, for the appalling weather of the 1987 racing season. The wetter the ground and the greater the distance he was asked to race over, the more he seemed to like it. He ploughed through the mud like a tractor, and seemed to be given an engine that would never falter and never run out of fuel.

For Hosgood up in the boxroom, the horse was a dream. The rating kept going up: 80, 82, 87, and now 95, but everything he was entered in, he won. He was doing more than any horse in the yard to keep things ticking over, and providing a source of beer money. Every race he ran, he seemed to bring in a dividend.

But would the fourth dividend come up at Newmarket? Hosgood decided he had already staked quite enough on the race. The horse was loaded into the horse-box, with Scobie to look after him, and that was the day the *Racing Calendar* always arrives. Not by coincidence, but through careful planning, the Newmarket race was to be held on the day the new ratings were announced, but the day before they actually came into force. Hosgood naturally ripped it open the second he saw it, turned to the letter A, and ran his eye down to Angel City. And his blood froze in horror. The handicapper had only penalized Angel City two pounds for his win. The race conditions penalized him four pounds. Hosgood's scheme now meant that Angel City was racing with an extra two pounds on his back: two pounds that could easily make the difference between winning and losing. Hosgood checked the runners in the race from the morning's racing paper: all the horses that might be a danger were standing their ground. Was Angel City really going to beat In Dreams and Sudden Victory with an extra two pounds on his back?

The race was run at six that evening, and Hosgood went down to the bookies in Rustington to listen to the race commentary. He was not remotely tempted by the idea of a bet. The commentary began: Hosgood was in too deep and what was worse, the commentator did not make a single mention of Angel City. Where the hell was the horse? What the hell was the jockey, Newnes, playing at?

At last, three furlongs out, the commentator announced passionlessly that Angel City was making his move. The plan with the horse was always pretty much the same: to make the challenge a good way out, and with two still to run, to go for it, and see what happened. Angel City slowly built up his head of steam, and started to bowl merrily along towards the front.

He came alongside In Dreams and Sudden Victory, and threw down his challenge. This, surely, was the point at which the extra weight would tell.

Who had the turn of foot now? The expressionless voice of the commentator continued: 'And with a furlong to go it's Angel City, followed by Sudden Victory and In Dreams, Angel City in the lead . . .' Was it too soon? Was it too late? Marcus stood there surrounded by Rustington punters, and silently willed the winning post to appear.

And then all at once the sun began to shine and a heavenly choir of angels began to sing. Angel City. By a length. Thank you, God, thought Marcus, and returned humbly and gratefully back up the hill to Castle Stables.

31

THERE WAS A growing feeling of amazement out on the gallops. And it concerned Alwuhush, the white-faced two-year-old, otherwise known as 'the Nureyev'. And it was not that he was beating everything out of sight on the gallops: quite the reverse. But everyone was absolutely delighted.

Alwuhush was going very well indeed. He had run his first race in July, and was runner-up to Emmson. He had run very green that day, not surprisingly, since he had no idea what it was all about. He led, but got pipped on the line, a disappointing result to a pleasing race. On the gallops he looked magnificent, strong, handsome and able to cruise past just about anything. Nothing could keep with him up the long slope in Arundel Park.

But in August he stopped having it all his own way. He was put to do his Work alongside a horse called Alquoz, otherwise known as 'the Caerleon colt'. This was a big black thing (racing people pretend that a black horse is actually brown, so for official purposes Alquoz, as black as night, is a br. c.). Alquoz wasn't quite as showy looking as Alwuhush, but never mind that. In August he came to himself and simply set fire to the gallops. Alwuhush had got used to being cock of the walk, but now he found that Alquoz was going past him, moving easily, eating up the ground, and loving every minute of it.

And throughout Castle Stables, a light went on in everybody's brain. The light said: 'Derby!' And that was enough to give a special taste for all the rest of the season. The three-year-olds may have been a trifle disappointing this season: but what about the two-year-olds: Ashayer, Alwuhush – but you ain't seen nothing yet. Wait till you see the dark horse we have hidden away.

And the routine of stable life continued: hope garnished with winners.

But this horse business will always throw a few setbacks alongside the good news. Tommy Way, the previous season's Italian Derby winner, had his second race of the season, at Deauville in France, and broke a blood vessel again. He was beaten 14 lengths that day, and it looked as if it were the last race he would ever run.

There were still winners. The Castle Stables machine was gathering momentum: Wood Chanter, Moon Madness's brother, won his maiden, a couple more races were picked up, and, on the same day that Tommy Way broke down, Moon Madness delighted everyone by winning a race with immense courage, a great heartlifting ding-donger at Newbury. It all left Eddie Watt in most excellent spirits. His job is to keep the Castle Stables machine turning, and besides, he has a very soft spot for Moon Madness.

Every castle needs its ghost, to patrol the grounds at the spooky times of night, and at Arundel, Eddie Watt does his best to fulfil the role. In the pre-dawn half-light, he pads about the stable yards, a small, lone figure, moving from box to box. The horses stir and fidget as he passes, sending out little gouts of steam from their nostrils in the cold months, at warmer times simply giving out the wet, warm smell of contented horse. They pop their heads outside the v-bars above the stable doors to check him out as he passes: it is five o'clock, and when the horses see Eddie they know it is time to start the day. Their beloved routine begins with him and takes its time from him throughout the day until he passes by last thing at night.

Watt dishes out the first feed of the day, always a momentous event for a healthy horse. They greet his arrival with the deep-throated chuckling noise: that cheery, eager sound that all horsepeople know: the sound that means 'mealtime' in every stable in the world. The feed trolley makes its rattling journey, the more it rattles the more eager the chuckles, the horses stir and stretch and stamp the odd foot, shake an occasional head. Another day begins, same as the last day, same as tomorrow. If it's Eddie Watt, it must be breakfast.

Watt is John Dunlop's head lad. There are five head lads altogether: Watt is in charge of the main yard and is senior head lad over the other four: the entire stable is his area of responsibility. He is one of those small, utterly self-possessed men that racing specializes in, and he wears a special outfit to show that he has a special role in the stable. The lads wear flat caps, or woolly hats when the weather starts to bite, and various different interpretations of riding gear. Watt wears a knee-length buttoned brown cotton overall, and a porkpie hat, set at a distinctly jaunty angle. His expression is often distinctly unjaunty: he is very much a get-the-job-done-and-get-it-done-right sort of man.

He is a Scot, and despite spending most of his life in darkest Sussex, he still burrs his Rs and Scotifies his vowels. And in a rather Scottish way, he has elevated conscientiousness to the status of a personal religion. To goof off, to cut corners, would be blasphemous. But it would never occur to him to do so.

He is with the horses at five in the morning, often earlier. He checks them again in the evening, 'last thing as night' as stable people call nine p.m. 'I always walk round just before I go to bed. I have a walk round to make sure. I just want to see that they're all all right, that nothing's got cast – sometimes you'll find a horse cast, lying in the corner with his legs up in the air, can't get up.'

Finding a horse cast is yet another of those acts of God that are part of racing's rich pattern of disasters and frustrations. Horses like to roll on their backs for a good old scratch: when they do this in their boxes, they sometimes get stuck in a corner and can't get up again. They get frightened, flail about, and hit the walls by mistake: those million-pound legs start crashing about like demented pistons, collecting bangs, cuts and bruises against the walls, injuries that can affect them for a week, a season, or forever. It is perfectly possible for a horse to break its leg after getting cast. The sooner a cast horse is found, the sooner it can be righted: hence Watt's regular crisscross of the yard at the ghostly times of night.

Watt started in racing as a 14-year-old lad working for Hugh Barclay in Scotland. He arrived in Arundel to work as a lad in 1952 and has worked under the last three Arundel governors: Willie Smyth, Gordon Smyth, and now Dunlop. Gordon Smyth was the first to promote him, giving him the job of travelling head lad, the man who takes the horses to and from the racecourse. He did the job for 22 years: a life of extraordinarily long hours, all of them miles away from home. 'Every day is different, travelling, but you get to a certain age, you probably think you have done enough travelling. I've been head man here five years. Mr Dunlop asked me to do the job, give up the travelling. I'm happy.'

Every day is different for the travelling head lad, but for the head lad himself, every day is as much the same as he can make it: the regular feeding, the clatter of hooves, the summoning of the lads on the tannoy ('All right, everybody on the yards!'), the quiet afternoons, the rounds of evening stables with the trainer or his assistant, the main feed at six in the evening, the constant pacing of the yard, the checking and double checking. Watt lives in one of the estate cottages: when he is at home he is always just about to go and check on the horses. 'I've got a good home life. My wife's father was in racing, so she understands. It's an all-day job, and you've got to be there. Animals have got to be looked after. Somebody's got to be there.'

'So the hours must be the biggest problem about the job?' I asked.

'No. Staff. Getting good staff. That's the biggest problem. That's the biggest difference between racing when I first came into it, and racing today. Years ago you always had good staff, and they made the job easy. But getting good staff is a problem now. People just don't come into racing these days. They're not interested in the same way. They are not interested like the old-timers were – I think the pay's got a lot to do with it.

'When someone comes to me looking for a job, the first thing I do is size them up. Some people who come to me looking for work are just too big. You've only got to look at them to see if they're the right build and if they've got the right attitude. That's got a lot to do with it: they've got to have the right attitude to come and work with animals.'

Watt is not the hirer and firer – like everything else in the yard, that is done by and through Dunlop. But like every trainer, Dunlop relies immensely on the head lad. Watt's recommendations in the hiring and firing line are likely to be met favourably.

The principal thing the trainer demands from his head lad is rock solid reliability. The head lad is the fixed point of the yard, and everything revolves around him. Dunlop has his pupil assistants as well as his head lads: the relationship between them is rather like that between freshfaced subalterns and grizzled NCOs. And how often is it said that good sergeants run the army?

'So what are the satisfactions of running the yard?'

'Winners. Good winners. It all comes down to winners. Good winners make up for everything.'

'So what was it like during the 31-day lean stretch?'

'Depressing. Very depressing. It's hard to explain – it was just very depressing. Things just weren't going right. On the whole the staff were very good. They understood. They all sort of mucked in – we've got a pretty good staff. The majority of them are married, and living around the estate, rent-free. The girls, I don't know why, but I find the majority of them very good, really interested in their horses. And they take good care of them.

'I know every horse in the yard. I'm involved with every one of them. I start going round at half past four, and I check every horse we've got. I check their legs, make sure there are no cuts or swellings. I check every horse individually, and I've always got soft spots for some of them. There's always a character. Moon Madness has got to be the one at the moment. He's one of them that always seems to know what's going on, he's always alert. You've got to work with horses before you can understand them. And he's a character.

'But Shirley Heights was probably my favourite of all time. I was travelling head lad when he won his two Derbys – it was great at Epsom, it was a thrill you can't explain. It was a great feeling. I was right on the winning post, right on the rails on the nearside. It was a great feeling to see him come home.

'But I know all the horses. I know them all, as well as anybody could.'

32

MOST CASUAL PUNTERS like to follow the jockey in form, but it makes far better sense to follow the stable in form. Each horse is an autonomous animal, but the same thing can affect every horse in a yard. John Dunlop's horses all got a little backward in the spring, because the gallops were suffering under the appalling weather – there was so much appalling weather, an appalling winter, an appalling spring and an appalling summer, that it is easy to lose track, but it was the appalling spring which made the gallops boggy, and so made it impossible to get the Arundel horses working too hard too soon.

The horses are trained together as a team. The ability to give each horse in the string individual attention is one of the great skills of training, and Dunlop's magic memory system with his own massive cavalry is one of the great training feats of every season, but all the same, the horses exercise together, and will often tend to come good and find their peak form at round about the same time. This is the rhythm of the stable: some trainers will get their horses frantically forward in the spring, so they will be cleaning up before the roses are in bloom. Others will be masters at striking early with their two-year-olds in mid-season. Dunlop brings his own two-year-olds on more slowly, and ran the 1986 autumn as a one-man benefit. There were signs in the way things were going that a traditionally decent autumn might be on the cards. Angel City won yet again, and then Boon Point, Mike Huntley-Robertson's muscly colt, did his best to be a glorious horse and won in Ostend. Things were not going too badly. Now.

Looking back sanely and unemotionally at the terrible period of the Drought, it seemed obvious that there had been some kind of infection running around the yard. It was not the dreadful, rampaging virus that put the entire string out of action in 1985, but some weird little thing that did not even show up in the repeated examinations and tests. It was, however, just enough to take the edge off a horse's performance. A horse may be performing well in training but, stressful though training is, there is nothing like the effort that is asked for in a race. The old practice of running trials at racing speed is no longer done: it is too wildly profligate of a horse's resources. Better to bring it to its peak and to ask for the supreme effort in public, when a good performance really counts for something.

The downside of this is that when you ask for the supreme effort, you never quite know what is there. And a horse can disappoint horribly, as we know. Some lurking infection can knock a few per cent off a horse's ability, and that is enough to make the difference between winning and losing.

'The main difference between being a normal vet and being a vet to a racing stable is that we are not dealing primarily with sick animals,' said Robert Allpress, one of the vets in the partnership that looks after Castle Stables. 'We are dealing with athletes, and for the most part we are dealing with very small things that affect their ability to perform. And I think the trouble this season has been that some low-grade, almost subclinical disease has taken, say, the top five per cent off an animal's ability to perform.'

The problem of diagnosing so tiny a problem can be imagined. Eventually, it was done, but it took a terrible length of time to be discovered. In the end, the problem was traced to a bacterial infection, technically called streptococcus pneumonia.

It had probably been brought into the yard by a new horse, or been picked up at the races: who knows? And it spread slowly. The virus spreads 'like a stubble fire' Allpress said. But this weird little thing drifted here and there, picking off the odd individual here and there, mostly the young horses.

It had more or less cleared up, as the results showed, but it was still lingering, popping up in odd horses that had seemed to be clear, and with others who seemed to be taking an unconscionable time in getting rid of it. Spotting the ones who had it was a real headache: often there only seemed to be something wrong when one of them disappointed at the racetrack. 'It has been,' said Allpress, with some feeling, 'a very, very frustrating time.' Everyone connected with Castle Stables will say Amen to that.

Every trainer understands the frustration of the tiny, fractionally debilitating infections that affect the horses and the plans so horribly. The problem is what to do about it. Any obvious cure is totally elusive. The best thing that can be done is to reduce the stress: a bacterial infection cannot be wiped out at a stroke with antibiotics.

Even better: do not get the infection in the first place: prevention is what all trainers long for. More than anything, they yearn for a simple, magical solution: an injection against the virus and all the respiratory problems that affect racehorses in training. Dunlop has done a good deal of work to encourage research in this direction. But the researchers are finding it a problematic, frustration-filled task. As yet there is no solution, nor is the prospect of one imminent. 'In the end, it may turn out to be a blind alley,' Allpress said.

The other answers are less magical. If you cannot stop the horse getting the infection, you can at least reduce the effects it will have. You do this by taking the horse away from stress: no galloping, perhaps no cantering either. Certainly no racing. But to do this, you need to spot the infection very early indeed. 'The ultimate aim is to spot a horse that is *about* to succumb, and to avoid putting him under pressure, and that will avoid the long-term effects,' Allpress said.

'But that is not easy. Every racing stable brings a large number of young animals together. Young animals have not developed the immunities that older ones have, so by bringing them together you are setting yourself up for respiratory problems. The horse world was probably the last to realize that putting large numbers of young animals together was a recipe for trouble. Pig farmers and calf rearers have been aware of this for a long time.

'So the most useful thing that can be done, more useful than hoping for a vaccination to provide a miracle answer, is to work at improving stable hygiene. Clean air, good bedding: fundamental horse management. All very lowtech. It doesn't come out of a needle, but it still works: the more hygienic your stable, the fewer problems you are likely to get.

'We had an expert in stable hygiene who came around here after we had the virus, and he was quite satisfied. There are several different stable designs here, some purpose-built blocks, some made out of old cottages. The air flow is quite good. The point is to encourage the stable staff to participate, to take it very seriously indeed. We need the young assistants in particular to keep a close eye on this. You can have a horse in a good clean environment, who will get a small respiratory virus, and have very little problem from it. He will recover quickly, and not go down with a secondary infection. In these cases, the horse will just sail on without anyone noticing that anything was wrong at all – it is the secondary problems that are every bit as important as the actual virus.

'But I don't think it is possible to keep a stable wholly free from viral disease. All you can do is reduce its effect.' It seemed, however, that the worst of the problem had gone. Touch wood, touch it most fervently, but the thing seemed to have more or less run its course, barring a few stragglers. Three Tails tried to look like a totally reliable filly by winning a Group race at the Curragh, and on 30 August, a double-pronged raid abroad brought a win for Almaarad at Deauville and another for Harlestone Lake at Ostend. It was all as if the horrors of the Drought had never been.

33

THE MEMBERS OF Sue Abbott's Domino Fire syndicate were all in the jolliest form. Domino really did seem to have a good chance in her race at Lingfield, and what is more, it was a gorgeous evening. It was about the only occasion in the year that Michael Fish relented, and he sent us the kind of late summer evening that has racing gentlemen all over England reaching for their panamas.

Punters love evening meetings, and this one was packed and fizzing. Trainers and lads hate evening meetings, of course: people who start work shortly after six in the morning tend to go off the idea of work after six in the evening. But evening meetings always have a particular kind of jollity: slightly raffish, slightly downmarket, a feeling of having stolen a treat from the normal run of events.

The band of Mrs Abbott's owners was savouring the anticipation for all it was worth: after all, anticipation is so often the best part. The savouring of victory is a much rarer treat, but every owner in every race can revel in the prospect of a miracle, the never-wozzer coming good at last and beating the book at 100–1. Domino's owners were not all there: getting all ten owners to the course never quite happens, but there were about half a dozen of them, and that was certainly a quorum.

James Burns was there acting for John Dunlop: he is the amiable Irish subaltern or pupil assistant, and you could not wish for a nicer deputy. He told the posse of owners that Domino was in good shape and good heart, and, given luck in the running, should be there or thereabouts. They were putting up young Graham Foster, or Elvis, the apprentice from the Findon branch of the Dunlop empire. Foster had won on Domino Fire at Warwick and, with his weight allowance, he was taking seven pounds off the horse's back. It was all very promising, just as it should be at the races when the sun shines: panamas, pretty dresses and your horses worth a bet: the dream was in full motion down at Lingfield.

Burns himself was not at his happiest, however, for all his smiling, informed chat with the syndicate members. His day had been a stinker. For a start, he had forgotten his binoculars, which was going to make reading the race a trifle difficult. The trainer's representative has to say all kinds of wise things to the owners afterwards: 'Ah well, it was the weight that beat her.' 'She got a bump coming into the straight and never got going again.' 'She changed her legs coming down the hill and lost three or four lengths, so next time we won't run her on an undulating course.' These are the sort of excuses a trainer or his representative can offer, but when your principal owner is as knowledgeable as Mrs Abbott, it helps if the excuse is the right one.

And then the gatekeeper questioned Burns's authority to act as Dunlop's representative. Funnily enough, most gatekeepers on racecourses are reasonably pleasant, considering what that species is normally like. But Burns had probably got the man from Lords cricket ground on his day off: 'It's all very well you saying this, but how do I know you are who you say you are?' A brief brush with the more-than-my-job's-worth brigade puts years on you, and doesn't help a young subaltern when he has to be charming to owners.

However, Burns eventually persuaded them that he was James

Burns, and he was able to give Foster his leg-up and his instructions. Foster set off once again to meet his future, eaten up with ambition, the desire to make a good impression, and the need to look like a real jockey.

The horses were loaded into the stalls, and with a bang, they were off. I hadn't forgotten my binoculars (honestly, I would have lent them to James had I known of his plight) and I raked through the field, a pretty large one, trying to find the blue and white colours of Domino Fire. It took a fair while: the horse seemed to be burrowing her way into a serious equestrian rugby scrum. It would take some inspired riding to get out of that lot.

Reading a race from the stands is a very difficult business, even if you haven't forgotten your binoculars. I am no good at it at all: I get far too excited. Anyone who has a bet tends to watch one horse only. To come up with a cool, accurate and dispassionate assessment of the race: why this horse won, where he made his move, why the favourite vanished from the reckoning, why this horse ran such a stinker, and how the outsider ran such a promising race for third spot: this is a tough and demanding task for the professional racereaders of the sporting press, and the trainers.

I didn't need to be a genius to work out that Domino Fire had run a stinker. She was not involved in anything at any significant stage of the race. In fact, I don't think the race commentator mentioned her name once. I recall a glimpse of Foster, wild-eyed and riding like a demon when the horse was in tenth position and making no headway whatsoever: a grim sight.

After the race, the horses were led to their various fates. I had an arrangement to meet Mrs Abbott after the race 'either in the winner's enclosure or at excuses corner' as she put it. There would need to be some pretty fancy excuses. The horse was led through the racegoers (for Lingfield is a very intimate little track) with Foster sitting hunched and round-shouldered in the saddle, injured innocence in every line of his body.

Burns approached the horse and the bevy of owners. And then the tannoy boomed out: 'Would Mr John Dunlop the trainer, or his representative, please report to the stewards.' That was precisely all that Burns needed. For a mild man, he looked a very great deal like Basil Fawlty: 'Thank you God! Thank you so bloody much!'

Mrs Abbott was saying things like: 'Ah well. It is the sort of thing you must expect if you put up a boy.' But she would have sounded a great deal more philosophical if she had un-clenched her teeth.

I spoke to Burns about it all when the dust had settled. 'I didn't realize how bad it was when I watched from the stands,' he said. 'Graham said afterwards that he was going for a gap when he got collared and was sandwiched. When I watched the head-on film in the Stewards' Room, it was clear that the gap he had gone for was in fact nonexistent. And so he had clipped the heels of the horse in front, and his own horse had fallen to her knees. He then showed his inexperience by hitting the horse and trying to ride a finish. He was cautioned by the stewards as to his future riding. And – well, I expect he will learn by his mistakes.'

All people learning every profession make terrible errors at some stage or another. The best make fewer, that is all. And they don't make the same mistake twice.

The syndicate members took their cue from Mrs Abbott, and were as philosophical as they could manage. If you put up a seven-pound claimer, you know it is a gamble: the weight you take off the horse's back might help her to fly, or the boy's inexperience might make for a disaster. All experienced owners know and understand this. It doesn't make the disappointment any the less. But at least you know how to behave in your disappointment.

Poor old Foster was very rueful afterwards. There was no way of avoiding the fact that this was an awful cock-up. Every apprentice makes them, you know that, but that doesn't stop the whole thing being acutely embarrassing, humiliating and totally horrible. 'I got myself into a load of trouble in the race,' he said. 'And I just lost my cool.' This was especially hard for Foster, who prides himself on his cool, to come to terms with. 'It's inexperience, I know. The stewards weren't too bad. I told them I didn't realize I was beaten that far, which I didn't. And I didn't realize I was being that hard on her. And when I saw the video, I realized how hard I had been.'

'And the owners?'

'They didn't say much.'

'Will they put you up again?'

'I don't know. I'll have to wait and see.'

34

ONWARD, THEN, INTO September. Autumn was beginning, and if anyone thought we were going to get an Indian summer after the horrors of the real summer, he was disappointed. And if John Dunlop was to have a golden autumn, it was time to start going. The strike rate since the Drought had been good rather than great, and the lads were wondering if there were going to be even as many winners as there had been in the virus season of 1985. There were 42 winners going into the September of 1987, and the 1985 total of 66 winners was still some way off.

Castle Stables had a double on 12 September, St Leger day, but unfortunately, neither of the winners was in the Leger. Love The Groom had his run in the race that Moon Madness had won the previous year, but it was a great disappointment. He finished last but one, and the wins from Tanouma and Freedom's Choice didn't really make up for it. 'In a way,' Jeremy Noseda said, 'it would be nice to stop this season right now and get cracking on the next. We have so much promise for next season, and have had so many problems in this one, that there is a part of me that wants to say: well, this one just didn't work out. Let's go straight on to the next.'

But there was a very pleasant joke to go with all this. The most trumpeted feat of the season was Henry Cecil's beating of all training records: with his 147th winner, he beat the 120-year-old record of John Day. This was celebrated with Reference Point's splendid battling win in the St Leger. But shortly afterwards, one of Cecil's previous winners, Quexioss, was disqualified retrospectively: because of an error it had been treated with a prohibited cream before its race. In the end, the magic winner number 147 was not Reference Point but Madam Cyn, winner of a humble seller in Yarmouth. And the trainer who benefited from the disqualification? None other than J. L. Dunlop of Arundel. Noble Bid was promoted from second to first in the Mayfair Graduation Stakes at Windsor, a race worth £1,184. And the belated win occurred, ironically enough, during the Drought.

But the season went on, and the winners didn't dry up, even if they failed to arrive in packages of a dozen at a time. Chilibang got up again, and on 24 September, Dunlop had a treble. Panienka won at Beverley, and Moon Madness won a Group race at Ascot, to pick up another £34,000. And the same day, Graham Foster (the apprentice) rode Tanouma to another win, which cheered him greatly. In fact, he rode rather well that day, really looked the part. He was at one with the world again.

As autumn comes, so the Sales season starts: the Highflyer again, Keeneland, Goffs in Ireland. The new year of racing begins as the old season is still going on: Dunlop has to make prolonged absences to talk to owners, to buy horses, to feel horses' legs. While he is away, Castle Stables has to look after itself. It does so very adequately indeed.

Delegation is vital, Dunlop is always insisting. It is the key to the enterprise when there are 200 horses to look after. But in racing, there is a snag to delegation that other businesses don't have. Every owner is paying to have his horse trained by J. L. Dunlop. Not by some person they have never heard of.

The multiple owners, such as the Arabs and the del Bonos, are different, of course. For a start, they act through agents, and this makes the relationship far more conventionally businesslike:

not that either the Arabs or the del Bonos are in it for the money, simply that they pursue their sporting dreams in a more detached and methodical way than the owner with but a single horse.

When most owners reach for the telephone for news of their beloved beast, it is Dunlop's voice they want to hear. A trainer, especially a trainer of some celebrity, is selling not just his yard's machinery, but also his personality. When owners choose Dunlop's yard as the home for their horse, they are motivated not just by his record but also, frivolous as this may sound, by his charm. Throughout the racing season, owner after owner, as we stood watching the string beside the Japanese Range Rover, took me to one side to tell me how marvellous Mr Dunlop was, what a phenomenal memory for horses he had, how they would never choose another yard. Dunlop effortlessly makes his owners feel wanted, part of the set-up.

It is an education to hear Dunlop in action on the telephone, bantering with belted earls in his patrician drawl, teasing wealthy ladies, reporting instantly on the wellbeing of any member of the 200-strong cavalry: 'Well, Suffolk, what's all this whingeing about these horses of yours?'

He somehow gives the impression that every single task in the stable is done by his own hand: that he feeds, grooms, rides and adores every horse in his charge. He is diplomat, public relations man and jolly good fellow. No one seriously believes that Dunlop does everything, but his aura of omniscience, his ability to put a personal touch into everything, are immense assets. But in sober fact, his number two, Tony Couch, carries a mighty share of the load, and Dunlop would never wish to minimize the reliance he places on him.

If you wanted to pick a man as a complete contrast to Dunlop, then Couch would be your man. Dunlop is languid and laid-back, and his patrician speech is quite unaffected. He will even tend to end sentences with a drawled 'hwaat?', as in: 'Have to do something about all these lame horses, hwaat?' But Couch is a bustler, and you can tell him for a Yorkshireman at about 50 paces, more on a still day. 'I'm from Malton, the Newmarket o' the north.'

Couch was born into a racing family, like so many racing people. His father trained at Malton. Couch has worked just about everywhere, and in every capacity: head lad here, assistant trainer there, travelling head lad somewhere else. He spent two years in German racing. He has been with Dunlop since 1978: 'I joined about six weeks before Shirley Heights won the Derby for us. I wish I could say it were some of my doing.'

Couch has made himself into the perfect number two for this kind of operation. He is not pushy or over-ambitious, but nor is he stretched by his responsibilities. He can stand in for the governor on every occasion it is necessary, never wishing to overshadow him. He is a man of stature. The two know each other well.

'My main purpose here is to run the yard. To make sure that everything works here at home.' This involves acting as number one all the time Dunlop is away from Arundel, racing, or at the sales or even, for a few snatched weeks in the winter, on holiday.

But in the dark weeks that followed Tim's death, there was something of a role reversal. Dunlop decided to stay away from the races, and to run everything from Arundel. Couch went to the races in his stead, briefed the jockeys, chatted up the owners and answered the questions from the press. And as the losers kept piling up, this task became more and more unpleasant. 'Yes, we are concerned about this losing streak. No, we do not think we have the virus, but we are checking every horse and taking every precaution. The poor performance of our runner in the last race is a mystery to us, because he had been going very well at home.'

'Oh, it was a bad time all right,' Couch said. 'I wish I could have saddled up a few winners for him in that time. But it just didn't happen.'

Couch has done just about everything in racing bar train himself. He is terrific, responsible and capable, but he has never sought out the ultimate responsibility of being the trainer. Being assistant trainer to a string of 200 horses involves more work and more responsibility than any trainer in the land takes on, bar the real heavyweights. But there is still a vast difference between being number two to 200 horses, and number one with a string of ten.

'Well, since you mention it, I have sometimes wondered about setting up . . . taking a job as a private trainer, that is.' It takes a great deal of money and optimism to set up as a public trainer. Dunlop, remember, began as a private trainer to the late Duke.

Couch's stock-in-trade is his massive competence, his immense air of capability. He is the man who takes care of the nuts and bolts, who gives the trainer the elbow room to make the big decisions, the time to go to Ireland or Keeneland to wheel and deal. Being a number two is the least glamorous job in racing: even the lads get to appear on television when they lead their charges around the parade ring. But Couch somehow doesn't strike you as a man seeking glamour. He is happy enough being essential.

35

'EFISIO, YOU BASTARD, are you going to behave yourself today?' Efisio, quirky, cantankerous and the noisiest horse in the yard, walked into the horse-box with dainty steps and a mild eye, as if he were the sweetest and soppiest thing in Arundel, the old hypocrite. Perhaps his lad had belatedly learned the Crocodile Dundee art of quelling him with a glance: but Stuart Johnston – that is Angus – had good reason not to trust the sour five-year-old.

Efisio was going to Ascot for the Festival of British Racing, which had been proudly announced as the richest day in the history of British turf. He was making the journey with two stable companions, a pair of the two-year-olds from whom great things were expected. Lovely Ashayer minced into the box like a high-heeled princess stepping into her carriage, and Alwuhush, big, bay and butch with his great white face, swaggered in afterwards.

Racing stables spend the entire season moving horses all over the country, and when there are 200 of them, the operation naturally becomes smooth and polished. Even Efisio seemed chastened by all the slickness of the routine. It is so much a part of English racing, that it is a job in itself. It involves an enormous

number of small and irritating chores, and there is a great responsibility to be carried all day. It is a job done by the travelling
head lad. He does not do horses at home, or run any of the yards:
his concern is getting the horses to the track, and supervising all the
tasks necessary to get the horse into the race and then home again.
John Dunlop employs four travelling head lads, and the most
senior of these is Robert Hamilton, known as Rab.

Hamilton rides out, but most of his job is sitting doing nothing
in the cab of the horse-box humming along the roads of England
for hours at a stretch, or walking very rapidly from one place to
another with a harassed expression on his face and a cigarette
between his lips. He is the fixer, he is the trainer's hands. He
takes responsibility for all the niggling little details of racing.
Before the horse-box sets off, he collects the colours – preferably
the right ones – from the dozens that live in the front office in a
cupboard behind Sue the secretary, and the horses' passports.
The passports record every single detail of colouration on a
horse, from fleck of white on the near hind heel to a spot of
pink on the nose. It is not easy to get an impostor through the
complex checking that goes on at a racetrack. And it helps things
along if Hamilton remembers the tack, too: a job of niggles,
and it is Hamilton's job to tackle it anywhere in England, or
Europe, or the world. To be travelling head lad at Castle Stables,
you must be capable of dealing with anything in racing's global
village.

The lads need their passes too, to get into the security areas of
the racecourse. In the stabling blocks, not even owners are
allowed in unless they are escorted by the trainer. The horses are
kept away from the racing crowds until they step out into the
parade ring. Racing believes in making a parade of its security:
the industry desperately wants to be seen to be doing everything
within its power to make the game as straight and as honest as it
possibly could be.

The day of the Festival of British Racing, Hamilton was in
charge of three horses and three lads. Alwuhush had Scobie, or
Ken Bedford, light-boned and fiercely moustached. Jane Martindale was doing Ashayer. The female lads do not tend to get

nicknames, but they learn to handle an awful lot of good-humoured – well, mostly good humoured – banter.

It was time to leave for the races when Hamilton came to-wards the van with his quick-stepped walk, and jumped into the cab. The driving is done by Wally Watkins, a man of heavy build and placid temperament. He and Hamilton have organized the front cab with an eye to every possible comfort: they spend hours of every day together in there, adding up to days in every month and several weeks in every year, sitting in the cab and rolling all over the country with a million quid's worth of horses in the back. Each has a thermos within reach and cigar-ettes where a right hand will naturally fall on them. Watkins has his Rizla cigarette papers before him, and, a touch that impressed me, a real china mug to drink from.

Wally seemed like a man whom nothing on earth could ruffle. His driving style exuded oceans of calmness. 'You drive as if you had a cargo of unexploded bombs in the back,' I said. 'I have got a cargo of unexploded bombs in the back,' he replied. He has a large and complicated nose, and drives as if there were a two-foot spike protruding from the centre of the steering wheel. His progress around roundabouts is effortlessly smooth and at the approximate speed of a glacier.

'Horses love motorways,' he said. 'I stick to them whenever I can.' The journey from Arundel to Ascot is a fiddle across country, a succession of roundabouts, but even Efisio was pretty calm about it, under the soporific influence of Wally's driving.

'Efisio! Numero uno!' said Angus encouragingly, as the horse gazed forward at the lads with untroubled eyes. The lads have a compartment to themselves between the driver's cab and the horses. 'And it's Ashayer, it's Ashayer going into the lead as they pass the furlong marker, she's increasing her lead with every stride, it's Ashayer by four lengths!' Angus was predicting the racecourse commentary, shouting his money home in advance, getting into the mood.

'What I hate most,' Hamilton said, 'is to travel a long way for a horse with no chance at all.' But Ashayer had a chance all right, a great chance. Yes, he would put his money there. So would half the lads in the yard: they think a lot of the filly, and the way she has been performing on the gallops would have anyone reaching for his wallet. She surely had the beating of them all that day.

'And Alwuhush is gaining on them, Alwuhush has drawn level – and Alwuhush wins by a head!' A mere hangover was not going to stop Angus getting into the mood. 'And Efisio has gone crazy, he's racing in the wrong direction, he's jumped over the running rail. . . .' Efisio is something of an equine eccentric, so naturally Angus has a fellow-feeling for him. 'The bugger put me in hospital once. He double-barrelled me. I walked into his box one day, just as I have hundreds of times, and gave him a friendly slap on the backside, as I've done hundreds of times – complacency!' Efisio lashed out with both hind feet together. It is not easy to land a kick on a lad as fly and as experienced as Angus, but Efisio is the sort that knows what he's doing and he landed both. 'I've still got the scar on my knee.'

'Where did the other hoof get you?'

'I refuse to reveal that. But I'll give you a clue: I was singing soprano for a fortnight.' And though Angus makes a good story of it, he was on crutches for three weeks. 'Efisio! Numero uno! – Efisio, you see, is the patron saint of an Italian town.'

'Oh.'

'His owners were Italian.'

Hamilton was not taking part in these exuberances. He answered the banter goodheartedly enough, but he was not in an over-the-top mood. 'All the lads love to go racing, it's a great change in routine for them. But for me, well, it is the routine, isn't it?'

And quite a routine it is, as well, By the time we had left for Ascot, just before ten, Hamilton had already been working for three hours, and had ridden out first lot. 'I enjoy riding out, but it makes for a long day.' This was going to be something like a 12-hour day, but that was because Ascot is pretty handy for Arundel. It could have been much longer. 'It's hard on the wife, because the job is basically about being away from home.'

With so many hours in which there is nothing to do but

watch the white line disappearing under the bonnet, it is not surprising that Hamilton badly wants there to be a point to it all. And racing, being such a simplified world, can only offer one point to an outing to the racetrack. To take a horse a long way and to lose, because it is the wrong race or the wrong time, is a deeply frustrating experience. 'It is winners that keep you going. Sometimes you get a bit depressed, with all the long hours. Sometimes I look out of the horse-box as we drive to a meeting, and see a windowcleaner, say. And I feel a sudden envy for the bloke cleaning the windows. But then maybe you come home with a winner, and you feel a bit different. . . .'

We reached Ascot without incident, indeed, with scarcely a noticeable gear change from Wally. The horses were unloaded outside the stabling block, which is a generously proportioned area across the road from the racecourse. The horses were led from the van, and walked stiff-leggedly away to their temporary headquarters. 'Meet us in the lads' canteen,' said Angus.

The lads' canteen is rather like the students' union at a small polytechnic. The company tends to be a bit sparkier, even though it tends to talk on only two subjects, the other of which is horses. The prices are wonderfully low, and a meat pie and a cup of tea costs only about 30p or so. The lads put their horses in their temporary boxes, and then come to the canteen for a serious snack and a talk. All the lads from different yards know each other from the races, and many from working together. The lads' canteen is a marvellous place for gossip and meetings and banter: 'Your old stick's got *no* chance today.' 'How good is that two-year-old of yours that's never raced?' 'Alquoz? He'll win the Derby next year *no* problem. . . .'

'Don't think everywhere we go is like this,' Scobie said. 'You should come to Wolverhampton. This is the Hilton, this place. The best in the country.'

Angus said: 'I need a drink.' I joined him at the bar: two pints of lager, please. That'll be a pound, sir. Thank you very much. 'There's a best-turned-out prize in every race today,' Scobie was saying. 'They're great, we really love them. They're a real incentive.'

'I won £250 once – that's two weeks' wages,' said Angus.

'Remember when I won that five-pound salmon at Goodwood with Angel City?' said Scobie. 'He won the race too. That was a good day all right.'

'Is going to the races the best part of the job?' I asked.

'Seeing your horse win is the best part,' said Scobie. 'But it's always good to go racing.'

'Except evening racing,' said Angus.

Evening racing is the pits, for the lads. After a full morning's work, they set off to the races, missing out on their midday break. Often enough they are home after midnight. And the prospect of Sunday racing – well, don't ask a stable lad about that, it brings him out in a hot flush every time. 'No, the only thing really wrong with the job is the money,' Scobie said. 'I left racing for a year once, and got another job, so that I could pay all my bills. But now I'm back, and I've got a mortgage. You see, I run a mobile disco, take it anywhere at nights. Scobie's Disco, I call it. I get lots of bookings now I'm getting known, and that's how I manage to pay the mortgage.'

I caught up with Hamilton, who was involved in one of his frantic charges about the place, delivering colours to jockeys, and pieces of paper to officials. The weighing-room, full of slight, half-naked bodies topped by famous faces, had to be visited to arrange things with the valets, the men who look after the jockeys. Hamilton has a round of things to fix, 'and I also have to act as the trainer's representative when he isn't here. I've only had to go before the stewards once, though – and they were pretty nice to me.' Hamilton's job is one of rather tedious routines which might at any moment turn into serious dramas. When he is travelling the horses abroad, this is twice as likely to happen. It is job about coping.

'When you have a winner, people see you on television, you're the one who throws a blanket over the horse in the winner's enclosure. People think that is all a travelling head lad has to do – but that's the easy part. Oh, I wouldn't mind if the job was nothing but throwing blankets over horses in the winner's enclosure!'

The lads had left the canteen to prepare their horses for their appointments with destiny, brushing deep and beautiful shines into the already glossy coats, brushing complicated chequerboard patterns into the rumps to fancy the horses up. Before the horses paraded, the lads stepped out of their stable clothes and into something a little smarter: Jane changed into blue and white, with a blue ribbon in her hair to match Ashayer's colours, and Ashayer looked a world-beater alongside. I watched for a while with the pleasure that looking at Ashayer is apt to give one and then ducked off to Tattersall's. The lads had asked me to put the money on for them, and this was a sacred trust.

All the same, I wish I hadn't bothered. Ashayer was third, a sad sight. She was never happy, never greatly involved. Efisio, with Angus leading him in a jacket slightly too tight under the arms, was on his best behaviour, but he failed to put any of his legendary aggression into the race. He was, as that cruel line in the form book often has it, 'never a factor'.

Alwuhush looked handsome, and Scobie looked dapper as any disco man beside him in the paddock before his own race. When the race got going, Alwuhush looked rather remote and uninvolved, but right at the end he suddenly seemed to get the hang of it. He discovered that he possessed the most terrific turn of foot, and thundered mightily into third place, finishing fastest of all, and looking, to be totally biased, like the best horse in the race. If he had known what he was doing, he would surely have won it. Perhaps now he had learned. 'Very pleasing,' said Dunlop, meaning bloody great.

Next time out, he would surely show them all. Next time out, Efisio might think about winning. Next time out, Ashayer might race like Ashayer. Next time, we might even have a winner. 'Ah, but it's not just about winning, is it?' said Angus. 'When you collect your horse after the race, and he's knackered, and he says, like, I've done me best, Dad – well, that's good enough for me. Winning is good, but it's horses, that's what's it's all about. They call this the sport of kings, right? Well, let me tell you, it is the horses that are the bloody kings.'

36

ALQUOZ PEERED AT the cobbles with the deepest suspicion, convinced there were dragons lurking beneath. Angus, something of a dirty jobs specialist, was at his head encouraging him to step off the safe tarmac and on to the ever-so-frightening cobbles.

It was looking as if at long last, Alquoz was going to make his entry on to a racecourse. Enormous things were – expected? No. I had learned too much during the year to say that. Hoped for. But still – Alquoz. Robert Allpress, the vet, was giving him a check-over to see if he was free of infection. Two or three times, Alquoz had been all primed up for his first race, but each time he had shown some lingering trace of a respiratory infection. And you do not want to run any horse with such a thing, let alone Alquoz.

It always amazes me that horses who show such a hysterical reaction to the horrors of stepping from one underfoot surface to another, from tarmac on to .cobble, can put up with scoping as if it were a mere nothing. I am fairly sure that I would not react so amiably if someone attempted to stuff a couple of yards of black rubber tube up my nose.

But Alquoz, with his black face and his white star, stood

there as serene as one could wish while Allpress fed the seemingly endless tube into his nose. Allpress then raised the eyepiece, peered through it, and said resignedly: 'Oh no. He's mucky again. He's a two again.' He was looking deep inside the horse: the tube goes through the nostril and right down the windpipe to the point where it divides towards the two lungs. And he was looking at clots of phlegm and mucus, not a frightfully attractive sight. Actually, the view through the eyepiece is not quite as throw-up-making as you would expect: the image seems unconnected with flesh and blood: a Jackson Pollock abstract in patterns of bright scarlet with jolly patches of yellow. In a healthy horse, the pattern is pink, with no yellow at all. No doubt about it, then: there was something amiss with Alquoz, and he would not be running that week for sure.

Of course, he wasn't ill, he wasn't coughing, he was in no discomfort whatsoever. If he were a human, he would go to the office, and would not even complain to his secretary that he had a slight cold, it would be so trivial. A normal horse, a hack or a hunter or a dressage horse, could do his normal quota of work without any problem: a racehorse could still gallop, and could still race. But with one slight problem: he would not go quite as fast as usual. When asked for his supreme effort, he would have nothing to give. And without the magic black tube, the scope, you would have no idea what was wrong: I thought he was better than that, I just don't understand it, it was too bad to be true. But with the scope and modern veterinary science you can at least cut down on the number of variables, and at least you won't run a horse when its tubes are all full of muck.

The scope has been a great boon to racing vets, and to trainers. The device costs around £15,000, and was developed as a colonoscope for doctors to use on humans. Apparently they used it on Ronald Reagan. For doctors as for vets, it is a marvellous tool. It operates on glass fibre optics, which means you can see round corners with no distortion of the image. It has a light, so that you can see in the dark. And as a bonus, you can also use it for flushing out a sample of whatever you are looking at.

Scoping the horses is a regular pattern at John Dunlop's yard. They have developed a special jargon for the results: a zero is clear and pink, a one has a few yellowish specks and is turning scarlet, a two will have, as Allpress said, 'great blobs of muco-muck', and a three will have 'a continuous stream of really foul-looking material.'

'The surprising thing is that they don't cough,' Allpress said. 'Even with a colossal amount of discharge plus the scope in their throats – well, you or I would be gasping, eyes watering. They don't. Horses just don't seem to have a very efficient cough mechanism. Occasionally, when a horse *does* cough when I am scoping it, you can see that the cough hardly shifts the stuff at all. The cough just isn't productive.

'I think this is because in the wild, a horse spends such a lot of time with its head down, grazing, and this provides a natural drainage. They don't need to rely on a cough, as a more upright animal does. But we have brought them into stables, and put their mangers and water up high, and often they have haynets up high as well – so they never need to put their heads down at all. I think a lot of debris accumulates because of that.'

Despite the mounting number of winners, this had never quite stopped being a year of frustrations. The vets had spent most of the year peering at horrible stuff in horses' throats. This was the Year of the Mucus. At least some disasters had been avoided with the constant monitoring. Alquoz had not had to go out and disgrace himself or overstrain himself: and perhaps he would be right for the Futurity at Doncaster later in the year. But all this was pretty much of a negative thing to gain. And as we know, there is no easy answer when it comes to treatment and cure.

Allpress is all for doing everything he can: 'If you snag your knee, it will get better by itself. But if you put Savlon on it and protect it, it will get better a little bit quicker.' The thing about a racehorse is that its racing life is so short. A horse with the lineage and the hopes of Alquoz ought to make its mark at two, and certainly must prove itself in the Classics at three. And every day that a horse can't race, or can't Work, you hear the clock ticking its racing life away. Alquoz would have to set all convention aside if he was going to win the Derby without having raced as a two-year-old. The dreaded snuffles had made his season one of almost unbearable frustration. Angus took Alquoz back to his box: un-tested: untried: rocket or damp squib, nobody knew. And so long as his throat was full of nonsense, nobody ever would.

37

B Y OCTOBER IS seemed obvious that Castle Stables had modelled its season on its most wayward inmate, Three Tails. Three Tails made a habit of coming good too late: too late in the Oaks, when she started racing only after she had made certain she would lose the race, and too late in the season, when she learned how to race properly slightly too late to set the world on fire. By the end of September, Castle Stables really found its stride: far too late for John Dunlop to be champion trainer or anything like that, but certainly enough to have everybody singing as they marched towards the close season.

The first weekend in October, Dunlop made yet another raid abroad, picked up two Group wins in an afternoon and, with them, more than £80,000 in prize money. This was pleasant enough, but it gets better. The Prix Marcel Boussac in Longchamp had been won the previous year by Miesque, who became one of the outstanding racehorses of the year. Dunlop decided to send lovely Ashayer to contest the race, and she won in grand style. The fifty grand was nice, but nicer still was the way she showed that the beliefs and hopes invested in her had all been worthwhile. The same day, Sergeyevich, who had won in May, and who had won again at Goodwood in August with his tongue hanging out, completed a long season by winning the Italian St Leger in Milan.

The rhythm of winners continued: Highland Chieftain suddenly gave notice that he was coming to form by winning a small race at Warwick. Two more winners came on 14 October, and five days later Castle Stables struck four times at two different meetings, a small triumph in the art of finding the right race at the right time, and it all left Marcus Hosgood quite delighted with life.

And on into the declining autumn. The yearlings were beginning to arrive, David Kitcher was getting them organized, and lads like Chris Blyth and Raymond Baker were getting the long reins fixed to the new boys. Michael Fish had thrown in his final devastating blow of the year, though this time, perhaps, he was blameless. 'A woman has just telephoned to ask if there was a hurricane on the way,' he told us smiling. 'Well, don't worry, there isn't.' That should have been a sign for everyone in England to bolt the doors and retreat to the cellars: that night the hurricane struck at southern England, and Arundel Park seemed to be its prime target. Hundreds of trees, what the Duchess called 'important' trees, were ripped out of the ground. The morning after, there was devastation across southern England. There were so many fallen trees that it was impossible to get the horses out into the park, and they were restricted to walking round and round the yard. The park itself was devastated, the trees literally decimated, the work of centuries destroyed in a single night of meteorological caprice.

But as ever in this business, life goes on. Highland Chieftain next went to Düsseldorf, and picked up a Group Three race, a big step up from the modest company he had kept in his previous outing. On the last day of October, Dunlop lunged abroad again, and this time came back with three winners. Patriach, good ol' Reliable himself, won in Ireland, and there were two wins in Milan. One of these was – yes – Highland Chieftain, who picked up another Group Three race. But going one better, to the surprise and delight of Angus, was Efisio: the old rogue galloped up to win a Group Two race worth £21,000, and to give Angus what looked as if it would be a farewell present. Efisio! Numero uno!

And on into November, with the season declining fast. Alquoz had still been unable to run. Alwuhush had finished a dreadfully disappointing last in the Futurity. But in successive weekends, Dunlop made a couple of raids on Rome, and each time won a Group race. Patriach did his stuff again, and so did Highland Chieftain, winning his fourth race off the reel and still looking full of running: the season just wasn't long enough for him. At the end of this dirty, golden autumn, training racehorses suddenly looked like a fairly easy and comfortable way to make a living: nothing to it really. Everyone at the stables was full of himself.

'I gather we're going to win the Derby next year, anyway.'

'And the Oaks, don't forget that!'

'Of course, how could I?'

And so the season ended, not with a whimper, but with a bit of a bang. The English season was over: there were a couple more to be raced abroad, and that would be it. Moon Madness had been invited to go to Tokyo to race in the Japan Cup, and Highland Chieftain was to have one more swing at glory on 13 December in Naples: positively the last race of the season. But things had more or less stopped for the annual stocktaking. Some of the fillies had moved out to studfarms, to spend some time turned out 'on their holidays'. The yearlings were still arriving, and some of the older horses were moving on.

There had been 28 horses sold on in the Horses in Training Sale, some of the fillies as potential broodmares, some of the colts as jumpers. Sheikh Hamdan and Sheikh Mohammed had each sent nice batches of yearlings to Castle Stables: a new collection of potential world-beaters, sheikhs' dreams at stratospheric prices. Perhaps there was a Shirley Heights among them, perhaps a Snaafi Dancer. They came from all the usual places, from the Highflyer Sales, from the States, from the Arabs' own burgeoning breeding concerns. Dunlop had, of course, been to all the sales, feeling legs as religiously as he had when I had been with him in Newmarket the previous autumn. Let us look back on the horses he had acquired at the Highflyer the previous year: Anhaar, Pretoria, Hi Lass, Charme The Nickle, Gamble On, Picaroon, Dreadlock, Baltic Bay, Jabrut and Sergeant At Arms. Of these, only Pretoria and Picaroon had won races. Hi Lass, Dreadlock, and Baltic Bay didn't even race. But there is always another season.

And the 1987 season? Well it was, you may say, satisfactory. An unsuccessful season in some ways, but there are a good few trainers who would be pretty happy with an unsuccessful season with total winnings of £1,153,968. In the end, the season was only fractionally down on the best ever season of 1986, in which there was a total of £1,315,085. But there was a lot of difference between the two seasons. In 1986, Dunlop had 119 winners, more than any other trainer in England. This year the total was 77, which, by his standards, was poor.

But the prize money was up to scratch. This was because, of the 77 wins, there were 18 victories in Group races. In other words, more than one in five, or 23 per cent, of the wins were in Pattern Race company, which is remarkably good in any season, and particularly remarkable in a season so beset with troubles. The overseas strike rate was nothing less than splendid. Dunlop contested 35 races overseas and from them had 16 winners. A strike rate of 45 per cent is what trainers dream about. Only nine of these 35 raiders finished unplaced.

The failure of the stable, then, was only in the bread-and-butter department. The moderate horses had simply not pinged in as they ought. Overall, the season was something of a triumph: something of a victory. But another victory like that I don't think Castle Stables could stand it.

38

IT WAS NOVEMBER, and English racing was over. The lads had dug out their foul-weather gear: Scobie was dressed head to foot in oilskins, another lad had adopted German army surplus fatigues, Chris Beavis the workaholic wore his woolly hat so that it covered his eyebrows, one of the girls had acquired an enviable pair of leather chaps. Graham Foster was riding out at Arundel, and was as dapper as ever. He had ended up with six winners from 28 rides, and was far from displeased with the way things had gone. Next year the breakthrough? Foster was full of hope.

Because of the hurricane devastation around the cricket pitch, the warm-up walk was now taking place round and round the main stable block. The new yearlings were walking about in the park, and a good few of them had already been ridden. Angus had a sweet-natured Shirley Heights yearling to look after, as a compensation for four years of Efisio. The horse was called Murango, and was a half-brother to Efisio – but he seemed much less quirky. Sue the secretary said that Paul Coombes had been applying for jobs in England, and using Castle Stables as a reference: obviously things had not worked out for him in Holland. I was sad to hear this of such a nice chap. Scobie said his disco was booked solid until Christmas: good news for the mortgage.

The seasons had turned their full circle, and I was back where I had started, out on the gallops beside the Japanese Range Rover with a waterproof zipped up to the chin and a cap over my eyes against thin driving rain, savouring the routine and the atmosphere of hope, indeed, savouring the routine of hope. Racing is perhaps the world's most expensive celebration of the constant triumph of hope over experience. The gates of Castle Stables should carry the legend 'Abandon expectation all ye who enter here'. But a racing stable is ever the stronghold of Hope.

And where there is Hope there is life. Even in a year of professional problems and personal sadness, the presence of 200 horses insists that life goes on: there is no getting out of it. And in the end, there was plenty to cheer about. Deluge had followed deluge throughout the year, the sun had scarcely ever shone, but all the same, the year had ended with a small flood of winners for John Dunlop's stable.

The racing year had been one of disappointment seasoned with triumph, like most people's racing years. The picture of Shirley Heights still hung in the secretaries' office: perhaps in another year there would be a picture of another Derby winner. Every autumn has that possibility, however faint. Perhaps it would be appropriate if there was a picture of Snaafi Dancer to complement the Shirley Heights one, but it would be unnecessary. No trainer of racehorses ever needs to be reminded about disappointment. All he needs to do is look out of the window. Disappointment is a daily fact of life in racing. That is the point, in fact: disappointment is the setting for the glittering triumphs that occasionally come your way. The rarity value of triumph is perhaps racing's most seductive trait. And at least at Castle Stables we – no other pronoun will do – had had a triumph or two to savour.

'Well, it's difficult not to compare it with the season just gone,' John Dunlop said. 'But when you make comparisons from year to year, it is always misleading. We had an exceptional year last year – and the year before that, we had an exceptionally *bad* year. So which do you compare this last season with? If you compare it with Cecil's, it's been a bloody awful year. He has had an exceptional year. We have had ... a *moderate* year.

'We started off fairly quietly as we usually do, and then we had that awful spell that knocked a major hole in the season. And there has been this constant dribbling problem with the two-year-olds, which has stopped us running quite a lot of them. And I think that our three- and four-year-olds really were a very substandard lot. We were held together by some very promising two-year-olds, and the likes of Moon Madness, Almaarad and the older horses. Not a great year, really, but it could have been a lot worse. Indeed, it *looked* like being a lot worse.

'The basic weakness of the three-year-olds was a problem, and I think because of that, we are a little down on numbers right now. On the other hand, I was pleased with the two-year-olds in several ways – though I can't claim to have the top two-year-old as such. Ashayer was very much a plus, especially her win in the Group One race in Paris in October.'

'But she has had an up-and-down year, really, hasn't she? Beautiful as she is.'

'Well, she has and she hasn't. She won first time out, the day before the Diamonds. She was third in that race at Doncaster and should have won it, but she didn't get going until it was all too late. At Ascot, at the Festival of British Racing, I tried her in blinkers, and she got all in a muddle. It was not totally her fault, she got bumped a couple of times and then finished very well. But I took them off her again, and she won in Paris. She's won twice and been third twice, and you can't call that a total disappointment. She is certainly *one* of the top fillies, even though she can't claim to be number one.'

'So you'll hope to have her fit for the 1,000 Guineas and the Oaks?'

'Probably. Maybe even the French Guineas. She has whistled round Longchamp very successfully.'

'And the colts? I know you think a lot of Alquoz.'

'Yes, Alquoz who never ran. He always looked like a very good horse indeed. But he suffered from this wretched respiratory problem. We couldn't get him right, and we couldn't get him right, and we got him right and he deteriorated again. But it's not the end of the world: perhaps he is better off not having had a race this year. Though I have a feeling that if he had, he would have shown something fairly startling.'

'And Alwuhush, with the big white face?'

'He ran that marvellous race at Ascot, again at the Festival of British Racing, but he ran a stinker in the Futurity at Doncaster. I'm not actually certain, but I think he's got an odd sort of floppy palate. It flops down every now and then and interferes with his breathing. You can have something done surgically. Some horses have a palate that is just not quite as tense as it should be. I think what happened at Doncaster was that he was going all right, and then suddenly it slipped, cut off his wind, perhaps for as little as a couple of strides – and frightened him to death.

'So naturally he lost all momentum. I think that is what happened – impossible to tell, of course. The jockey, Tony Ives, didn't notice anything wrong with his breathing – but it was such an out-of-character race for the horse, and he was rather distressed afterwards, which is also out of character. And the horse that won was behind us at Ascot – so it was, in fact, a major disappointment.

'There are some things you can do about this. You can get a special bit that lies over the tongue or you can go a step further and actually tie the tongue down. The principle of this is that the muscles that control the tongue and the palate are the same. So fixing the tongue should help the palate. If that race had worked out as it should have done, we would have had one of the top colts as well as one of the top fillies.

'Love The Groom did very well, but he was another sufferer from the respiratory problem. And as you know, we only began to get this properly cleared up by October, and indeed, it is still not wholly cleared up now, at the end of November. But Love The Groom won for us at Goodwood and at Royal Ascot, and we decided to let him take his chance in the St Leger. There was only one horse to beat, as we saw it, and that was Reference Point, and we wondered if he wasn't on the blink by then – there was some suggestion of this, and in the end as things turned out, when he ran so disappointingly in the Arc, this was not totally unfounded. But Reference Point won, and Love The Groom ran very disappointingly indeed, and came back coughing. Either the infection had re-established itself, or he had picked up something else.

'But the point is that he hasn't done a lot of racing, and he will be an interesting one for next year. Because I think that apart from Reference Point, this year's crop of true mile-and-a-half horses is pretty weak.' And of course, Reference Point went off to stud after his year of heroics.

Almaarad and Sergeyevich, both useful Stakes horses, were to stay in training. Angel City, who ended up winning five off the reel (and almost giving Marcus Hosgood a heart attack in the process), was also to stay in training for another year. He had improved enough throughout the year to earn a crack at the French St Leger (along with Sergeyevich), but then found the ground too soft for him. Both were possible Cup horses for the following season.

But the disappointments still stuck out from the year. Perhaps the greatest of these was Three Tails in the Oaks: 'A disappointing and *surprising* performance. Especially as afterwards, she did everything she was asked. I really did think she would win the Oaks. She ran so well at Newbury first time out. But for some reason, she just didn't compete at Epsom. She just went walkabout, like the tennis player Evonne Goolagong. I was sitting at home watching, and I just couldn't believe my eyes when I saw that Willie was riding her head off after six furlongs. She won the Lancashire Oaks, the Meld Stakes, and was unlucky to get beaten in a Group One race. In the end, she had a good season – but at one stage I thought she was going to be a star. She really looked like that.'

But Three Tails left the yard, and went to the States to become a broodmare. Dunlop was sad to see her go. She was a nearly horse, a frustrating horse in a year of frustrations, but he felt that she might have matured in mind and body as a four-year-old. She was due to visit the stallion Blushing Groom, and perhaps her foals will end up winning the races in which their dam had shown so much ability and, when it suited her, delivered the goods. 'She was a lovely filly,' Dunlop said. 'She did some funny things, but she was a lovely filly despite all that.'

Efisio had finally left the yard, doubtless giving one last black look at Angus, and giving him cause to remember his career as soprano. Boon Point, Mike Huntley-Robertson's ever-glorious horse, had won his race in Ostend but had come back with a slight injury to his tendon. As we know, that front tendon is the crucial bit of a racing animal, and the injury was enough to end Boon Point's career on the track. A new career as a stallion was opening up for him: Dunlop had had enquiries from Chile, India and Yugoslavia. Huntley-Robertson had not, at that stage, bought into a new horse.

Perhaps the greatest training feat of the season was Dunlop's triumph with the weird, dipbacked monster, Promise Kept, the Señora's darling. Dunlop did actually manage to get a win into the horse. 'He showed a measure of ability,' Dunlop said. 'A fairly small measure.' But he won his race at the end of September, in a seller, which means that he was auctioned afterwards, and he actually found a buyer. So the Señora had a winner to her broodmare, and had got rid of that oddity into the bargain. She sent two yearlings to Castle Stables, both of them with straight backs, so things were improving.

Despite the incredible and magnificent triumph of Promise Kept at Nottingham (prize money of £1,139), there were a couple of moments that were even better. Ashayer's win in Paris gave the entire stable something to look forward to and to get excited about for the following season. The victory was one of the sweetest moments of the season for Castle Stables.

But the best, Dunlop said, was Moon Madness's win at Saint-Cloud. 'The Duchess came when she was really very ill, you will remember,' Dunlop said. 'I was seriously worried that she might not see the day out. But thank the Lord, it all worked out, the horse won, and from that day on, the Duchess started to improve herself. It was a great relief, and it was probably the highlight of the year for me. The win with Ashayer was great. But the Grand Prix de Saint-Cloud gave so much pleasure to the person involved, and that really is one of the most important parts of being a trainer. It is very satisfying – to be able to give real pleasure to people.'

39

I T WAS TIME for the last hurrah. Moon Madness had been invited to run in the Japan Cup in Tokyo, and the Duchess had accepted with great delight. 'He looks as though he is ready to start the season,' the Duchess said happily. 'From his coat you would think he was ready for Ascot.'

The Japan Cup not only invites its contestants, it also pays for them. There is an appearance fee, which the Duchess with magnificent vagueness said was 'several thousand yen'. The flight and the accommodation were also paid for, not only for the horse, but for owners, trainers, jockeys and lads as well: the organizers do their very best to attract real quality to the race. The Duchess catalogued this with all the delight that only the very rich can feel at such a freebie. 'No expense at all!' she said. 'Isn't it *extraordinary?*'

'I think he's got a chance,' Dunlop said. 'They have run this race for the past seven years, and for five of them the going has been dry and firm: it is frosty and quite sunny out there now, so let us hope it stays that way, since that is just the thing to keep it dry. Moon Madness is in good shape physically, which is especially important at the end of a long season. He enjoys competing, that is the great thing. The Duchess has decided to keep him on in training for another season, as a five-year-old, and I think he should do all right in Japan.'

Robert Hamilton – Rab, the travelling head lad – supervised the horse's trip out, and he endured it well enough and settled in when he got there. Rab rode his preparation work himself, and reported back: 'Moon Madness has never been better.' Conditions were firm and looked like staying that way.

The main danger was Triptych, a terrific racemare, strong and gutsy, but never quite consistent. 'Only she knows when she is ready to go,' said her trainer, Patrick Biancone. 'But I can tell she is in the right mood at present.' Pat Eddery flew out to join Moon Madness, and the plan was to blunt the mare's renowned finishing speed with front-running tactics. 'There is no point in playing into Triptych's hands,' he said.

The Tokyo course is a good open galloping track. Dunlop walked it, and agreed that there was no point in keeping Moon Madness hanging about. The betting made Triptych favourite at 5–4 on, with Mood Madness 7–2 and a French horse called Le Glorieux at 7–1. To my eyes, and to many others, Moon Madness looked a cracking good bet.

More than 80,000 people turned up for the race, and they bet more than £70 million at the meeting, several thousand yen, in fact. They bet £34 million on the big race alone.

Then they were off, and Moon Madness missed his break from an outside draw, and had no option but to run all the way round the outside. He went blazing away and finally scorched into the lead at the first turn. Eddery kicked for home as they turned into the straight. He had set the most amazing early pace, and Le Glorieux moved into second place behind him, and then set sail for victory, moving past Moon Madness, setting a new course record and winning the race quite emphatically.

Oh.

'Moon Madness had to burn up his speed too early from his bad draw,' Dunlop said afterwards. Perhaps Eddery went too fast too soon, certainly some people thought so. But I had intended to make the Japan Cup a resounding last chapter, a last hurrah, a last memory of triumph to take into the winter, and to close my book with. A final taste of victory from the ever-splendid Moon Madness. I felt that Dunlop, and all Castle Stables were owed that: a happy ending. But racing stories are never quite as predictable as fairy stories. Still, there is always another race, though, in fact, the season had ended. But there is always another season.

Oh, but there was Highland Chieftain as well. He was due to run his final race of the season, positively the final race of the year for Castle Stables, in Naples on 13 December, a Group Three race, the Premio Unire. He had been boarded out in Italy for three weeks, following his win in Rome at the end of November.

John Reid went out to ride him, and Tony Couch went out to represent Dunlop. A horse called Melbury Lad looked like the main danger, and he set off at a scorching pace, and went well clear. Highland Chieftain was back in fourth or fifth spot, and eventually set off in pursuit. In the end he managed to get up in the last couple of yards. Victory! That is the way to finish, all right. A slight tang of luck in it: but a win, a win by a neck, and there is nothing like a win. And after spending a year or so as the guest of Castle Stables, revelling in the horses, feeling the disappointments, delighting in the company of the ever-urbane John Dunlop, the banter of the lads, the hospitality of the secretaries, the knowledge of Marcus Hosgood, the helpfulness and kindness of everyone in the yard, I had, I think, learned the point of the operation. And so I rejoiced, just as I had whenever a win came throughout the year. What is more, from now on, every time a winner is trained at Castle Stables, I will rejoice with everyone there, wherever I am, and at the races I will drink a toast after every winner from John Dunlop's yard: to victory, to horses, and to life.

APPENDIX 1

Horses trained by John Dunlop 1987

Note: the breeding in this appendix is all on the distaff side. An expanded version would read:

Bold Pillager
- Formidable (USA) *Sire*
- Pilley Green *Dam*
  - Porto Bello
  - Phoenicia
    - Premonition

FOUR YEAR OLDS AND UPWARDS

Dexam International Ltd.	Bold Pillager	5 b.g.	Formidable (USA) – Pilley Green by Porto Bello – Phoenicia by Premonition
Lord Granard	Bold Rex (FR)	5 b.c.	Rex Magna – Lady Bold (IRE) by Bold Lad (IRE) – Egerie by Vieux Manoir
Mrs M. Landi & G. Jabre	Efisio	5 b.c.	Formidable (USA) – Eldoret by High Top – Bamburi by Ragusa
Ogden Mills Phipps	Freedom's Choice (USA)	5 ch.c.	Forli (ARG) – Full of Hope by Bold Ruler – Lady Be Good by Better Self
J. L. Dunlop	Harlestone Lake	5 gr.m.	Riboboy (USA) – January (FR) by Sigebert – Just Windy by Torbido
P. S. Winfield	Patriach	5 b.c.	London Bells (CAN) – Julip by Track Spare – Jacine by Owen Tudor
Dana Stud Ltd.	Siyan Kalem (USA)	5 ch.c.	Mr Prospector – Lady Graustark by Graustark – Inyala by My Babu
P. S. Winfield	Aitch 'n' Bee	4 ch.c.	Northfields (USA) – Hot Case by Upper Case (USA) – Chili Girl by Skymaster
Hamdan Al Maktoum	Almaarad	4 ch.c.	Ela-Mana-Mou – Silk Blend by Busted – Silken Yogan by Ballyogan
Hamdan Al Maktoum	Al Salite	4 ch.c.	High Line – Delicia by Sovereign Path – Relicia by Relko
N. M. Avery & M. Robertson	Boon Point	4 br.c.	Shirley Heights – Brightelmstone by Prince Regent (FR) – Sweet Reason by Elopement
J. A. Haverhals	Flower Bowl	4 b.f.	Homing – Anzeige (GER) by Soderini – Ankerkette by Nearco
D. R. Hunnisett	Highland Chieftain	4 b.c.	Kampala – La Primavera by Northfields (USA) – Eos by Sovereign Path

Mrs M. Landi	Ichnusa	4 b.f.	Bay Express – Skiboule (BEL) by Boulou – Skitor by Torbido
Lavinia, Duchess of Norfolk	Moon Madness	4 b.c.	Vitiges (FR) – Castle Moon by Kalamoun – Fotheringay by Right Royal V
Magnus Berger	Senor Tomas	4 b.c.	Sparkler – Pearlemor by Gulf Pearl – A. I. by Abernant
D. R. Hunnisett	Silver Dragon	4 gr.g.	Dragonara Palace (USA) – Penitent by Sing Sing – Under Canvas by Winterhalter
H.R.H. Prince Faisal	Tanouma (USA)	4 b.f.	Miswaki – Diffusion (FR) by Habitat – Dress Uniform by Court Martial
Lady Cohen, Ettore Landi & A. Baxter	Tinterosse (FR)	4 b.c.	Kenmare (FR) – Dressed In Red by Red Alert – Double Type by Behistoun
Gezio Mazza	Tommy Way	4 b.c.	Thatch (USA) – Tilia (ITY) by Dschingis Khan – Coralba by Kythnos
P. M. Brant	Tout Ensemble	4 b.c.	Shergar – Snobby Kate by Snob – Kate's Intent by Intentionally
H.H. Sheikh Mohammed	War Hero	4 b.c.	Troy – Bahariva (FR) by Sir Gaylord – Barbara by Le Fabuleux

THREE YEAR OLDS

Mrs A. V. Ferguson	Adanus	ch.c.	General Assembly (USA) – Mirkan Honey by Ballymore – Honey Bend (USA) by Never Bend
Dana Stud Ltd.	Al Farabi	ch.c.	Be My Guest (USA) – Lady Graustark (USA) by Graustark – Inyala by My Babu
Cyril Humphris & J. L. Dunlop	Angel City (FR)	gr.c.	Carwhite – Kumari by Luthier – Kashmiri Song by Kashmir II
Ogden Mills Phipps	Arabian Sheik (USA)	b.c.	Nijinsky II (CAN) – Arabian Miss by Damascus – Lady Love by Dr Fager
H.H. Sheikh Mohammed	Battalion (USA)	b.c.	Vaguely Noble – Blazon by Ack Ack – Too Bald by Bald Eagle
Hamdan Al Maktoum	Bawareq	b.c.	Mill Reef (USA) – Regal Heiress by English Prince – Hardiemma by Hardicanute
Erik Penser	Beauchamp Buzz	b.f.	High Top – Buss by Busted – Miss Klaire II by Klairon
Erik Penser	Beauchamp Lady	b.f.	Niniski (USA) – Jubilee by Reform – Golden Ivy by Sir Ivor
Mrs B. Lynott & E. J. Price	Betty Jane	ch.f.	Morston – Indulgence by Prominer – Perennial Twinkle by Continuation
J. A. Haverhals	Black Love	b.f.	Windjammer (USA) – Sodina by Saulingo – Red Rag by Ragusa
A. Stirling	Bracorina	b.f.	High Line – Premiere Danseuse by Saritamer (USA) – First Round by Primera

Sir Thomas Pilkington	Bronzewing	b.f.	Beldale Flutter (USA) – Starlust by Sallust – Welsh Star by Welsh Abbot
A. J. Struthers	Buchan Ness	b.c.	Hittite Glory – Ruddy Duck by Dicta Drake – Cheongsam by Tantieme
Lady Cohen	Cas-en-Bas	b.f.	Good Times – Ariadne by Bustino – Zerbinetta by Henry the Seventh
Lavinia, Duchess of Norfolk	Castle in the Air	b.f.	Castle Keep – Skiboule (BEL) by Boulou – Skitor by Torbido
H.H. Sheikh Mohammed	Castle Ward	ch.c.	Castle Keep – Super Anna by Super Sam – Rondone by Fighting Don
Lavinia, Duchess of Norfolk	Celtic Ring	b.f.	Welsh Pageant – Pencuik Jewel by Petingo – Fotheringay by Right Royal V
J. L. Dunlop	Charity Day	gr.g.	Connaught – January (FR) by Sigebert – Justy Windy by Torbido
Mrs H. J. Heinz	Chilibang	gr.c.	Formidable (USA) – Chili Girl by Skymaster – A. I. by Abernant
H.H. Sheikh Mohammed	Darley Knight	b.c.	Formidable (USA) – Yelney by Blakeney – Yelda by Crepello
H.H. Sheikh Mohammed	Devon Lass	ch.f.	Bustino – Stogumber by Habitat – Another Daughter by Crepello
Mrs P. Lewis & Partners	Domino Fire	ch.f.	Dominion – Enlighten by Twilight Alley – Hakoah by Palestine
H.H. Sheikh Mohammed	Don't Knock It	ch.f.	Tap on Wood – Compliment by Tudor Music – Flattering by Abernant
Mrs V. Gaucci del Bono	Employ Force (USA)	b.f.	Alleged – Maratona by Be My Guest – Oh So Fair by Graustark
Midhurst Farm Inc. & Mrs B. Allen	Fah So Law (FR)	br.f.	Trepan – French Minuet by Jim French – Muscial II by Prince Chevalier
K. M. Campbell	Final Rush	b.f.	Final Straw – Iona by Kalydon – Island Woman by Kings Troop
J. O. R. Darby, M. J. Blackburn & M. J. Arnold	Fleet Lord	b.c.	Lord Gayle (USA) – Penna Bianca by My Swallow – Acknowledgement (USA) by Fleet Nasrullah
Ahmed Mutawa	Frasquita	ch.f.	Song – Trickster by Major Portion – Lady Jester by Bleep-Bleep
R. G. Percival, T. G. Warner & D. Gibson	George James	gr.c.	Mummy's Pet – Pariscene by Dragonara Palace (USA) – Rennet by King's Bench
Cyril Humphris	Gianotti	b.f.	Sharpo – Clymene by Vitiges (FR) – Siraf by Alcide
Ettore Landi	Gilberto	b.c.	Runnett – Natasha by Native Prince (USA) – The Chaser by Fighting Don
Mrs Veronica Gaucci del Bono	Go Henri (USA)	b.c.	Sharpen Up – Quacker by Creme de la Creme – Quillion by Princequillo
Dexam International Ltd.	Hajji Baba	ch.c.	Persian Bold – Merry Yarn by Aggressor – Wharfedale by Wilwyn

P. G. Goulandris	Hollomoore	b.f.	Moorestyle – Glebe Hollow by Wolver Hollow – Azurn by Klairon
A. J. Struthers	Hotel Lotti	b.f.	Relkino – Lune de Miel by Kalamoun – Dauphine by Pampered King
Ahmed Mutawa	Hyatti	ch.f.	Habitat – Cutie Kiss (FR) by Luthier – Arctic Wave by Arctic Slave
H.H. Sheikh Mohammed	Kalia Crest	b.c.	Shirley Heights – Dankalia by Le Levanstell – Deodota II by Relic
Ahmed Mutawa	Kawther	ch.f.	Tap on Wood – Field Day by Northfields (USA) – Royal News by Sovereign Path
D. R. Hunnisett	King Richard	ch.c.	Try My Best (USA) – Penny Halfpenny by Sir Ivor – Wise Countess by Count Amber
H.H. Sheikh Mohammed	Klarara	b.f.	King's Lake (USA) – Imbrama (USA) by Imbros – Alabama Gal by Determine
H.H. Sheikh Ahmed Al Maktoum	Lagta	b.f.	Kris – Ivory Girl (USA) by Sir Ivor – Treacle by Hornbeam
Mrs Veronica Gaucci del Bono	Love the Groom (USA)	b.c.	Blushing Groom (FR) – Nell's Briquette by Lanyon – Double's Nell by Nodouble
Mrs Veronica Gaucci del Bono	Lyphard Ace (USA)	b.c.	Lyphard (USA) – Reina Real (ARG) by Escudo Real – Tres Reinas by Isaac The Angel
Hamdan Al Maktoum	Mahafel	b.c.	Kris – Royal Meath by Realm – Hill of Tara by Royal Palace
Lavinia, Duchess of Norfolk	Maid Maleen	b.f.	Castle Keep – Escape Me Never by Run the Gantlet (USA) – Parolee by Sing Sing
H.H. Sheikh Ahmed Al Maktoum	Maksab	b.c.	Mill Reef (USA) – Hayloft (FR) by Tudor Melody – Haymaking by Galivanter
Hon. David Montagu & J. L. Dunlop	Marienbourg	br.g.	Belgio (FR) – Ma Carte (FR) by Gift Card (FR) – Matushka (GER) by Orsini
Mrs D. Abbott & Partners	Mislay	b.f.	Henbit (USA) – Miss Slip (USA) by Coursing – Am Stretchin' by Ambiorix II
C. Humphris & Partners	My House (FR)	b.f.	Open House – Kiphissia by Baldric II – Cyparissia by Philius
A . Stirling & The Earl of Suffolk	Noble Bid	b.c.	King's Lake (USA) – First Round by Primera – Gun Play by Wilwyn
Sir Robin McAlpine	Norfolk Lily	b.f.	Blakeney – Cecilia Bianchi by Petingo – Cendres Bleues (ITY) by Charlottesville
Julian Byng	Panienka (POL)	b.f.	Dom Racine (FR) – Pointe Rousse (FR) by Margouillat – Pointe d'Onyx by Exbury
Earl of Halifax	Piffle	b.f.	Shirley Heights – Fiddle Faddle by Silly Season – Fiddlededee by Acropolis

The Hon. David Montagu, Lord Soames & Edward Rayne	Pour L'italie	ch.f.	Posse (USA) – Crosmieres (FR) by Lyphard (USA) – Renee Martin by Crepello
Señor M. Machline	Purple Rose	ch.f.	Sharpman – Ensnarer (USA) by Bold Ruler – Embuche (FR) by Le Haar
Count Roland de Chambure	Raw Energy (FR)	b.c.	Habitat – Satu by Primera – Creation by Crepello
D. R. Hunnisett	Rob Roy MacGregor	ch.c.	Ballad Rock – Sovereign Bloom by Florescence – Sovereign Game by Sovereign Path
Ahmed Mutawa	Royal Pageant	b.c.	Welsh Pageant – Copt Hall Royale by Right Tack – Sauce Royale by Royale Palace
H.R.H. Prince Faisal	Sanam (USA)	ch.c.	Golden Act – Rose Goddess (IRE) by Sassafras (FR) – Cicarde II by Red God
A. J. Struthers	Sea Island	b.f.	Windjammer (USA) – Sule Skerry by Scottish Rifle – Ruddy Duck by Dicta Drake
P. S. Winfield	Seek To Win	b.c.	Dalsaan – Woo by Stage Door Johnny (USA) – Covey by Rustam
Mrs D. Riley-Smith	Sergeyevich	b.c.	Niniski (USA) – Rexana by Relko (FR) – Parthian Queen by Parthia
Dana Stud Ltd.	Shore Lark	b.f.	Ela-Mana-Mou – Sweety Grey by Young Emperor – Cassowary by Kashmir II
Mrs K. M. Campbell	Spanish Melody	br.f.	King of Spain – Carry On Singing by Derring-Do – Sing by Sing Sing
A. J. Struthers	Strathblane	ch.f.	Castle Keep – Mother Brown by Candy Cane – March Brown by March Past
The Duke of Marlborough	Stubble Fire	ch.c.	Thatch (USA) – Explosiva (USA) by Explodent – Whispering Willow by New Providence
Mrs Veronica Gaucci del Bono	Sweet Reef	br.c.	Mill Reef (USA) – Sweet and Lovely by Prince Tenderfoot (USA) – Full of Flavour by Romulus
Mrs Veronica Gaucci del Bono	Taiana (FR)	b.f.	Bellypha – Tarilla by Ribero – Teresa Tibaldi by Hornbeam
Lady Hardy & R. G. Percival	Tallow Hill	b.f.	Dunphy (FR) – Lover's Rose by King Emperor (USA) – Nonnie by Dumbarnie
Mrs A. V. Ferguson	Temple Reef	ch.c.	Mill Reef (USA) – Makura by Pampered King – Eye Shade by Anwar
H.H. Sheikh Mohammed	Three Tails	b.f.	Blakeney – Triple First by High Top – Field Mouse by Grey Sovereign
Hesmonds Stud Ltd.	Tiquegrean	b.f.	Great Nephew – Helvetique (FR) by Val de Loir – Helvetie II by Klairon
Mrs Anne Clabby	Traniski	ch.f.	Niniski (USA) – Tranquilly (USA) by Sea Bird II – Mill House (USA) by Basis

Señor M. Machline	Tropical Flower	b.f.	Brigadier Gerard – Longest Day (FR) by Lyphard (USA) – Rough Sea by Herbager	
H.H. Sheikh Mohammed	True Gent	b.c.	Lord Gaylord – Glamour Girl (ARG) by Mysolo – Esbeltez by Grass Court	
Prince Ahmed Bin Salman	Uptothehilt	b.c.	Kris – Karine by Habitat – Dialora (FR) by Diatome	
G. R. Rickman	Very Droll	b.g.	Comedy Star (USA) – Hartnell Dream by Grundy – Scarlet Thread by Joshua	
H.H. Sheikh Mohammed	War Brave	gr.c.	Indian King (USA) – Kizzy by Dancer's Image (USA) – Dialora (FR) by Diatome	
Lavinia, Duchess of Norfolk	Wood Chanter	gr.c.	Vitiges (FR) – Castle Moon by Kalamoun – Fotheringay by Right Royal V	

TWO YEAR OLDS

Dana Stud Ltd.	Ali Mourad	ch.c.	Final Straw – Paper Sun by Match III – Vivien by Nearco	2/5
Hamdan Al-Maktoum	Alquoz (USA)	br.c.	Caerleon – I Understand by Dr Fager – Native Street by Native Dancer	17/5
Mrs Veronica Gaucci del Bono	Altamos	br.f.	Priamos (GER) – Altara (GER) by Tarim – Alaria by Kaiseradler	27/3
Hamdan Al-Maktoum	Alwuhush (USA)	b.c.	Nureyev – Beaming Bride (IRE) by King Emperor – Khazeen by Charlottesville	10/3
Ettore Landi	Aaghelu Ruyu	br.f.	Rusticaro (FR) – Song Grove by Song – Grove Hall by Hook Money	10/3
Hamdan Al-Maktoum	Anhaar	b.f.	Ela-Mana-Mou – Chilblains by Hotfoot – Chiltern Red by Red God	9/4
Hamdan Al-Maktoum	Arfjah	b.f.	Taufan (USA) – Thit-Kho by Irish Love – June Minstrel by Will Somers	1/2
Hamdan Al-Maktoum	Ashayer (USA)	b.f.	Lomond – Good Lassie by Moulton – Violetta III by Pinza	20/3
H.R.H. Prince Faisal	Ashshama (USA)	b.f.	Arctic Tern – Sheer Fantasy by Damascus – Bold Bikini by Boldnesian	27/3
Hamdan Al-Maktoum	Asl (USA)	gr.f.	Caro – Call Me Goddess by Prince John – Marshua by Nashua	29/5
Gezio Mazza	Aulogellio	ch.c.	Tap On Wood – What A Pity by Blakeney – Scarcely Blessed by So Blessed	19/2

Mrs S. P. Hornung	Aunt Blue	ch.f.	Blue Refrain – Cranberry Sauce by Crepello – Queensberry by Grey Sovereign	28/3
Mrs H. J. Heinz	Baby Marie	b.f.	Jalmood (USA) – Chili Girl by Skymaster – Al by Abernant	13/4
Prince Yazid	Baltic Bay	ch.c.	Irish River (FR) – High Galaxie (USA) by Irish Castle – Avanti Girl by Royal Levee	11/2
Earl of Halifax	Banket	b.f.	Glint of Gold – Bempton by Blakeney – Hardiemma by Hardicanute	3/5
Hamdan Al-Maktoum	Basirah	br.f.	Persian Bold – Lochboisdale by Saritamer (USA) – Hecla by Henry The Seventh	28/3
Erik Penser	Beauchamp Cactus	b.f.	Niniski (USA) – Buss by Busted – Miss Klaire II by Klairon	12/3
Erik Penser	Beauchamp Crest	b.f.	Jalmood (USA) – Jubilee by Reform – Golden Ivy by Sir Ivor	30/1
Señor M. Machline	Brazilian Boy (FR)	b.c.	Formidable (USA) – Longest Day (FR) by Lyphard (USA) – Rough Sea by Herbager	26/4
Lavinia, Duchess of Norfolk	Castle Moat	b.c.	Jalmood (USA) – Fotheringay by Right Royal V – La Fresnes by Court Martial	5/6
Mrs Veronica Gaucci del Bono	Charme the Nickle	b.f.	Plugged Nickle (USA) – Charmina (FR) by Nonoalco (USA) – Very Charming (USA) by Vaguely Noble	27/3
Lady Cohen	Comedy Mask	b.c.	Comedy Star (USA) – Ariadne by Bustino – Zerbinetta by Henry The Seventh	27/2
N. M. Avery	Defiantly	b.f.	Bold Lad (IRE) – Corona Bay by Targowice (USA) – Bay Tree (FR) by Relko	6/3
Ahmed Mutawa	Djlah	b.f.	Glenstal (USA) – Sipapu by Targowice (USA) – Nakomis (USA) by Sky High (AUS)	4/3
Mrs Veronica Gaucco del Bono	Don Fiorenzo (USA)	b.c.	Green Dancer – Synclinal by Vaguely Noble – Hippodamia by Hail To Reason	23/4
Mrs Veronoca Gaucci del Bono	Dongiulio (USA)	b.c.	Nijinsky II (CAN) – Ack's Secret by Ack Ack – Escandinhas by Binkil	6/4
Dr J. A. Hobby	Donner Und Blitzen	ch.c.	Connaught – Foudroyer by Artaius (USA) – Foudre by Petingo	14/3
H.H. Sheikh Mohammed	Dreadlock	b.c.	Formidable (USA) – Habella by Habitat – Galana by Reform	25/2

Aubrey Ison	Dust Devil	b.b.	Horage – Witch of Endor by Matador – Oracabessa by Alycidon	8/3
J. A. Haverhals	Dutchess Best	b.f.	Blakeney – Just A Dutchess (USA) by Knightly Manner – King's Darling by King of the Tudors	14/3
H.H. Sheikh Mohammed	Ever Welcome	ch.f.	Be My Guest (USA) – Ghaiya (USA) by Alleged (USA) – Proud Pattie by Noble Commander	19/2
Duke of Marlborough	Fast Chick	ch.f.	Henbit (USA) – Hasten by Northfields (USA) – No Delay by Never Say Die	9/3
Dana Stud Ltd.	Fes City	br.f.	Caerleon (USA) – Nancy Chere (USA) by Gallant Man – Nancy Jr by Tim Tam	28/3
Mrs Veronica Gaucci del Bono	Fluorescent Star	b.f.	Fluorescent Light (USA) – Flinging Star (USA) by Northern Fling (USA) – Staretta by Dark Star	22/3
Mrs D. Riley-Smith	Flying Buttress	br.f.	Castle Keep – Princess Log by King Log – Kessall by Stephen Paul	6/5
H.H. Sheikh Mohammed	Gamble On	b.f.	Beldale Flutter (USA) – Edwinarowe by Blakeney – Lucyrowe by Crepello	11/5
R. G. Percival & Partners	Game Try	gr.c.	Mummy's Game – Pariscene by Dragonara Palace (USA) – Rennet by King's Bench	21/5
A. Stirling & R. E. Sangster	Gun Lady	b.f.	Thatching – First Round by Primera – Gun Play by Wilwyn	8/4
Miss Cynthia Phipps	Hawaiian Bloom (USA)	b.f.	Hawaii – Frost Flower by Jacinto – St Bernard by Hill Prince	19/3
Lavinia, Duchess of Norfolk	Height of Folly	b.f.	Shirley Heights – Criminelle by Crepello – La Fresnes by Court Martial	1/4
D. R. Hunnisett	Hereward	b.c.	Aragon – Dastina by Derring-Do – Omentello by Elopement	26/4
A. M. Budgett	Hi Lass	b.f.	Shirley Heights – Good Lass (FR) by Reform – Derry Lass by Derring-Do	14/1
H.R.H. Prince Faisal	Irnan	b.c.	Valiyar – Nawara by Welsh Pageant – Bright Decision by Busted	8/2
Hamdan Al-Maktoum	Jabrut	b.c.	Young Generation – Migoletty by Oats – Loch Leven by Le Levanstell	7/4
Lavinia, Duchess of Norfolk	Jinga	b.c.	Castle Keep – Eldoret by High Top – Bamburi by Ragusa	22/3

— 220 —

Dr K. T. B. Menon	Juno Moneta	gr.f.	Deep Roots – Strathdearn by Saritamer (USA) – Shenachie by Sheshoon	4/6
Señor M. Machline	King of Art	b.c.	Artaius (USA) – Ensnarer (USA) by Bold Ruler – Embuche (FR) by Le Haar	20/4
P. G. Goulandris	Lavender Deed	gr.c.	Known Fact (USA) – Lavender Dance by Dance in Time (CAN) – Sea Lavender by Never Say Die	22/1
Sir Thomas Pilkington	Le Cygne	b.f.	Pas de Seul – Star Life by Star Appeal – Alive Allivo by Never Say Die	14/3
Mrs Veronica Gaucci del Bono	Live Image (USA)	b.f.	Riverman – Spanked by Cornish Prince – Won't Tell You by Crafty Admiral	15/5
Mrs Veronica Gaucci del Bono	Lord Gramy (USA)	b.c.	Naskra-Gramy (FR) – by Tapioca – Gracile by Silnet	19/4
Captain John Macdonald-Buchanan	Llyn Gwynant	b.f.	Persian Bold – Etoile des Galles by Busted – Welsh Star by Welsh Abbot	11/4
The Hon. David Montagu & J. L. Dunlop	Mariano	b.c.	Aragon – Ma Carte (FR) by Gift Card (FR) – Matushka (GER) by Orsini	23/3
Hamdan Al-Maktoum	Matlub	b.c.	Valiyar – State Ball by Dance In Time (CAN) – Crystal Palace by Solar Slipper	6/4
Sheikh Ahmed Al-Maktoum	Mawzoon (USA)	b.c.	Danzig – Dare To Be Bare by Grey Dawn II – Topless by Gallant Man	12/2
Julian Byng	Midnight Mariner	b.c.	Pyjama Hunt – Figure de Proue (FR) by Petingo – Bel Paese (USA) by Forli (ARG)	2/5
Mrs S. Rogers	Mild Intrigue (USA)	b.f.	Sir Ivor – Mild Deception by Buckpasser – Natashka by Dedicate	1/5
Dana Stud Ltd.	Milieu	b.c.	Habitat – Lady Graustark (USA) by Graustark – Inyala by My Babu	9/3
Mr D. Greedy & T. J. Allen	Moon Warrior	b.c.	The Brianstan – Briannie Moon by Brigadier Gerard – Castle Moon by Kalamoun	8/3
Cyril Humphris	Mother Courage	ch.f.	Busted – Never A Lady by Pontifex (USA) – Camogie by Celtic Ash	13/3
Hamdan Al-Maktoum	Mutarid (USA)	ch.c.	Kris – Voie Lactee (FR) by Amber Rama (USA) – Pinap II by Relic	27/5
Mrs Veronica Gaucci del Bono	Nasr Moon (USA)	b.f.	Al Nasr (FR) – Fairs Fair (USA) by Ribot – All Beautiful by Battlefield	13/5
P. Vela & Partners	Nebula Way	ch.c.	Aragon – New Way by Klairon – New Move by Umberto	2/4

I. A. D. Pilkington & M. C. C. Armitage	Night Pass	b.c.	Pas de Seul – Bid For Freedom by Run The Gantlet (USA) – Fotheringay by Right Royal V	14/5
A. J. Struthers	Old Kilpatrick	br.c.	Touching Wood (USA) – Mother Brown by Candy Cane – March Brown by March Past	13/3
Lavinia, Duchess of Norfolk	Petavious	b.c.	Mummy's Pet – Pencuik Jewel by Petingo – Fotheringay by Right Royal V	9/3
P. S. Winfield	Picaroon	br.c.	Taufan (USA) – Get Ready by On Your Mark – La Corsaire by Pirate King	24/4
Earl of Halifax	Poffle	b.f.	Beldale Flutter (USA) – Fiddle Faddle by Silly Season –Fiddlededee by Acropolis	25/4
H.H. Sheikh Mohammed	Pretoria	b.f.	Habitat – Diamond Land by Sparkler – Canaan by Santa Claus	15/4
Windflower Overseas Holdings Inc.	Promise Kept	b.c.	Castle Keep – Gay Fantasy by Troy – Miss Upward by Alcide	5/3
H.R.H. Prince Faisal	Ranyah (USA)	b.f.	Our Native (USA) – Mineola (FR) by Tyrant – Miss Minny by Mincio	8/3
Mrs D. Abbott & Partners	Restless Wave	ch.f.	Ballad Rock – Hollow Reef by Wollow – Roselyn by Mill Reef (USA)	24/3
Mrs Veronica Gaucci del Bono	Rivereel (USA)	b.c.	Riverman – Irish Reel by Irish Lancer – Night of Nights by Johns Joy	12/4
Lord Chelsea & Partners	Royal Borough	b.c.	Bustino – Lady R.B. (USA) by Gun Shot – Ribbons and Bows by War Admiral	2/5
Dana Stud Ltd.	Saneena	ch.f.	Kris – Northern Valley (USA) by Northern Dancer – Green Valley II (FR) by Val de Loir	13/3
I. A. D. Pilkington & M. C. C. Armitage	San Roque	b.g.	Aragon – Arch Sculptress by Arch Sculptor – Effervescence II by Charlottesville	15/2
Gezio Mazza	Scipione	ch.c.	Jalmood (USA) – Spimpinina by Be My Guest (USA) – Pagan Queen by Vaguely Noble	29/4
H.H. Sheikh Mohammed	Sergeant at Arms	b.c.	Shirley Heights – Sunningdale Queen by Gay Fandango (USA) – Lisabella (FR) by Right Royal V	16/3
Mrs A. Clabby	Sharp Celine	b.f.	Sharpo – Celina by Crepello –Rose of Medina by Never Say Die	29/4

Lavinia, Duchess of Norfolk	Shingle Ridge	b.f.	Blakeney – Red Ruby by Tudor Melody – Ruby Laser by Red God	22/3
Mr S. Khaled	Smart Roberto (USA)	b.c.	Roberto – Night Fire by Cannonade – La Griffe by Prince John	19/4
Sir John Prideaux & Sir Rex Cohen	Smokejack	gr.c.	Jalmood (USA) – Oakwoodhill by Habat – Tomboy by Sica Boy	2/4
Mrs Veronica Gaucci del Bono	Stop Day (USA)	b.f.	Stop The Music – Yellow Serenade by Graustark – Yellow Train by Olden Times	4/3
Ettore Landi	Sulcis	ch.c.	Castle Keep – Skiboule (BEL) by Boulou – Skitor by Torbido	15/4
H.H. Sheikh Mohammed	Swooping	b.c.	King's Lake (USA) – High Hawk by Shirley Heights – Sunbittern by Sea Hawk II	25/1
Ahmed Mutawa	Terrain	b.c.	Jalmood (USA) – Be Merry by Charlottown – Mabel by French Biege	29/3
J. L. Dunlop	Thirty First	gr.c.	Castle Keep – January (FR) by Sigebert – Just Windy by Torbido	4/4
Aubrey Ison	Thorn Bush	ch.c.	Sharpo – Red Roses (FR) by Roi Dagobert – La Theve by Red God	2/5
T. D. Stoner & Partners	Thunderflash	b.f.	Runnett – High Explosive by Mount Hagen (FR) – Blonde Bomb by Worden II	18/2
Ettore Landi	Tirso	b.c.	Niniski (USA) – Lady of the Manor by Astec – Fotheringay by Right Royal V	29/4
Mrs Veronica Gaucci del Bono	Topsider Man (USA)	b.c.	Riverman – Donna Inez by Herbager – Banja Luka by Double Jay	30/3
H.H. Sheikh Mohammed	Tutor (USA)	br.c.	Mr Prospector – Love of Learning by Hail to Reason – Cosmah by Cosmic Bomb	24/3
Gilbert Jabre	Very Sober	b.c.	Noalcoholic (FR) – Cupids Hill by Sallust – Sweet Jewel by Will Somers	5/3
H.H. Sheikh Mohammed	Victory Torch (USA)	b.c.	Majestic Light – Victory Songster (CAN) by Stratus – Victory Chant by Victoria Park	5/5
H.H. Sheikh Mohammed	Village Talk	br.f.	Known Fact (USA) – Stogumber by Habitat – Another Daughter by Crepello	6/4

Sir Robin McAlpine	White-Wash	b.f.	Final Straw – Cecilia Bianchi (FR) by Petingo – Cendres Bleues (ITY) by Charlottesville	5/4
Ogden Mills Phipps	Whitewash (USA)	ch.c.	Majestic Light – Clear Ceiling by Bold Ruler – Grey Flight by Mahmoud	3/3

APPENDIX 2

Winners trained by John Dunlop 1987

Date	Horse	Race	Course	Jockey	Prize	Odds
30.3.87	Darley Knight	Rochester Graduation Guaranteed Sweepstakes (Division 2)	Folkestone	Pat Eddery	£684	8/15 fav
25.4.87	Bronzewing	Esher Cup Handicap	Sandown	W. Carson	£12,350	8/1
25.4.87	Flower Bowl	Holsten Pils Trophy European Breeders Fund Stakes (Listed)	Leicester	W. Newnes	£7,661	10/1
29.4.87	Almaarad	Chobham Apprentice Handicap	Ascot	G. Foster	£3,987	6/1
4.5.87	Uptothehilt	A. F. Budge Handicap	Doncaster	W. Carson	£4,416	8/1
6.5.87	Piffle	Druids Graduation Stakes	Salisbury	B. Rouse	£1,283	100/30
12.5.87	Lagta	T. I. Creda Electric Stakes (Handicap)	Chepstow	B. Rouse	£1,867	16/1
16.5.87	Sergeyevich	Shaw Maiden Stakes (Division 1)	Newbury	B. Rouse	£3,043	6/1
18.5.87	Noble Bid	Mayfair Graduation Stakes	Windsor	W. Carson	£1,184	14/1
16.6.87	Love The Groom	King Edward VII Stakes (Group 2)	Royal Ascot	Pat Eddery	£51,534	7/1
25.6.87	Sea Island	Arundel Claiming Stakes	Goodwood	B. Thomson	£3,096	7/1
26.6.87	Betty Jane	Whitbread Best Bitter Handicap	Lingfield	W. Carson	£2,369	9/2
30.6.87	Angel City	Rockhold Handicap	Newbury	W. Carson	£3,044	9/4 fav
4.7.87	Three Tails	Harp Lager Lancashire Oaks (Group 3)	Haydock	T. Ives	£29,457	6/4 fav
4.7.87	Gilberto	Gedling Stakes (3.y.o)	Nottingham	W. Carson	£1,826	1/14 fav
5.7.87	Moon Madness	Grand Prix de Saint-Cloud (Group 1)	Saint-Cloud	Pat Eddery	£126,926	11/2
9.7.87	Bronzewing	Addison Tools Handicap Stakes	Newmarket	W. Carson	£16,674	8/1
10.7.87	Cas-En-Bas	Truman Maiden Stakes	Lingfield	B. Rouse	£1,104	11/1
10.7.87	Chilibang	Lin Pac Handicap	York	W. Carson	£1,104	4/1
11.7.87	Almaarad	The Curragh Cup	Curragh	Pat Eddery	£13,800	8/13
15.7.87	Bold Pillager	Insider Handicap	Kempton	W. Carson	£2,712	100/30 fav
17.7.87	Angel City	White Horse Handicap	Newbury	W. Carson	£4,000	15/8 fav
17.7.87	Ranyah	Somersham Maiden Stakes	Newmarket	W. Carson	£3,353	9/2
17.7.87	Domino Fire	South Bank Manton Apprentice Claim Stakes	Warwick	G. Foster	£1,820	4/1

Date	Horse	Race	Course	Jockey	Amount	Odds
18.7.87	Irnan	European Breeders Fund Findon Stakes	Lingfield	J. Reid	£1,354	12/1
24.7.87	Ashayer	Virginia Water Maiden Stakes	Ascot	W. Carson	£8,656	11/8 fav
25.7.87	Don't Knock It	Largs Maiden Guaranteed Stakes	Ayr	G. Duffield	£959	2/1
28.7.87	Love The Groom	Gordon Stakes (Group 3)	Goodwood	W. Carson	£23,192	6/4 fav
29.7.87	Angel City	Scottish Salmon Handicap	Goodwood	Pat Eddery	£8,285	15/8 fav
30.7.87	Sergeyevich	The Goodwood Cup (Group 3)	Goodwood	W. Carson	£22,710	Evens Fav
7.8.87	Angel City	Headland Overseas Properties Handicap	Newmarket	W. Newnes	£3,954	3/1
8.8.87	Wood Chanter	Bank of New Zealand Maiden Stakes	Newmarket	Pat Eddery	£3,444	8/11 fav
9.8.87	Almaarad	Prix Kergorlay Group 2	Deauville	W. Carson	£23,984	4.8/1
11.8.87	Castle Ward	Hemlock Stone Maiden Guaranteed Stakes	Nottingham	W. Carson	£1,279	4/1
14.8.87	Freedom's Choice	Tom Caxton Home Brew Handicap	Newbury	T. Ives	£7,086	9/1
15.8.87	Moon Madness	Geoffrey Freer Stakes (Group 2)	Newbury	Pat Eddery	£33,546	11/8
17.8.87	Picaroon	Newholme Graduation Guaranteed Stakes	Windsor	Pat Eddery	£1,102	9/4 fav
18.8.87	Angel City	Lonsdale Stakes (Listed)	York	W. Carson	£7,648	5/2
23.8.87	Boon Point	Grand International d'Ostende	Ostend	T. Ives	£16,722	3.1/1
29.8.87	Three Tails	The Meld Stakes (Group 3)	Curragh	J. Reid	£13,176	4/5 fav
30.8.87	Almaarad	Grand Prix de Deauville Lancel (Group 2)	Deauville	W. Carson	£38,212	3.7/1
30.8.87	Harlestone Lake	Gladiateur d'Ostende	Ostend	J. Reid	£8,361	7BF/10BF
5.9.87	Pour L'Italie	Falcon Claiming Stakes	Thirsk	J. Lowe	£2,607	9/2 fav
12.9.87	Tanouma	Holsten For Ladies Stakes	Doncaster	Carolyn Eddery	£3,993	11/2
12.9.87	Freedom's Choice	Battle of Britain Handicap	Doncaster	W. Carson	£13,091	11/2
16.9.87	Castle In The Air	Jim Taylor Memorial Handicap	Brighton	W. Carson	£2,662	9/2
22.9.87	Sea Island	Charnwood Claiming Stakes	Leicester	Pat Eddery	£2,506	11/4 fav
23.9.87	Chilibang	Raffingora European Breeders Fund Sprint Stakes	Beverley	W. Carson	£2,905	11/8 fav
24.9.87	Moon Madness	Hoover Cumberland Lodge Stakes (Group 3)	Ascot	Pat Eddery	£34,058	6/5 fav
24.9.87	Tanouma	Bishopsgate Apprentice Stakes	Ascot	G. Foster	£4,045	4/6 fav
24.9.87	Panienka	Sancton Graduation Stakes	Beverley	G. Duffield	£1,951	12/1

Date	Horse	Race	Course	Jockey	Prize	Odds
25.9.87	Bronzewing	Taylor Woodrow Team Charity Stakes (Handicap)	Ascot	Pat Eddery	£11,843	6/1
28.9.87	Promise Kept	Sibthorpe Selling Stakes (Division 1)	Nottingham	Pat Eddery	£1,139	6/4 fav
29.9.87	Lagta	Nottingham Goose Fair Handicap	Nottingham	W. Carson	£2,011	11/2
29.9.87	Gun Lady	Winthorpe Fillies Nursery Handicap	Nottingham	W. Newnes	£2,251	7/1
30.9.87	Chilibang	Rous Stakes (Listed)	Newmarket	W. Carson	£9,146	5/1
4.10.87	Ashayer	Prix Marcel Boussac (Group 1)	Longchamp	W. Carson	£50,656	13.4/1
4.10.87	Sergeyevich	St Leger Italiano (Group 2)	San Siro (Milan)	B. Rouse	£34,736	7/10
7.10.87	Dust Devil	Marlborough Maiden Stakes (Division 1, part 2)	Salisbury	W. Carson	£1,199	10/1
12.10.87	Highland Chieftain	Arden European Breeders Fund Stakes	Warwick	S. Cauthen	£2,562	7/1
14.10.87	Smart Roberto	Whitebeam Maiden Stakes (Division 1)	Haydock	Pat Eddery	£2,182	4/5 fav
14.10.87	Topsider Man	Whitebeam Maiden Stakes (Division 2)	Haydock	W. Carson	£2,176	Evens Fav
19.10.87	Baby Marie	Hare Maiden Fillies Stakes (Division 1, part 2)	Leicester	Pat Eddery	£964	5/4 fav
19.10.87	Asl	Hare Maiden Fillies Stakes (Division 2, part 1)	Leicester	W. Carson	£964	3/1
19.10.87	Pretoria	Hare Maiden Fillies Stakes (Division 2, part 2)	Leicester	M. Roberts	£964	14/1
19.10.87	Dust Devil	Whitbury Manor Grad Stakes (Division 1)	Chepstow	J. Reid	£1,055	4/11 fav
21.10.87	Night Pass	Ruswarp Maiden Guaranteed Stakes	Redcar	Pat Eddery	£1,700	11/2
25.10.87	Highland Chieftain	Preis der Speilbanken-des Landes Nordrhein-Westfalen (Group 3)	Dusseldorf	T. Ives	£12,280	3.4/1
27.10.87	Temple Reef	Full Choke Handicap Stakes	Nottingham	J. Reid	£1,346	100/30 jt-fav
31.10.87	Patriach	Solonaway Race	Curragh	D. Gillespie	£9,750	7/4 fav Irish
31.10.87	Highland Chieftain	Premio Carlo Porta (Group 3)	Milan	J. Reid	£16,008	22/10
31.10.87	Efisio	Premio Chiusura (Group 2)	Milan	J. Reid	£21,826	37/10
2.11.87	Celtic Ring	Wysall European Breeders Fund Stakes	Leicester	J. Lowe	£3,118	9/4 jt fav
7.11.87	Night Pass	European Breeders Fund Armistice Graduated Stakes	Doncaster	Pat Eddery	£1,647	7/4 fav
15.11.87	Patriarch	Premio Ribot (Group 2)	Rome	J. Reid	£21,574	56/10

| 22.11.87 | Highland Chieftain | Premio Roma Vecchia (Group 3) | Rome | W. Carson | £16,190 | 14/10 |
| 13.12.87 | Highland Chieftain | Premio U.N.I.R.E. | Naples | J. Reid | £15,115 | 1/5 |

Grateful thanks go to Marcus Hosgood for preparing the appendices.